Antique Collecting for MEN

Books by Louis H. Hertz

Advanced Model Railroading
Antique Collecting for Men
Collecting Model Trains
The Complete Book of Building and Collecting Model Automobiles
The Complete Book of Model Aircraft, Spacecraft, and Rockets
The Complete Book of Model Raceways and Roadways
The Complete Book of Model Railroading
The Handbook of Old American Toys
Making Your Model Railroad
Mechanical Toy Banks
Messrs. Ives of Bridgeport
Miniature Railroad Service and Repair Manual
Model Railroad Conversion Manual
New Roads to Adventure in Model Railroading
Riding the Tinplate Rails
The Toy Collector

Antique Collecting for MEN

by
LOUIS H. HERTZ

HAWTHORN BOOKS, INC.
PUBLISHERS / NEW YORK

Designed by Harold Franklin

To Helen,
whose witticisms provided
the idea for this book

An outstanding example of sports statuary: John L. Sullivan knocking down Billy Mitchell in the thirty-nine-round World's Heavyweight Championship bareknuckle bout, March 10, 1888, at Chantilly, France. A 14½-inch-high bronze by Émile Hébert, commissioned by Baron Rothschild, on whose estate the fight was held, for distribution to his friends.

Mark Haber

Contents

Contents

x   *Contents*

Introduction

The basic concept that led to bringing this book into being is obvious and requires no further explanation here. Whether in the long run this concept properly may come to be regarded as a serious commentary on a situation of recent and current times, or perhaps only as a hinge or assembly point for the gathering together and presentation of treatments of various types of collectables—some long and firmly established as such; some to a great extent still unplumbed—is something concerning which the writer does not feel qualified or certain enough to express a definite opinion. There are other equally and perhaps even more important themes running through this book that may or may not prove wholly acceptable to every reader. Certainly the writer must admit having taken advantage of the opportunity afforded by the bringing into being of the book to coalesce and express in print a number of thoughts that have long been held, if largely until now unheard, by a number of individuals including himself.

If, particularly to those who regard themselves as familiar with the usually accepted mores of antique collecting, a number of seemingly new ideas and outlooks are expressed herein, it is not so much that they actually are novel but rather that the previously somewhat unorganized, unexpressed, and even in some cases subconscious thoughts of a great many men are for the first time assembled and enunciated upon these pages.

It has always struck the writer as somewhat grotesque to examine a book supposedly directed to collectors and potential collectors and to find the pictorial material made up completely, or at least almost entirely, of specimens whose counterparts, or even substantially similar items, the average reader could hardly ever hope to obtain for himself. There are indeed some rare specimens illustrated in this book, along with many far commoner articles. Nothing shown herein—or at least in terms of things of a similar type and quality—is beyond possible acquisition by a reader. True enough, in a number of cases, illustrations are of specimens in museums or the collections of manufacturers. However, in most instances, identical or similar articles are known to exist in private collections.

Indeed, it is only in the case of a few items shown from private collections that a reader may find the available supply so sadly diminished as virtually to be nonexistent or at least of an availability impossible to pinpoint on the present-day antiques market. Even here, however, there may well be pleasant surprises in store for some, for it is possible only to express amazement at what can and does continue to come to light. Recently, for example, a fine old steam fire engine was discovered in a corner of a barn where it had been hidden ever since its use as a stationary boiler to heat a greenhouse had been abandoned a good number of years ago. Similarly, the writer refuses to be convinced that there may not still remain a few ancient plantation or industrial steam locomotives surviving undiscovered, awaiting the search of collectors possessed of sufficient diligence and enthusiasm.

Experience has shown that a word of caution is desirable in any collectors' book, even though experience has also shown that it will be ignored by many: Merely because a particular article is selected as the subject of an illustration or for discussion in the text does not in itself mean that it or a similar specimen is therefore automatically very rare, highly desirable, and valuable. Contrariwise, the fact that any given article or type of article is not pictured or mentioned in a collectors' book does not mean that it is perforce very rare, highly desirable, and valuable. This may all seem so obvious to many as to make this paragraph appear not a little ridiculous and certainly superfluous. Such readers may feel happy that they have avoided that substantial area of collecting, buying, and selling where the bywords are "It must be very rare because it is illustrated in the book" or, alternatively, "It is so rare it is not illustrated in the book."

Having made these few seemingly necessary comments, the primary task here is to thank the many individuals and organizations who have been of assistance in preparing this book. The writer wishes to express his deep and sincere appreciation:

To Mrs. Helen C. Harris, whose sparkling remarks first gave the writer the idea for this book.

To G. William Holland and George S. Indig, both enthusiastic collectors themselves, for making numerous special photographs of both their own items and those of others, including a number of specimens belonging to owners who wish to remain anonymous. The differentiation is made clear in each of these two gentlemen's credit lines; the name followed by the word "Collection" indicates that the article pictured is owned by the photographer himself; the word "Photograph" indicates that the subject or subjects of the illustration are owned by another.

To five other outstanding collectors of wide-ranging interests in particular for so generously making available photographs of specimens in their collections, a plethora that if anything resulted in an overabundance of photographic riches more than sufficient to make extremely difficult the final selection: Mark Haber, Ward Kimball, A. J. Koveleski, W. van Roosbroeck, and W. Porter Ware.

To W. B. Thorsen, of *The American Book Collector;* the Bausch & Lomb Optical Company; Charles Bragin; Captain Ralph S. Barnaby, U.S.N. (Retired), of the Franklin Institute; Mrs. M. S. Cook, of the Bishop Historical Room, Bridgeport Public Library; Thomas J. Turner, of Colt Industries, Colt's Firearms Division; Wilbur J. Kurtz, Jr., and Mrs. Margaret Hopper, of The Archives, The Coca-Cola Company; Miss Helen Comstock and Mrs. E. Smith, of *Antiques Magazine;* Alexander L. Murphy, of E. I. Du Pont de Nemours & Company; Miss Felice Davis; Edward J. Maas, of the Glass Container Manufacturers Institute, Inc.; Robert E. Mayer, of the General Aniline and Film Corporation; Martin Siegel, of the General Foods Corporation; Mrs. Julia Gunsbury; Andrew B. Haber; Mrs. and the late L. C. Hegerty; Harry K. Hudson; William A. Hall; Charles E. Crandall, of the Herkimer County Historical Society, Inc.; Freeman Hubbard and Roger Arcara, of *Railroad Magazine;* Frank McMenamin, of the Hillerich & Bradsby Company; Robert C. Lietz, of the Milwaukee Public Museum; Mrs. A. J. Koveleski; Mrs. Michele Selcon, of Michele's Antiques; Gus

Metz; Ben McCready, of *Playthings;* Rev. Richard E. Matera; Thomas Matera; Frederick J. Dockstader, of the Museum of the American Indian, Haye Foundation; Captain Dale Mayberry, U.S.N. (Retired), of the United States Naval Academy Museum; James J. Keeney, of Old Sturbridge Village; R. E. Fitzwater, of the National Cash Register Company; F. A. Nichols; Mrs. Dorothy Reville, of the New York Zoological Society; Cole Palen, of Old Rhinebeck Aerodrome; Mr. and Mrs. Charles A. Penn, of the Bumble Bee Trading Post; Horace Smith; Howard Coulson; J. W. Mc Kennon, Curtis G. Coley, and Mel Miller, of the Ringling Museum of the Circus; S. M. Alvis, of the Remington Arms Company, Inc.; Robert W. Coburn and Miss Judith Ferreira, of the Royal Typewriter Company, Inc.; Dr. G. A. Robinson; Kenneth M. Newman, of the Old Print Shop; Mike Saisbury, of *West Magazine;* Norman F. Schaut; Ralph T. Buckley; Earl T. Strickler, of the National Association of Watch and Clock Collectors; Mrs. L. W. Slaughter; Frank A. Taylor, Edwin A. Battison, John H. White, Jr., Warren J. Danzenbaker, Don H. Berkebile, M. L. Peterson, and Richard E. Ahlborn, of the Smithsonian Institution; Wallace E. Tompkins, of Smith & Wesson of Bangor Punta; Thomas W. Sefton; Sterling D. Emerson, of the Shelburne Museum; E. C. Benfield and R. F. West, of the Stanley Works; W. C. Rockwell, of the Sperry Rand Corporation, Remington Rand Office Machines; F. C. Straw, of the Seth Thomas Division of the General Time Corporation.

Also to: Charles F. Stevens, of the United States Playing Card Company; Bill Wilson, of B & B Enterprises; Richard E. Kuehne, Philip M. Cavanaugh, and Gerald Slowe, of the West Point Museum; Richard J. Greene and Mrs. Young Hi Quick, of Western Electric; Albert Reese, of Kennedy Galleries, Inc.; L. A. Maxon, of Revere Copper and Brass, Inc.; the Winchester Gun Museum—Olin—New Haven; John C. Fountain, of John C. Fountain's "Ole" Empty Bottle House; the Bell Telephone Laboratories; Miss Carol A. Nixdorf, of the Hamilton Watch Company; Ernest L. Pettit; Leon J. Perelman; George A. Hawkins and Richard W. Felthousen, of the Brown & Sharpe Manufacturing Company; Ken Smith, of the National Baseball Hall of Fame and Museum, Inc.; I. Warshaw, of the Warshaw Collection of Business Americana; Adrian D. Lyons; Mr. and Mrs. Kenneth D. Roberts, of the American Clock and Watch Museum; Paul F.

Rovetti, of the Mattatuck Museum; Howard Shavelson, of the Benrus Watch Company, Inc.; C. C. Nordmark, of the L. S. Starrett Company; Colonel Thomas E. Griess, U.S.M.A.; Jay Irving; Alexander H. Weinberg; Mrs. Dorothy M. Ginn, of the Free Public Library, Atlantic City, New Jersey; Alfred Zari; Alfred Zari, Jr., and Peter Zari, of Zari Brothers' Washington Garage; Albert O. Roth; George L. Larned; G. R. Bouck, of The Bitters Bottle; Harold Carstens, Naomi Drake, and Steven Ahlstadt, of Carstens Publications; Mrs. A. Peterka; Frederick P. Fried; Mrs. Louis Walton Sipley, of the American Museum of Photography; Dr. and Mrs. Franklin A. Earnest; Charles A. Stenman; Wayne Boulton; Mrs. Barbara M. North; William Gowan, of the Bulova Watch Company, Inc.; Helmut Nickel, of the Metropolitan Museum of Art; Norman Richards; Miss Pearl Winick, of the Madison Square Garden National Antiques Show; Mrs. Sue Hutchinson, of the Sessions Clock Company; John S. Kebabian and Raymond R. Townsend, of the Early American Industries Association, Inc.; O. K. Bourgeois; Q. David Bowers, of Hathaway and Bowers, Inc.; Mrs. Grace Kendrick; Mrs. Mary W. Baskett, of the Cincinnati Art Museum.

Also to: David Golden; Charles Terwilliger; John T. Pierson, Mrs. Gladys Schmuck, and Hal Quinn, of the Vendo Company; Mr. and Mrs. Harry W. Hartman, of Vernon Antiques and Decorators; Miss Anne Adams, of *The Lamp;* Mrs. Hugh Nelson, of Essex Institute; Chester F. Stevens, of the United States Playing Card Company; Gerald W. Groglio, Jr.; Joseph N. Shure and Richard M. Shure, of the Strombecker Corporation; Lewis L. Graham, of the Museum of Music; John Miller, Walter Zervas, R. L. Allen, Mrs. Carmen Memberg, and Miss Elizabeth Roth, of the New York Public Library, Astor, Lenor, and Tilden Foundations; S. Lawrence Whipple, of the Lexington Historical Society, Inc.; Andrew Wittenborn; Mrs. Arline G. Maver, Museum Curator, Connecticut State Library; and Robert Weinstein.

L. H. H.

Scarsdale, New York
July, 1969

One man's collecting interests. Representatives of a number of popular categories of collectables used decoratively in the home of Mr. and Mrs. G. William Holland. Included are trade signs, weathervanes, prints, toys, and a tambourine once used on an early Lake Champlain steamboat.

G. William Holland Collection

CHAPTER I

Do Antiques Have Gender?

Do antiques have gender, much perhaps as do Latin nouns?

After several decades of association with countless collectors, vendors, and commentators, the writer has come to the conclusion that the answer most definitely is yes.

Furthermore, it seems apparent that many men shy away from any admitted interest in antiques and antique collecting because of an association it has in their minds with hobbies for women, and they attempt to conceal their own collecting enthusiasms altogether, or else disguise them under some "euphemism" that will seemingly somehow separate them from what they so evidently regard as a stigma connected with antiques and antique collecting.

Yet this outlook is actually one of relatively recent date and, from a historical standpoint, rather startling. Up until well into the nineteenth century antique collecting was almost universally regarded as primarily a man's game. From Roman times onward, the great recorded collectors, whether of ornamental or useful artifacts, almost without exception were men. They might at times have been criticized for the excesses to which their collecting mania led them—not excluding, in the case of those who were in a position to impose them, onerous taxes to secure revenue with which to further their hobbies—but no one faulted them for their inclinations toward collecting as such. Antique collecting was regarded as a thoroughly masculine avocation. If any-

1

thing, the gathering and preservation of relics of the past was regarded as a rather saving grace; no one who collected antiques, not even a Caligula or a Nero, it was thought, could be "all bad."

When women collectors were recorded, they were viewed rather as exceptions. And, for the most part, these were regal ladies who, upon coming into their inheritances, merely retained the good old family treasures, much as today's widow hangs onto her A. T. & T. When they did actively collect, it was usually in such popular but limited areas as books and paintings, items of accepted "cultural value." Even as late as 1918, A. Edward Newton, in *The Amenities of Book Collecting*, patently found it unusual and not a little disconcerting that there should be a woman collector of sufficient stature to possess a particularly rare association copy of Boswell's *Life of Johnson* that Newton coveted, and he tipped his hat in passing to Miss Amy Lowell of Boston, "America's most distinguished woman collector."

By 1918, however, the concept of a woman collector in almost any field of antiques should not have seemed unusual to anyone. For between Lee's surrender and Kaiser Bill's abdication, the ladies, most especially in America, had gradually apportioned unto themselves practically the whole of antique collecting. Admittedly it cannot be said with precise accuracy that they had stolen antique collecting lock, stock, and barrel, for, despite the tradition of such weaker vessels as Molly Pitcher, Calamity Jane, Annie Oakley, Lizzie Borden, and the gal who advised

> You can pass my door,
> You can pass my gate,
> But you cannot pass
> My thirty-eight

(a verse to which an advertising man is claimed once to have tacked on a terminal line, "Barbasol!"), firearms and edged-weapons collecting—and little else—had been left to men.

Later, this neat campaign of piracy will be examined in a little more detail; suffice it for the moment to observe that even to this day many men, figuratively speaking, have not been able to recover from the initial shock.

An Antiques Grammar

Generally speaking, men and women have entirely different outlooks on antiques and antique collecting. Men are for the most part interested in different types of antiques than women, or, in categories commonly collected by both, men have a different and usually more complex outlook. In short, antiques definitely do have gender in the minds of men and women collectors.

An antiques grammar, which must always allow for exceptions and variations, might start out with something like this:

> Firearms, *masculine*
> Clocks, *masculine and feminine*
> Embroidery, *feminine*

Here, with the third entry, we immediately start to run into trouble. Not only is needlework accepted therapy at times for wounded soldiers, but from the standpoint of antique collecting, we would have to add to the entry something like this: "Except when depicting historical personages or events, inventions and machinery, sports, etc." However, the basic principle involved and the general thesis of this book are exemplified by the above.

Clock collecting is a good illustration of an area of interest to both men and women, although there are almost certainly a far greater number of men who seriously collect and study clocks than women. Aside from its possible value as a working timepiece, which may be of interest and practical value to both sexes, feminine interest in old clocks is largely from a decorative or external standpoint. Masculine interest goes deeper, and while it would definitely be incorrect to say that men are not concerned with external values, most particularly when these relate to model changes and development, it certainly would be proper to state that externals are in themselves seldom a primary concern. A man is usually interested in and intrigued by the design and mode of construction, and the workings of the internal mechanism. At a further remove, masculine interest reaches to the industrial and technical history of the clock and of the clockmaking business.

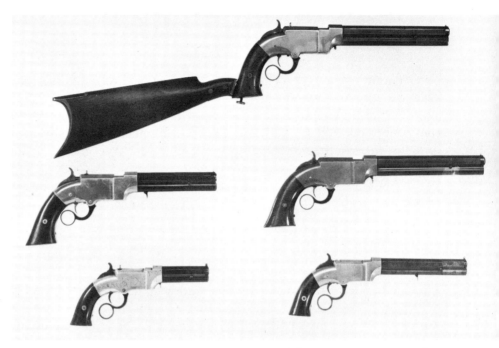

Volcanic repeating pistols. The upper three, .38 caliber, were manufactured in 1856–57 by the Volcanic Repeating Arms Company; the lower two, .30 caliber, were made in 1858–60 by the New Haven Arms Company.

Winchester Gun Museum—Olin—New Haven, Connecticut

Old Chauncey Jerome summed up much of the spirit involved here in his combined autobiography and narrative of the clockmaking industry, *History of the American Clock Business for the Past Sixty Years.* This book was published in 1860 when Jerome was sixty-seven years of age. Some of the passages are sheer romance to the average man; it is a hardy soul indeed who can read something like the following without conjuring up a vision of illimitable technical skill and mass-producton know-how:

I will venture to say that I can pick out three men who will take the brass in the sheet, press out and level under the drop, there cut the teeth, and make all of the wheels to five hundred clocks in one day; there are from eight to ten of these wheels in every clock, and in an eight-day clock more. This will look to some like a great story, but is one of the wonders of the clock business. If some of the parts of a clock were not made for almost nothing, they could not be sold so cheap when finished.

Most women will not think much of the foregoing; they will not find very much at all of poetic imagery in it, and, in most cases, they probably would not have liked Chauncey Jerome anyhow, essentially

A restoration of an old railroad station, including a number of items illustrated separately in this book, and also housing a general collection of railroadiana. Since this photograph was made the stove has been replaced by the one illustrated in Chapter XII.

Ward Kimball

because he manufactured clocks by the tens of thousands and not, as an artist supposedly should, one at a time. On the contrary, most men find a definite artistry and romance invoked by the hum of the machine and of the factory as an entity, in the whole concept and output of the so-called Machine Age. Having a practical understanding and appreciation of such things, men for the most part hold a firm conviction that there is usually as much, if not more, true artistry and craftsmanship involved in the process of taking a mass-produced article through the successive designing, tooling up, and fabricating stages from initial conception to finished product as there is in the making by hand of a single unit. In effect, therefore, any machine-made, mass-produced article of an even recently bygone day is a masculine antique.

Determining the Gender

Thus, some antiques are obviously feminine; others are with equal certainty masculine. Some, as in the case of clocks, as noted above, may be of both masculine and feminine interest but in such cases the basic outlook on the subject is almost invariably different. For the most part it might be said that decorative articles or those whose primary use is decorative are essentially feminine antiques; operating and functional articles are for the most part inherently masculine antiques. This, as is the case with all broad generalizations, can undoubtedly be found faulty in spots; a likely demurrer would concern the fantastically elaborate extent to which men at one time decorated their weapons and hunting pieces. Admittedly, to the modern mind, there was often something at once grotesque and childlike in all this, much showing off and status symbolism. The baron expected to carry a much better-looking fowling piece than his steward, and in turn he expected, in the natural way of things, that his overlord would possess a still better piece than he. Nevertheless, the primary purpose of the artifacts in question was, in theory at least, functional.

Neither does the sex of the original owner or user of an article necessarily play the determining role in deciding whether or not anything is, as an antique, masculine or feminine. For example, many early kitchen appliances, such as mechanical apple peelers with their inge-

Two Connecticut shelf clocks, ca. 1830, showing transitional or competition-inspired departures from the pillar scroll-top case design. The specimen at the left, which includes a second hand, was manufactured by Eli Terry & Sons; that at the right, by Boardman & Wells.

Old Sturbridge Village Photo

nious gears and blades, may well today be of far more interest to men as mechanical antiquities than to women. This holds true for many early household appliances, gadgets, and containers; to a large extent old iceboxes, washing machines, stoves, coffee grinders, scales, sewing machines, and the like are essentially if not almost totally masculine antiques. A woman might employ one or two old coffee grinders, quite possibly converted into lamps and thereby in men's eyes rather absurdly ruined, as decorative items; it is improbable that anyone but a man would attempt to gather dozens or even hundreds of coffee grinders in an endeavor to trace, illustrate, and preserve their history. Then, too, the typewriter, one of the greatest of all masculine antiques, is not only a device that almost from its inception was used far more often by women than by men, but historically it is to a large extent the very means by which women were emancipated.

Some other generalities might be made to shed still more light on the line of thinking involved here. For example, women are more inclined to the fragile rather than to the substantial: glass, china, cloth, and so on; while men lean toward the more substantial materials, such as iron and tin. Again there are exceptions; there certainly can be no more masculine an article in conception, original use, and as an antique than china shaving mugs. As already intimated, women usually collect with decorative values or a definite decorative purpose in mind; men, for study from a technical or historical standpoint. Women's collections usually are displayed in their entirety as part of the general home decorative scheme, while men's collections, with their multiplicity of variations and damaged or incomplete specimens, are often housed in closets or cellars, or their display limited to the owner's den or hobby room. Women lean toward the handmade and are attracted by stories—real or imagined—of hand craftsmanship; even in the 1920s, for example, it was not considered in good taste by many to collect pressed glass because, no matter how beautiful and decorative it might be, it was admittedly machine-made.

Men, on the other hand, tend toward the manufactured article and are aware, as already pointed out—though the principle perhaps cannot be iterated too often—that there is as much and very often more true craftsmanship involved in the creation of the original design, drawings, tracings, patterns, molds, dies, jigs, and fixtures, and what-

Smoker's metal novelties of the late nineteenth and early twentieth century. At the top is a counter cigar lighter as used in cigar stores; at the bottom are five cast-iron animated cigar cutters.

ever else may be required for the bringing into being of a mass-produced article as in a handmade piece. Then, too, mere age alone tends to be much more of an influence upon what properly is collectable as an antique with women than with men. While for various reasons, often emanating from both practical and commercial considerations, the generally accepted dates marking the arrival of collectability on all articles of the past constantly are being moved forward, a woman almost always will place more importance on date than will a man. A woman will reject something that she otherwise finds greatly appealing simply because it is not old enough to stand scrutiny as a proper "antique" in her view and in that of her friends. Or, optionally, a woman often will simply suspend disbelief and profess not to be aware of the age of an article when she knows perfectly well it is of comparatively recent date, or else she will assert and perhaps even eventually convince herself it is much older. A man confronted with the same situation will—although this does not mean he is immune to the common fault of predating—merely laugh and move up the date that in his mind marks an article as an "antique" in order to accommodate that which he desires to collect. As a result, men frequently, if ridiculously and unjustly, have been censured for collecting as "antiques" articles made perhaps but a quarter of a century earlier.

One need not speak glowingly in specific terms of the attributes of the fair sex or their necessity to men in any seemingly called-for effort to soften or make amends for anything that may be said here. Intelligent women will agree substantially. Most fortunate indeed is the man who can share a collecting partnership with his wife, or, at least, whose wife looks with interest and even with enthusiasm upon his collecting pursuits and who will eagerly share in the gathering, study, and housing of his collection, and in the placement and display of at least a portion of it as part of the decor of their home. Obviously, this latter felicitously is the case with some of the collections of which portions, as displayed in the homes of their owners, are illustrated herein.

Quite apart from that, it must also be allowed that in some instances wives look with favor upon their mate's collecting activities in the expectation that these interests will help keep them out of mischief. The hope—if by no means necessarily the realization—may well be that the man who collects old typewriters, for example, will possess .

less time and energy to expend in the pursuit of "type-writers"—as the young ladies who operated these machines were initially designated when they first were permitted to enter the sacred and masculine precincts of commerce.

The Favorites of His Majesty

To expand upon some of the points already suggested or specifically noted, first, what are some of the favored categories of antiques for men, or, if you prefer, masculine antiques?

The titles of Chapters III through XIV will in themselves provide a broad description of some of these categories, and the subheadings within these chapters clarify and enunciate these interests still further. On the other hand, neither these nor the comments that follow profess to be exhaustive, although certainly all of the presently recognized high points are covered. Furthermore, it should be kept in mind that the intended scope of this book deliberately omits from inclusion such extremely popular masculine collecting hobbies as stamps, coins, and

An early nineteenth-century two-speed bow drill, operated by pushing the bow back and forth and thereby imparting rotary motion. The speed was varied as desired by moving the bow string from one pulley to another.

Old Sturbridge Village Photo

those relating to the natural sciences, such as geology, mineralogy, archaeology, and the like. It is generally understood and accepted that these represent long-established and favored masculine avocations, as indeed do some of the topics covered herein, but they are more or less manifestly beyond the intended bounds of the present volume.

In the area of things that can most readily be recognized as properly classifiable as antiques, however, men are particularly interested in:

anything mechanical, electrical, and scientific;

anything relating to business, commerce, and advertising;

tools and machinery and anything employed in craftsmanship and manufacture;

toys and models;

anything to do with processing and packaging;

anything relating to tobacco and spiritous liquids;

anything relating to the theater, motion pictures, the circus, or the world of entertainment in general;

anything to do with politics;

sports, games, and gaming;

anything to do with transportation;

printed and graphic materials;

clocks and anything operated by means of a clockwork mechanism;

weaponry;

anything produced by sand casting, or forged;

anything to do with ships and the sea, as above and beyond these things as a facet of the already mentioned topic of transportation, such as the craftwork done by sailors on long voyages. This is perhaps an unfair distinction, for with equal or even greater validity it could be said that there exists an enormous specific interest among men for anything that is connected with aeronautics, automobiles, and railroads and railroading.

The above listing presents many possible cross interests, a point that will be enlarged upon in the next chapter.

Above all, perhaps, it should be said that men are interested in anything that presents or is capable of action, and anything that is an example of unusually fine or especially interesting workmanship—although, as already seen, this well can be mass-production workman-

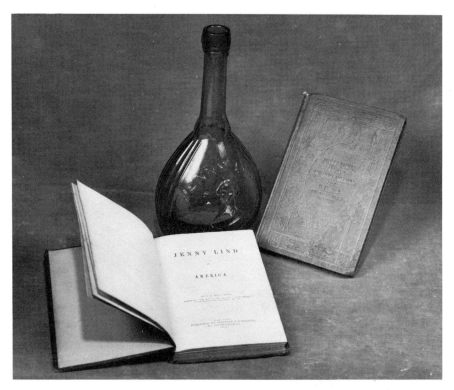

Collector's items resulting from Jenny Lind's famous visit to the United States; two copies of Jenny Lind in America *showing both title page and cover, and a calabash bottle, a form of pocket flask, bearing her name and picture.*

W. Porter Ware

ship rather than handcraftsmanship. Men do not—often to a degree that greatly surprises newcomers to collecting and outside observers—insist that their artifacts all actually work in the manner in which they originally performed, but any collectable that at any time was capable of working is almost always of particular interest.

This is merely one aspect of the beauty men customarily see in mechanical movements and in the fact that things are well made. Women often accuse men of being crass and unappreciative of purely esthetic values. This is not true in itself, but what women frequently fail to understand is that most men see a particular kind of beauty in objects and actions and their inherent designing and manufacturing backgrounds that women fail to perceive. An old typewriter, even when cleaned of the accumulation of a half century or more of dust and dirt, may well seem a rather ugly thing to a woman. To a man it is quite probably a thing of beauty, first as an entity, but even more so as an example of a manufacturing process that had reached a high state of perfection for its day (and may well claim merit or even superiority from that standpoint today), and as an inordinately inge-

Two disc record phonographs, a table model Victrola ca. 1915, and a floor-model Edison of the "Official Laboratory" model with double spring in a cabinet designated as William and Mary style, ca. 1919.

W. van Roosbroeck

nious design combination of levers and other mechanical movements. A man may well find as much beauty in the gears and mechanism of an old clock or music box as in the article as a clock or music box. To most men there is sheer beauty in the japanned cast-iron field, the green silk-insulated wire used to wind the coils, the nickeled bearing plates, and the copper commutator of a seventy-five-year-old electric motor; he sees a beauty of color, form, and function.

To a man there is beauty in the fact that the eight or ten or more intricate and separately cast iron components involved in any of thousands of Victorian artifacts neatly slip together into an integral whole with what was obviously a minimum of cleaning and fitting. An old lithographed coffee can or toy railroad car may well appear not merely an old can or toy and important for that in itself, but as a shining example of the all too often underrated art of lithographing in color on metal surfaces. In short, a man is likely to look upon and appreciate almost any antique article of interest from two or three or even more separate viewpoints, one or more of which may well involve specific, if largely unperceived and unappreciated by women, esthetic factors of a particularly masculine nature. Furthermore, and of considerable importance to note, they represent the outlook of a man of these times, a man who is the product of the cumulative industrial and scientific development that was born in the early decades of the nineteenth century. A man of the eighteenth century, or one born at any earlier date, could not possibly have had this same outlook on things. For better or for worse, modern man's outlook on such matters is the cultivated product of the Machine Age.

There is nothing arcane in all this, although it is by no means impossible that at least some of this outlook was subconsciously developed as a definite masculine defense against some of the outlooks and mores with which the opposite sex had colored almost the whole field of antiques. Neither, it should be emphasized, is there very much, or any at all in this, of the supposed attitude toward what may pass under various transitory names, such as pop art, in ill-advised attempts to give a sort of special status or legitimacy to things that never required nor now require special explanations or acceptability. To most men an old coffee can may be an example of packaging, of lithographic art, or the can manufacturer's production know-how, but it certainly does not represent "pop art" or "camp" or whatever odd term some may attempt to apply and make fashionable next week or next year.

To understand fully why the male may well have had to adopt defensive outlooks where antiques are concerned, and, in any event, to put the whole subject of antique collecting in its true historical perspective, it is worth examining in a little greater detail exactly what happened to antiques in the late nineteenth and early twentieth century to cause the shift in emphasis from the masculine to the feminine.

THE GREAT ANTIQUES STEAL

As we have seen, the collecting and study of objects of antiquity had for centuries been accepted unquestioned as being almost exclusively a man's prerogative. Then, along in the late nineteenth century, men invented, mass-produced, and placed in the hands of women a great number of artifacts that lightened their workload and led to their attaining that status usually referred to as "emancipation." The most important and noteworthy among these inventions were the sewing

Small electric motors with cast-iron fields and housings from the late 1880s to the 1920s. Motors of these types were used as toys, for classroom demonstration, and to perform useful light work. The motor at the upper left is five inches high.

George S. Indig Photograph

Standing before a statue of Jake Kilrain, Nat Fleischer shows James J. Corbett's old Indian clubs to W. Porter Ware. The latter has on the high silk hat that Bob Fitzsimmons wore when he arrived in San Francisco in 1890.

W. Porter Ware, Howard Coulson Photograph

machine and the typewriter, but actually there were uncountable lesser gadgets ranging from apple peelers to washing machines. At the same time, this Machine Age, which many women with newfound leisure on their hands were to decide was unpalatably gross and materialistic, placed in the hands of the average female household partner a great many objects of both usefulness and beauty whose appearance satisfactorily simulated that of wares that previously had been the province only of the wealthy, such as pressed glass, britanniaware, and china.

While the presentation of a mechanical washing machine in place of a wash board and tub may not seem to many, either then or today, as a particularly altruistic gift (nor were such artifacts by any means the lot of the majority) the ever-widening possession of these things provided women with leisure and with time to think, and, perversely, to yearn for the simpler days of their forebears when supposedly everything was made at home or purchased from an artisan craftsman, and most preferably, of course, from one bearing some such name as Paul Revere.

About the time of the Centennial in 1876—it is unnecessary to try to particularize the date too closely, and it is in fact possible to detect some signs of what was coming as early as the 1850s—there came upon a portion of the American people an awareness and appreciation of the historical implications of old things. These included both articles used in Colonial America, and of the European and especially British antiques that were to some extent the cultural heritage of the inhabitants of the United States. What had previously been largely regarded as so much dross, to be relegated to the attic if not actually discarded, suddenly became important and historic; closely tied in with the nation's birth. It was realized—for it was being stated and restated in the ladies' magazines—that America had reached an age when she had her own antiques and that, in the East at least, they were still relatively easily obtainable.

Virtually all of the articles that thus seemed worthy of attention were household furnishings—glass, china, furniture, silver, pewter, and the like—and the task of furnishing and decorating homes in a manner that employed such articles either for use or for display naturally fell to the distaff side. As a result, although there were some notable exceptions, the collecting of antiques became a feminine avocation. Furthermore, this was the age of contemporary furniture, which, whatever its faults—and the faults of Victorian furniture undoubtedly have been grossly exaggerated by antiques snobs—was comfortable. Overstuffed men accustomed to easing themselves into comfortable overstuffed furniture wanted no part of the spindly pieces that many of their wives sought to thrust upon them because they were Colonial or Federal—although many then and to this day fail to recognize the distinction and in their references to antiques thereby technically attribute a "Colonial" status to the United States approximately up to the time of the Presidency of Andrew Jackson! "Antiques" therefore became a bad word to many men and they were quite willing to denounce or renounce, as a particular instance might appear to require, any interest in them in exchange for a little accustomed comfort.

The matter continued to be one of friction and debate, or else abject surrender, in an increasing number of homes through the remainder of the nineteenth century and into the early years of the twentieth. The World's Columbian Exposition at Chicago in 1893, which commemorated one year too late the four hundredth anniver-

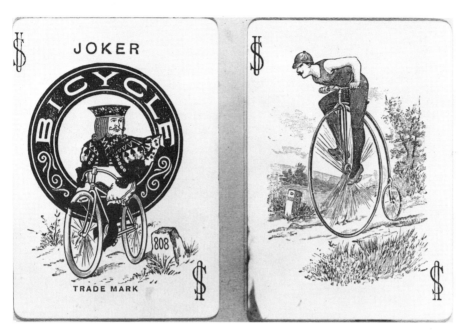

Two jokers from decks of Bicycle brand playing cards manufactured by the United States Playing Card Company in the late 1880s and early 1890s.

The John Omwake Playing Card Collection on Permanent Loan to the Cincinnati Art Museum from the United States Playing Card Company

sary of the landing of Columbus, even more fully than the 1876 Centennial Exposition emphasized the artifacts and household furnishings of the past, and its accompanying publicity added still more to the feminine awareness of and interest in antiques. At the Chicago Fair itself, while their spouses found some excuse to absent themselves and tried to catch a glimpse of Little Egypt's cooch dance on the midway, thousands of antique-conscious housewives naïvely suspended disbelief and purchased a Connecticut-designed clock bearing Columbus' portrait and the date "1492" under the impression it was the veritable clock carried on the *Santa Maria* or at least an exact duplicate thereof, a belief furthered by the manufacturer's clever omission of a minute hand. Still more fuel was added to the fire by the Trans-Mississippi Exposition in 1898, the Louisiana Purchase Exposition in 1904, and the Jamestown Exposition in 1907. By this time genuine old spinning wheels and Colonial cradles really were somewhat scarce, but of course the fakers—yes, undeniably males—already had long been at work.

A correlative factor that at once spread from this feminine takeover of antiques and at the same time fed it was the so-called arts and

Knowledgeable automobile enthusiasts are aware that cars need not be markedly old or initially elaborate to provide the basis of collecting enjoyment. Pictured here are beautiful specimens of the 1930 Ford Model A and the 1947 Studebaker.

William A. Hall *(top)*

Zari Brothers' Washington Garage Photograph *(bottom)*

crafts movement that beguiled a substantial portion of literate and leisure female America in the 1890s and early 1900s. The ladies looked about them at the imagined horrors of mass production and decided that the best way to counter them was to bring back an imagined nation of handcraftsmen that never had existed in actuality. The economics of the thing were somewhat dubious, but the general idea was to set up workshops in which old workmen would again make the old things in the old-fashioned way. While it was admitted that subsidization would be required at first, the ladies had so convinced themselves that masses of people would prefer to buy, even if at higher prices, the handmade artifacts that in no time at all the whole system would be put on a paying basis. Little workshops sprang up all over. In one town, for example, there was an old tradition of the community's once having been a center of berry-box manufacture. This was true enough, but even in the 1830s and 1840s the berry boxes had been made there by the tens of millions. It can hardly be asserted that the old craft of berry-box making was revived when two or three old carpenters were set to work making berry boxes by hand, and certainly the berry growers remained curiously uninterested in their output.

The arts and crafts movement as such died out in the face of these realities, but it left behind an even more deeply imbued feminine conviction that the machine was evil and that instinct and logic combined to provide a faith glorifying the handmade as opposed to the mass-produced. It continues to play its disconcerting and contentious role in antique collecting and studies down to the present day, and its patent absurdity has done much to prejudice men against antiques.

Perhaps it is not fair to claim outright, as some have suggested, that the ladies deliberately stole antique collecting for their own, much as the James brothers relieved an express messenger of the cargo entrusted to his care. Perhaps it would be fairer to say that, in the decades referred to above, most men gave up interest in antiques by default, as it were, but this in turn would seem to be carrying things to the opposite extreme. In any event, something happened and the ladies found themselves largely in firm possession of something that previously had not been for the most part theirs. It is a rather hard thing for a man to swallow. The ladies stole antique collecting, insofar as they did steal it, while their men were out building and running

A finely crafted ¾-inch scale model of a Baltimore & Ohio Railroad locomotive. This miniature, a working steam replica, was constructed between 1890 and 1900. Framed above it is a nineteenth-century instructive jigsaw picture puzzle of a locomotive.

Ward Kimball

what their wives and sweethearts looked upon as horrible iron and steel smoke-belching machines and thereby providing leisure time and spending money to a greater number of the gentler sex than had possessed them in any previous era of history. Today men can at last look back at these things objectively and analytically. It is possible to see what did happen when their backs were turned, and to a certain extent at least, an attempt can be made to reclaim a share of what was once honestly men's own. Whether we can get back a fair portion, or, indeed, just how much, all things considered, we might even want back, is, of course, another question altogether.

"Humble, Pious Workmen"

As the male collector pursues his endeavors, he is likely to encounter instances where his fellows, either deadpan or with a wink, depending on the circumstances, will mention one Schimmel or a certain Friend William Smith, or refer knowingly to something as having been made by a "humble, pious workman." Thereby hangs a tale for, applied as it is, this is a part of the special argot men have adopted for antiques.

Men generally are matter-of-fact in their dealings with antiques; they want bare-boned facts, regardless of how difficult it may be to dig them out and authenticate them.

Women, on the other hand, delight in stories about their antiques. It is not so much that they are fond of tales per se; what is revealing in this matter is that the most efficacious stories with the ladies are those wherein the drift is such as to suggest minute production or folk-art origins to the item or items in question, albeit in all candor it must be confessed that many of these stories are deliberately fabricated and circulated by male antique dealers as aids in selling goods to women. It is no accident that what is perhaps the all-time classic anecdote of antique collecting and one that each successive group of collectors and dealers repeats as its very own concerns a lady who expresses interest in a certain item toward the close of a hectic day at an antique show:

"How much is it?" she asks.

"Fifty dollars, ma'am."

"Is there a story that goes with it?"

"Lady, I'm dog-tired. You can have it for twenty-five dollars and do your own lying!"

At times the stories that are retailed on such occasions are so conducive that they take on a more than transient vitality, are repeated and cited, and in time end up as accepted segments of what passes as folk history. Two examples stand out as worthy of special mention because, as already implied, sooner or later anyone who presses into antique collecting is almost certainly going to hear about them!

From the so-called Pennsylvania Dutch country—actually Pennsylvania German—comes the story of the gentle wandering woodcarver, Wilhelm Schimmel, who supposedly gave lovingly crafted carvings in reciprocation for farmhouse hospitality or as gifts to children. Even cast-iron artifacts require, in many minds, a folk-art attribution; from New England comes the equally rapturously delineated saga of Friend William Smith, "a humble, pious workman at the J. & E. Stevens foundry" at Cromwell, Connecticut, who supposedly was permitted by a generous and nonefficiency-minded management to

The Tiffany lamp at the left would be of primary interest to many men collectors as an electrical antique rather than as an example of art glass; the Hotpoint electric plate and vaporizer kettle of the 1920s would be an almost equally interesting electrical collectable.

Madison Square Garden National Antiques Show *(left)*
George S. Indig Photograph *(right)*

halt work whenever the mood served him, cast a few religious-oriented toys and other artifacts, and then take off to peddle them to Connecticut farmhouses. Even the dialogue has been imagined and quoted at times—"Good morrow, madame, I am Friend William Smith, a humble, pious workman doing the good work."

According to the researches of the late Carl W. Drepperd, who himself was denounced by many as a dangerous "popularizer" of antiques—about the worst thing anyone can be called in certain collecting quarters—gentle Schimmel was a habitual drunkard of terrifying mien who would stomp into the saloons of Carlisle, Pennsylvania, and its environs and pound on bars, often exchanging a carving for a drink; he undoubtedly would have frightened the wits out of any housewife or child he approached. The funniest part of the Schimmel business was that, after numerous commentators and dealers had waxed ecstatic over his pure creative folk art, Drepperd demonstrated that there was nothing even original about Schimmel; he had copied his famed carved "folk art" eagles from mass-produced pipes and cast-iron building ornaments! Some people were very unhappy. They need not have been, for legend always is fleeter of foot than fact.

As for Friend William Smith (actually one Friend William Smith, Jr.—"Friend" was his given name and not a religious epithet, although some have even gone so far in attempting to merchandise things attributed to him to describe in detail the frock coat and broad-brimmed Quaker hat he supposedly wore on his back-road peregrinations, evidently deriving them from the picture on a well-known breakfast-cereal package), he may well have been pious, but he hardly was either humble or an employee of the Stevens foundry. At the time he supposedly was basking in their genial permissiveness he actually was the wealthy president of his own large Bridgeport, Connecticut, manufacturing concern, enjoying among other things the contract for all the United States Post Office Department's mail locks. He employed one hundred to two hundred workmen, and when he had occasion to deal with Stevens, it was on the basis of equals, to say the least.

Notwithstanding that these facts had been exposed in the 1940s, when in the 1960s there was identified among a number of old Stevens patterns secured by a collector the one illustrated in Chapter VII, which produced the front of what Stevens cataloged in the 1860s as a

"Church Book Rack," there was much excitement in certain quarters. Tempting offers to buy or rent the pattern so that castings could be made from it were proferred and declined by the owner. Here, certainly, was just the thing that might have been made and sold by the famed "humble, pious workman" of Stevens, and the cause of the excitement generated and the intention behind the offers were manifest.

Both the Schimmel and the Smith stories have become rather bywords of derision among knowledgeable collectors, although it must be admitted they have by now attained a sort of engaging half-life of their own since first aired in the 1930s. When you hear a man, upon being shown some antique, agreeably say, "Yes, it must have been made by Schimmel," he usually means that the article actually is of little or no importance whatsoever. When under similar circumstances a man says, "Yes, it must have been made by Friend William Smith" or "by a very humble, pious workman," the meaning generally is that the article in question is a mass-production piece, a fact that may well greatly enhance rather than detract from its interest and value in the view of discerning collectors.

THE ARTISTRY OF MASS PRODUCTION

The feminine zeal for folk-art and handmade attributions is at once awe-inspiringly wondrous and seemingly almost without any conceivable limits of logic. This does not mean that the thoughtful male collector is completely lacking in interest in and appreciation of the individually crafted article or even of folk art, although the latter name itself certainly is by no means classifiable as a masculine noun. However, men usually possess an innate sense of production facts and quantities, and are aware that probably far better than ninety-five percent of the so-called American folk art is, to say the least, sailing under false colors in the sense in which it customarily is so designated. A very good case could be made out for the fact that the really true American folk art is not at all the art of individual craftsmanship but, rather, the art of the machine, which most assuredly evolved to maturity at the hands of residents of the United States in the nineteenth century. (This is not to suggest, however, as some with peculiar

Comprising as they do the primary business antique, typewriters are among the articles of greatest interest to men collectors. This is a Hammond Multiplex of the World War I period.

W. van Roosbroeck

reasoning have done, that Americans engage in some sort of cold worship of the automated.) It is not the purpose of this book to attempt to make out a detailed case for the mass-produced as the true native folk art other than to the extent that the concept consciously or subconsciously, to a considerable extent at least, does most definitely influence the masculine outlook toward antiques. However, if only as a result of this fact, material will undoubtedly be found throughout the present volume that tends to advance this thesis.

The mere thought will no doubt horrify many of the gentler sex, but even in the early nineteenth century there were factories that turned out immense quantities of the types of utensils and other goods that now so often are erroneously thought to have been handmade and are classed as folk art. It will horrify them even more merely to suggest that it is a fact that, when such factory-made articles could be secured, our ancestors vastly preferred them to the homemade! People usually made things for themselves only when there was no available source of supply—as frequently happened as the frontier moved west, whether "west" was what is now Ohio or Oregon—

Old cameras are another favorite among men collectors. At the top is a typical amateur's camera of the 1880s, an Anthony dry-plate model. The camera at the bottom is a folding Premo model of 1893, also designed for the use of plates.

American Museum of Photography

when they could not afford the manufactured goods, or, although the thought may at first seem a little odd, as what we would today call a hobby. Much primitive painting, quilting, sampler making, and the like was undertaken in precisely this spirit of recreation even at a comparatively early date. Much of the foregoing may strike some as being offered in a sort of believe-it-or-not context, but it is in fact relatively easy to believe once you stop thinking as you have been taught to think by some decades of feminine command of the outlooks on such things, and simply start afresh with a clean slate and an open mind.

Bear in mind throughout this book, save in such references as do bear specifically on actual handcraftsmanship, that from a very early date the manufactured article was preferred. That is why New Englanders fought like cats and dogs in the late eighteenth and early nineteenth century over water rights on fast-flowing streams. That is why a man who possessed a steam engine in the 1830s was by that fact alone a little king. That is why, before the railroads came, we projected and dug canals by the score, in order to carry manufactured goods inland where an eager market awaited them. That is why there was—although at times it has unquestionably been overemphasized and overromanticized—such an extensive peddling traffic in the United States.

The canal fever of the first decades of the nineteenth century possibly provides the best tip-off to what really was happening. They were not dug merely to bring produce from the West—actually a comparatively minor factor at the time. Neither were they dug for the convenience of settlers moving westward, although once in existence they played their parts and bore a substantial portion of this traffic. A primary purpose, if not *the* primary purpose, was to carry manufactured goods to or at least part way toward the Western settlements with greater ease and economy. Many, if not most, of the manufactured goods they carried are things which, when we see surviving specimens today, we are informed are handmade folk art, presumably fabricated on the frontier in the old blockhouse during slow times between Indian attacks!

It is possible that what all this really adds up to is simply that many things that previously have been looked upon and collected as folk art should now properly be regarded and collected as examples of early mass-production manufacturing. To some this suggested alteration in outlook may seem a little pointless. Perhaps this is substantially true in a way. Nevertheless, to the man who is interested in collecting and studying the artifacts of the past it is a very important and essential change in outlook; in a sense it represents and signalizes a distinct alteration from a heretofore prevailing feminine mode of thinking about such matters to a distinctly masculine one.

CHAPTER II

The Rules
of the Game

In antique collecting the enthusiast will encounter many themes but few widely accepted standards or guidelines to which he can repair for reliable direction. At one time or another in their lives, most men have collected stamps, or at least are somewhat familiar with that hobby, including the existence of catalogs that provide a guide, even if not always an entirely satisfactory one, to values. With a few limited exceptions, antique collecting is an entirely different kettle of fish. If stamp collecting might be likened to a neatly laid out and labeled botanical garden, then antique collecting can be said to be a largely unexplored and uncharted wilderness, even in many instances a jungle complete with pitfalls and predators.

This fact, once it is realized, however, seldom proves discouraging, and certainly the less so to men. Many men would like nothing better than to contend with and explore a wilderness, and many aspects of antique collecting as pursued by enthusiasts will be found to present a similar if perhaps somewhat tamer challenge. Many a man has enjoyably hacked his way through the collecting and study of a category of antiques to emerge with results of substantial interest and value to numerous others. Some paths have been well trod by now, but still prove interesting and still offer a field for gaining further knowledge— firearms and clocks, to name but two. Yet even to this day, although there are helpful monographs on various types and makes, there is no such thing as a comprehensive catalog or check list of all firearms or

*Electrical relics from the era of polished wood cases. Left, a combination am-
meter and voltmeter. Right, a four-drop annunciator. Both were produced by the
Voltamp Electric Manufacturing Company in the early 1900s.*

George S. Indig Photograph

all clocks, in the sense that there are such worldwide catalogs of postage stamps.

The ready availability of information may affect a man's choice
of what he will collect in either direction. Without doubt, it is of great
aid and value to be able to refer to fairly comprehensive reference
works dealing with a particular category and be able to use them to
some extent as guides in forming a collection. On the other hand, to
many it is equally if not more rewarding to enter relatively little
plowed fields and look toward being able to make a sizable contribution themselves.

This, too, may be remarked: Specimens as such are usually much
more readily come by in categories that are already rather broadly
collected. Until such time as you may decide to specialize in a particular subdivision, it is fairly easy to assemble rapidly at least a commendable nucleus of a collection of, say, clocks or guns, although it
is to be hoped that the natural enthusiasm of a beginner will be re-
strained to the extent that you do not find yourself a few years later
possessed of a medley of overpriced material or sheer dross.

If you want to collect clocks or guns or some other type of widely collected material, you can start on your way simply by visiting almost any antiques shop or show. On the other hand, if your inclinations turn to a category or categories that are as yet relatively little collected, you will almost certainly have to do a considerable amount of exploration and digging, not only to learn something concerning your selected subject, but also to locate your initial specimens and continue to find more at a satisfying rate of speed. Many beginners automatically assume that, simply because they decide to collect something they regard as "antiques," they will find examples of the desired articles available in any shop or show that includes the word "antiques" in its name. On the contrary, they may archly be advised that what they seek are not considered antiques, that no proper antiques dealer would handle such trash, and that if the inquirer really is so lacking in taste as seriously to consider collecting such things, he should look for them in junk shops, Salvation Army stores, and the like. Such information can be and often is imparted in a very snobbish and disdainful manner.

A locomotive cab clock built by the Seth Thomas Clock Company. It was origi-
inally mounted in the cab of a Southern Pacific Railroad locomotive built about
1870.

Ward Kimball

The aware collector knows that he often can find numerous promising examples of things he seeks in precisely the type of outlets mentioned above. It is always satisfying to take up the collecting of such once-scorned categories and find, a decade or so later, that the very shops that once disprized them now avidly are seeking and featuring them. Then, too, in the natural course of things, a collection usually can be built up at considerably less expense if it is based on items not widely collected at the time it is commenced, although this, as with all fiscal matters pertaining to antiques, should, theoretically at least, not enter into calculations pertaining to collecting choices. Antique collecting undergoes a continual progression; yesterday's junk becomes today's acceptables and tomorrow's prizes, usually with consequently paralleling increments in value. This book covers many categories of collectables only recently come into their own, just now coming into their own, and others that, insofar as such things accurately can be predicted, will be collected widely in the future. In the last third of the twentieth century many potentially interesting, valid, and worthwhile categories eventually destined for widespread popularity are still open to the novice collector. Because of the inevitable progression mentioned above, there will always be additional categories opening up in the future.

It's Fun . . . If

There really are no hard and fast rules to collecting antiques, but if there plausibly might be, rule No. 1 probably would be not to take yourself or your collecting too seriously. Hobbies such as antique collecting are advocated as healthful and generally relaxing and beneficial. On the other hand, if pursued to extremes they can and almost invariably will have the exactly opposite effect.

The collecting of antiques can be good fun and relaxation, if:

you are willing to accept the personal validity of your own tastes and preferences and not take as absolute and exclusive truth the dictum of the so-called experts and pace setters—or writers, specifically not excluding the writer of this book;

you do not approach it primarily from the standpoint of an investment in the expectation of immediate or eventual profit;

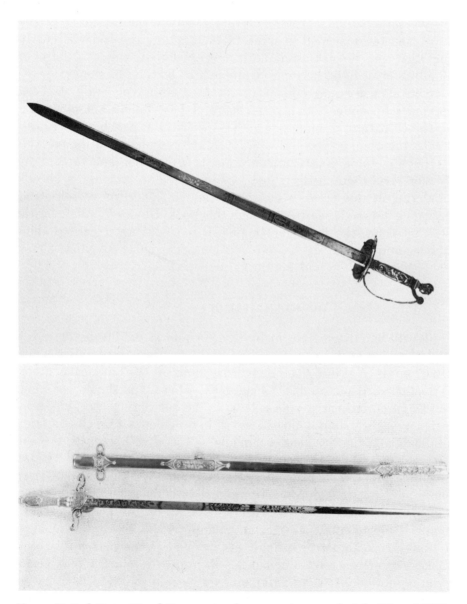

Top, a United States Naval Congressional presentation sword of the War of 1812.
Bottom, a United States Army paymaster sword, model 1840.

United States Naval Academy Museum *(top)*
West Point Museum *(bottom)*

you possess sufficient self-control not to allow yourself to be carried away and overextended in terms of time, effort, and financial outlay; and that you do not assemble a collection that, either in terms of numbers or of bulk, becomes a problem of housing or storage;

you conceive and adhere to—at least until you really feel the ground solid under your feet—a more or less definite but practically restricted pattern of interest whether wholly or in part based on historical, utilitarian, or decorative grounds, or a combination thereof.

Each of these points probably merits elaboration and further discussion, but there really should be no need to provide a specific rendering at this point. Much of the above should prove self-elaborating as the reader carries through this book. However, whatever the starting point, the intelligent man will soon discern a curious thing about antiques that all too often is overlooked, namely, that almost everything overlaps and interlocks to a startling degree.

Choosing a Subject or Subjects

It will be obvious that many things could as readily be described and classified under one or several headings than those under which they appear. A prime example will be found in the Studebaker transformation card pictured in Chapter IX, where it is shown, as seems most appropriate, as a political item. Put out during the 1912 campaign, a slight manipulation of the slide provides in turn photographs of the three main Presidential candidates, Theodore Roosevelt, William Howard Taft, and Woodrow Wilson. This is a piece that might well fall within several categories of antiques. It is a photographic antique. Even more, perhaps, it is an optical antique. It is an advertising antique, either for a collection of advertising materials or as a part of a collection relating to transportation in general or to horse-drawn vehicles. It is also an automotive antique, even though, somewhat curiously, it makes no reference to Studebaker self-propelled vehicles. It is also a printing antique. It is an antique of the novelty business. It is by no means impossible that this list is not exhaustive. An alert collector in some other highly particularized category might well find it properly falls within his sphere of interest, for instance, a collector of things relating to the inventor, A. S. Spiegel, or a collector of the products of the manufacturer, the Republic Novelty Company, of Chicago.

Old books of mechanical interest. Left, The Book of Illustrious Mechanics of Europe and America *(Aberdeen, 1848); center,* The Artist's Guide and Mechanic's Own Book *(Boston, 1856); and, right,* A History of Inventions, Discoveries, and Origins *(two volumes, London, 1846).*

George S. Indig Photograph

Many of the things illustrated present potentialities for interest in more than one category. Often these variations in interest are expressed in terms of material, definition, function, application, and similar classifications. A collector's item may even at times be properly classified by implication. An old whiskey bottle is at once an example of glassware (material), a container (function), and a relic of the history of the liquor business. A pottery stout bottle or gin jug would not be of interest to a collector of glass objects, but it would certainly fall within the interests of those collecting in the second and third categories. On the other hand, an old glass telegraph insulator, apart from being of interest to hobbyists specializing in insulators as such, would also at once be a glass antique and an electrical antique. A cast-iron cigar cutter is at once of interest to collectors specializing in cigar cutters, tobacco and smoking relics in general, and old cast-iron artifacts. A Coca-Cola lamp is at once an antique lamp, an advertising antique, and a relic of the soft-drink business.

Other potentially multiple fields of interest will be apparent in the illustrations herein and in things the collector continually will run across as he pursues his avocation. It is always rather gratifying when

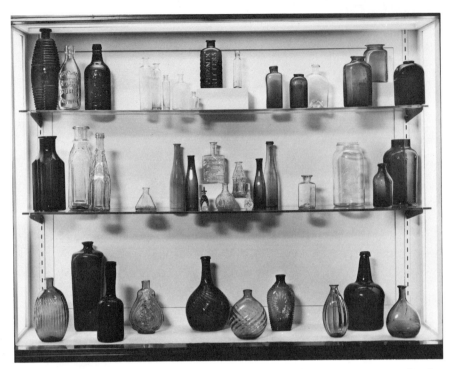

*The present-day trend toward the appreciation of the enormous promotional value
inherent in their antiques on the part of business and trade associations is typified
by this view of a display of free-blown and mold-blown bottles of the 1750–1900
period maintained by the Glass Container Manufacturers Institute, Inc.*

Glass Container Manufacturers
Institute, Inc.

a hobbyist can discern a connection with his own special interest in
an article that is being offered as something entirely different or that
at first thought apparently has no connection whatsoever with his
specialty.

Perhaps equally important to illustrating this point, the foregoing
will provide many indirect hints to a collector for selecting a particular subject or subjects of interest and for setting his own ground rules
and limitations. There is no particular reason why a collector should
not set rather broad bounds for himself. However, experience has
shown that most collectors eventually tend to limit themselves and
specialize, and there is much truth in the old adage about biting off
more than you can chew. For many hobbyists there is an enormous
satisfaction in getting together a good and comprehensive assemblage
of articles within a rather limited sphere—satisfaction both in the collection itself and for the opportunity it presents for serious study within
a narrow field and the consequent ability to contribute something
permanently meaningful to the total store of knowledge.

On the other hand, if the pattern appeals to you personally, there is in truth much to be said for a very broad and rather scatter-gun approach to collecting. This type of collecting is far less likely to become obsessive; the collector is less likely to awake one morning and find that instead of riding his hobby, his hobby is riding him. Many men find it pleasurable simply to collect whatever happens to appeal to them as a possession or a decoration: a few old bottles, a couple of old guns, an old typewriter, an old player piano, a few old toys, an old advertising lithograph, and so on. Many a parlor, den, game room, or office now is most interestingly decorated with some such general collection, some of which may be functional, or at least operative. It goes without saying, however, that when men specifically plan such collections with a decorative purpose in view, they must be wary of decorators' shops or booths at antique shows proffering such things as old sewing machines converted into bases for flower pots, which have about as much attraction as a culture of bubonic plague.

ANTIQUES AS AN AID TO BUSINESS

There is a question of long standing and one that in all probability can never be finally settled one way or another as to whether in choosing a category to collect a man is best advised and will find greatest satisfaction in collecting things associated with his business or profession, or in collecting things completely removed from his workaday affairs. Should a doctor collect old medical books, instruments, and bottles, or should he collect aeronautical materials, toys, or typewriters? Can a hardware store owner find relaxation in collecting old tools and ironwork, or would he find it more rewarding to collect anything other than articles directly or indirectly connected with the hardware business? Should a man who works in an office all day collect old typewriters; a man who drives a truck all day collect automobiliana?

At one time it was very widely held that for optimum benefits any hobby should be something completely removed, preferably as far as possible, from a man's breadwinning activities. The theory is still widely held and in many instances has validity. On the other hand, many men become interested in and begin actively pursuing a hobby because it relates to or is an outgrowth of their business interests.

A nineteenth-century Chinese carved-ivory group consisting of three figures representing sons showing off to their father.

Milwaukee Public Museum

Avocations of this type may prove just as relaxing, rewarding, and generally beneficial as the type that centers upon an interest totally removed from work. In recent years a great many men have taken up the collecting of antiques that relate to their trades and professions. It would appear that the really important and determining factor is just how interested a man is or can become in the history of his line of work and of the product or services he handles.

In some instances, collections of antiques relating to a given product or service possess definite and substantial commercial value. Displays of old products, packages, posters, and similar materials are not only interesting in offices, showrooms, and stores, but have enormous value as sales promotional aids when properly organized and packed so that they can be sent out as displays to conventions, retail outlets, expositions, and other affairs often not directly related with the business at hand. These collections are almost always creators of attention and traffic, and they can bring wide public notice to a company without cost other than that of shipping the display in places where, under other circumstances, such attention could not be purchased for any sum. As a result, many business and trade associations are today gathering and displaying collections of antiques. The man who collects antiques connected with his business may not only be pursuing an enjoyable hobby but also creating an extremely valuable promotional asset for his commercial endeavor. This applies equally to the owner of a store who garners free publicity by placing a collection on display in noncompetitive store windows throughout his area, and to the president of a large corporation who may keep several displays on continual nationwide move.

On the other side of the coin, many commercial enterprises that make use of such displays derive equal benefit by showing collections in no wise directly related to their businesses. As a result, there are today not only individuals who collect antiques connected with their

Two coin-operated vending machines for dispensing tobacco products. Left, a British brass "Honor Box," for snuff or perhaps rough-cut tobacco, circa 1800. The customer was honor-bound to reclose the lid, hence the name. Right, a machine that sold a single cigarette for a penny, manufactured circa 1915 by the Wilson Manufacturing Company, New York, N.Y.

The Vendo Company

business, but businesses that are building up collections of antiques, either or both for their purely historical interest or for their promotional value.

Collectors frequently find that arranging to display a portion of their collections in store windows or at local affairs is a good means

Old typewriters are a prime favorite among men collectors, both as mechanical artifacts in themselves and because of their importance in the history of business. Shown here is a portion of the old typewriters owned by David Golden, including late nineteenth- and early twentieth-century machines.

David Golden

of self-advertising and of locating and acquiring additional specimens. This can be overdone, however, and there is a definite point where results in terms of acquisitions are not worth the effort and the inevitable wear and tear on the articles displayed. Unavoidable damage and deterioration must be taken into consideration in permitting collections to be displayed, other than when permanently housed behind glass in the home or office. No matter how carefully a collection may be handled, either by the owner or his surrogates, it is virtually impossible to avoid wear and tear when a collection travels for display. As a result, many private collectors refuse to display their specimens under any circumstances, or retain a small group of duplicates specifically for this purpose. When a collection is especially set up for use in commercial promotions, however, fear of possible damage to specimens in transit and handling naturally is seldom considered an inhibiting factor.

BUYING: NOTES FOR THE BEGINNER

Once the intention has been established to collect one or more categories, there is scarcely anything in the world to equal the ferocious impatience of the new collector to acquire specimens in his chosen area. The only question is where and how to find and acquire the desired collectables.

Captain Kidd was, according to tradition, by way of being a collector. His method of acquisition is not to be recommended, although as the enthusiast moves out into the collecting world he may very likely find individuals who evidently have never taken such an injunction to heart. They can and often do give a hobby a bad name. Overt robbery and more subtle forms of con games apart, it may be said with a fair degree of accuracy that almost anything goes, or, at least, that there are those who will try to make almost anything go.

Buying antiques is at once a game of skill and a game of chance. The more a collector knows about his subject, the better prepared he will be to avoid pitfalls and defend himself. There are certain categories with fairly well established scales of rarity, desirability—which is not by any means synonymous with mere rarity as such—and values. But once a collector gets out into a relatively new field he is

Fire-station alarm bell manufactured by the Gamewell Fire-Alarm Telegraph Company of New York, measuring twenty-five inches in height. This specimen was removed from an old Los Angeles, California, firehouse, where this type of apparatus was used from the 1880s to the 1920s.

Ward Kimball

pretty much on his own. He may be offered articles at prices that represent real bargains, which may lead him into the error of believing that he can secure virtually everything he wants at substantially the same level and that anyone who quotes higher figures must be some kind of a swindler. He may well also be offered and buy specimens at prices that subsequent knowledge tells him were much too high, which does not necessarily mean that he has been deliberately victimized. The beginner, in fact, in his initial zeal to start building his collection is very likely to find later that he has paid too much for certain items; he will probably also run into the traditional and very-frequently-met-with beginner's luck and acquire some fine specimens extremely reasonably or even as gifts from people who either are sincerely interested in assisting him or who simply do not share his enthusiasm for certain items they happen to have long possessed.

On an uncharted sea and one where determinations of value, especially at the hands of dealers, are often matters of highly personal opinion, the collector may well be quoted widely varying prices for identical articles. On the other hand, he may fail to recognize that

seemingly identical articles actually display certain important variations, often recognizable by knowledgeable collectors or dealers but
of whose existence he is not yet aware, such variations as may mark
the difference between a common and a scarce version of substantially
the same thing, a slight change in design or a difference in color, for
example. The beginner may also find himself somewhat staggered by
the seemingly high prices quoted and presumably paid for certain
articles which appear to him neither particularly old nor prepossessing,
for, in the main, neither age nor intrinsic value is related to collectors'
values.

Buying antiques is not necessarily a continuous conflict between
buyer and seller, but often it does take on the aspects of a duel. It
must be remembered that in few instances is there such a thing as a
catalog price and in none a list price where antiques are concerned.
The fact that a dealer gives an item a certain price does not mean it
is worth that. For the most part, once outside categories with which
they are familiar, dealers are as much afraid of being taken as are
collectors. Many dealers automatically price articles with which they

*A portion of an extensive collection of druggist's antiques displayed in the home
of Mr. and Mrs. Warren Blair. Included among the articles pictured here are
show globes, apothecary jars, bottles, and scales.*

Mr. and Mrs. Warren Blair,
G. William Holland Photograph

are not conversant fairly high. It is up to the collector with time and experience to learn the subtleties of his category so that he can tell that one item is a splendid buy at X dollars while another and similar one is grossly overpriced. Overpricing is relative; what is high today may appear a great bargain at the same price in five or six years' time. Then again, it may not, although, generally speaking, the trend of antiques values and prices continually has been upward and, barring a major economic upset, in a basically inflationary economy probably will continue to be.

The collector, having in the last analysis no source of guidance in most instances other than his own knowledge, must decide whether he wants an item sufficiently to pay the requisite price, give or take a little bargaining on occasion. Having bought, he must be prepared to have no regrets and to chalk up to experience any disappointments that later experience and enhanced knowledge reveal.

In the main, a collector will acquire a substantial proportion of his specimens through purchase, whether from antique dealers, secondhand stores, other collectors, or private individuals. Trading

The proper application of the word "antique" is always comparative. Collectors recognize as an antique radio one manufactured in the 1920s or 1930s; as an antique television set, one made in the 1930s or 1940s. This is a General Electric television set of 1948.

George S. Indig Photograph

The Schreibkugel, the pioneer European typewriter whose name provides type-writer collectors with their favorite code designation for the object of their collect-ing: "kugels." This represents the simpler, non-electric form of the Schreibkugel, made in the early 1870's.

The Smithsonian Institution

with other collectors can be an important and rewarding mode of securing articles. In time the hobbyist may possess sufficient knowl-edge and enough duplicate or surplus items for such transactions to make up a noticeable portion of his acquisitions. But collectors pos-sessed of desirable duplicates not unnaturally want to exchange them only for articles of similar quality and in most instances the beginner is unlikely himself to possess much trading material at all, or at least of a nature that is of interest to a more experienced collector. When, on occasion, a novice does acquire something of rarity and value, he will probably find himself the recipient of many attractive offers to trade, frequently being offered a number of commoner pieces for the single article. Such offers usually are most attractive to novices, and here the beginner must confront and solve to his own satisfaction the classic collecting question of quantity for quality, and must decide whether he would rather possess several items which he quite prob-ably will again have opportunities to acquire later, or a single piece which, once disposed of, he may well never have an opportunity to obtain again.

A word should also be said here concerning antique price-guides, of which there has been a considerable proliferation in recent years. They usually appear to offer the beginner a shortcut to a comprehensive knowledge of relative values and specific prices; actually, it would seem quite accurate to say that, with the possible exception of a few highly specialized lists, knowledgeable collectors usually regard such price guides pretty much as a joke and, if anything, highly misleading, for the beginner most particularly. There are two reasons for this. The first is that antique prices, especially on the better items, tend to change so rapidly that many quotations become obsolete almost before the guides can report them. Furthermore, some quotations, while perhaps accurately enough reporting prices at which the items actually were sold, may be out-and-out flukes; they may represent a fantastically high price paid by an uninformed buyer or even by a knowledgeable collector who was aware that he was going overboard but wanted a particular item, perhaps to fill in a series or to use in a trade, enough to pay much too much. The second is that, within the space allotted, descriptions usually cannot possibly be sufficiently detailed as to variations, color, condition, and other factors of extreme importance in determining values for the quotations to be of any real use to an aware collector. This is particularly true within precisely those areas in which a male collector is likely to be most interested. In many if not most instances the sellers who report the transactions are themselves entirely unaware of what information is required or the actual points upon which the sale was made. Quotations may be much too high or much too low when related to similar but slightly different items.

THE SILENT COLLECTORS

As collecting interest inures, artifacts usually progress through various stages of dealer notice and acceptability. During the period before a category of antiques "arrives," knowledgeable collectors usually can have a field day, buying the better items and rejecting the lesser, all of them usually being priced about the same. Later, a new category will become so widely collected that their gradations of value will start to become recognized, although all too many novice collectors wantonly cut their own throats by circulating want lists

Pictorial material of interest to maritime enthusiasts. Top, an announcement of the departure of a steamboat of the late 1830s. Below, a French print of the mid-nineteenth century depicting the topsail schooner Balaou.

G. William Holland Collection *(top)*
The Old Print Shop *(bottom)*

and bid sheets for the better items, a foolish practice that invariably results in raising all prices too quickly above a normal development based on supply and demand. On the other hand, while monetary gains are properly far from the prime interest of any real hobbyist, there is little sense or merit in a long-drawn-out collecting endeavor and paying commendable prices at times unless there eventually is sufficiently widespread recognition of certain inherent values in the materials collected to assure that the individual collector is not merely quietly whistling in the dark, entrapped in a completely private world of distinctions and values which no one other than himself is prepared to recognize and accept. Somewhere along the line there must be found a suitable median between silent private collecting and a sudden boom in a newly "discovered," popular collectable. Nonetheless, in the initial stages of opening up new categories, the pioneers may properly be allowed a fair period to institute and develop a collecting area for themselves. All too often, to talk up a hobby interest too soon and too grandly has the result of an illogical and intemperate boom.

Having learned the hard way from previous experience, many men have acquired a measure of what might be regarded as cunning or adroitness, depending on one's viewpoint. In recent years a substantial body of male collectors has managed to conceal or at least to some extent obscure the degree of interest in such things as old electrical equipment, sporting goods, household appliances, photography material, typewriters, and so on. In a number of instances sagacious pioneer collectors have adopted code names or euphemisms in order to conceal their interest in certain categories, most particularly in discussing them with each other at antique shows and other crowded areas. For example, the code name for old electrical goods has been "sparks"; for old typewriters it has been "kugels," which is derived from Schreibkugel, the name of a very early European typewriter, the word literally meaning "writing sphere." With these and related deceptions, they have managed to conceal from many dealers the existence of a very substantial interest in many of these things.

Some would no doubt prefer to continue this state of affairs almost indefinitely, but, as pointed out above, there always must come a time when a popular collecting interest must be revealed and chronicled for what it is, or it is likely to take on too much of the air of merely an "in" joke or a personal conceit.

Nineteenth-century silver shaving mugs, including a repoussé "scuttle" mug with hinged top (left) and left- and right-hand utility shaving cups of the 1850s.

W. Porter Ware

The publication of the present volume unquestionably marks the time, and even the necessity, to reveal and admit some of the things that many collectors previously have preferred to hold to themselves. There will no doubt be many hobbyists who will object to these revelations and who would have preferred to enjoy silently strengthening their collections a while longer, although they may feel compensated for this deprivation by the thought that, as already pointed out, there are no real and accepted values without acknowledgment that the category or categories in question actually are fairly widely collected. No doubt some supposedly knowing commentators and dealers will feel chagrined at the way they have been, if not misled, at least mystified and perhaps somewhat thwarted. No one really need feel too disappointed, most especially collectors. There will be ample new categories to be similarly silently developed in the years and decades to come.

"Bird-Dogging" the Shops and Shows

The experienced collector—and this trait applies equally to men and women—can almost instantly recognize or sense whether there is any possibility that a given antiques shop or booth at an antiques show carries the type of article he or she is collecting. Such identifications can even at times be extended to complete antiques shows. Often the type of booth, shop, or show that is likely to prove most promising to a male collector is somewhat different from that of interest to a woman. Men who collect masculine antiques are quick to learn that they usually are not to be found in shops and booths that neatly array furniture, porcelain, glass, and the like. The customary designation for this type of material is "hottery and pottery," and men seldom bother to inquire for their wants at what they refer to as "hottery and pottery shops" or "hottery and pottery booths." Rather, they are aware that the shops and booths that fill every available foot of space with massed treasures of every kind are likely to prove the most fruitful hunting grounds for what they seek.

Although, to the uninitiated or to the less fastidious, such arrays are likely to seem so conglomerate as to be hopeless, the experienced collector soon learns that he will almost unerringly pick out examples of his specialty regardless of how much other material surrounds it. A man rapidly develops this ability almost to a level of instinctiveness equivalent to that of his hunting dog with a bird. For the novice collector, who assumes that because he is collecting antiques every booth at an antique show is likely to prove promising, and even somewhat naïvely believes that his specialty will be acknowledged to be a properly collectable antique by every dealer, a visit to an antique show

Left, china mule souvenir of the Pikes Peak Railroad, early 1900's. Right, carnival glass nut dish employed in the promotion of My-T-Fine pudding in the late 1920s, one of the few items used in such promotions that is definitely identifiable.

George S. Indig Photograph

made up of fifty or a hundred dealers in company with an old hand on the trail will prove a revelation. The experienced man will "bird-dog" a show in an hour or so while the beginner would spend a day and still miss something. If the experienced collector subsequently hears of an article being secured at the show that would have been of interest to him, he can usually feel assured that he did not miss it; it was brought in after his visit.

The beginner finds this difficult to believe, but after a surprisingly short time he will suddenly realize that he, too, has acquired the knack.

HOUSING A COLLECTION

Interesting as may be the use of antiques in displays or as decorations, the serious collector never worries if some or even most of his items must be kept packed away rather than on continual dumb show. The important thing is that he has studied them and learned from them, that they form their link or links in his overall collection. Indeed, it is often far better that articles be carefully packed away and protected than improperly exposed so as to require continual dusting and beset with all the risks inherent in careless handling. In the case of many articles, repeated handling even with the greatest care eventually results in wear and deterioration of finish. Of course, some categories stand open display and handling much better than do others, and there may always be some articles in a collection that it is desirable to keep out either for decoration or actual use. Comparative deterioration from exposure and handling is particularly high in the case of old items that the collector has been fortunate enough to obtain in brand-new condition.

How a collection should be housed and displayed naturally depends to a considerable extent on the type of antiques involved. There is not much point in securing and maintaining an old automobile unless it can be kept under cover; many automobile collectors are limited in their aspirations by available garage space. Many small and delicate articles make housing in glass cases or compartments a must. The average collector soon exhausts available proper display housing and packs things away to protect them. Specially built cases usually

Early whiskey bottles. Left to right, amber with applied seal, 1850s, "Chestnut Grove Whiskey C.W.," put out by Charles Wharton and made by the Whitney Glass Works; dark olive green, ca. 1855, B. Barstow and Company, made by H. Ricketts & Co., a British glassworks; and, pale olive green, 1860s, "Wm. H. Daly Sole Importers New York."

Bill Wilson

are expensive. Many collectors find relatively economical secondhand china closets, bookcases, or other glass-fronted furnishings ideal for at once protecting and showing off all or portions of their collections. Open shelving can be fairly inexpensively built and finished by most hobbyists themselves, but its use naturally carries with it the element of exposure.

Extremes of heat or cold are harmful to many categories of collectors' items, and direct sunlight is almost always an enemy, often fading even seemingly substantially finished articles before the damage is realized. In this connection, it ought also to be observed that fluorescent lighting has the quality not of fading artifacts, but of distorting colors and tones, often matters of extreme importance in collecting and in distinguishing variations. As a result, most knowledgeable collectors purposely eschew fluorescent lighting in areas where their collections are displayed or studied, preferring to employ regulation incandescent lights.

How Old Is an Antique?

While merely acquiring and perhaps displaying or using antiques is sufficient hobby activity for many antiques collectors, most men regard the ultimate satisfaction as studying their specimens and researching their backgrounds. They find this is particularly appealing in the case of mass-produced articles where there is obviously a definite product, manufacturing, business, advertising, and personal background to be charted if the facts can be secured. Research of this kind usually requires a great deal of time and effort, but most men feel the effort is well worthwhile and find it as enjoyable as the acquisition of the specimens themselves. It is also of considerable value insofar as it assists in arranging a collection by revealing the exact dates of specimens and the sequence of models and of minor variations.

As brought out in Chapter I, men are seldom put off by the discovery that something is not so old as it was initially thought to be. Men generally are not bemused by the supposed importance of "old" or "first," or whether correctly or erroneously attributed, or by either hasty or traditional attributions. The prudent and experienced collector seldom accepts at face value what he is told concerning an item unless he feels assured that the proffered information comes from a reasonably reliable source. He takes what he is told by the average seller with a grain of salt, buys the article if he feels it is worthy in itself, and then does his own research. Vendors' stories, even when true, may give little information regarding the age or value of an item. The fact that something came from "a family that settled here before the Revolution" or from a house or store that is "more than a hundred years old" does not, of course, guarantee the age of the object itself. Even personal stories from original owners are not in most cases particularly to be relied upon, although there never is any benefit in disputing them or pointing out such things as that an article asserted to be dated by the fact that it belonged to a forebear who died the same year as General Custer bears a 1907 patent date. The advisable procedure under all similar circumstances is to buy or not to buy as you choose, but never to argue; you will merely be taken for a sharper trying to pull a fast one in an effort to beat down the price.

For the most part, men are tolerant of the practical difficulties that must inevitably preclude anyone from becoming an expert on dozens or hundreds of highly specialized subjects simply because he has hung up a sign proclaiming himself a dealer in antiques. This does not mean that men cannot be self-deceived by wishful thinking or by the innocent or willful fallaciousness of others; the very word "sucker" somehow generally implies a male. Men usually like to think that they cannot be "taken"; as a consequence, they frequently are, and all that can be done here is to post a few warning signs.

Sooner or later the collector is likely to be archly informed that an antique as defined by United States law must be at least a hundred years old and that many or all of the things he has been happily collecting are not antiques at all and he had better not call them by that name. He may also be condescendingly informed that articles of lesser age may be referred to as "collectables," "collectors' items," or sometimes even as "courtesy antiques." It is in fact true that there is a statute on the books that defines an antique as an object at least a hundred years old; but it is a definition for customs purposes only. Initially, in 1930, the Congress of the United States permanently set the date as one hundred years previous, at 1830. This greatly delighted many slightly Neolithic types who felt it was the date roughly defining

A nineteenth-century boxed set of rack and pinion movable astronomical slides for a professional magic lantern, manufactured by Carpenter and Westley, London, England. The slide in the center foreground with seven concentric racks shows the eight-planet solar system as then known, Uranus and Neptune being on the same outer ring.

George S. Indig Photograph

the dawn of that ever-to-be-mentioned-with-horror Machine Age, forever cutting off from recognition anything produced during that crude and artless period or subsequently ever into the uncharted future. As the decades passed, it became increasingly obvious that a fixed date was ill-advised. Furthermore, many of those who had hailed it in the 1930s found somewhat later that it was limiting their latter-day importing efforts, not to mention having a generally inhibiting effect on sales. In 1967 the definition was altered to a progressive one hundred years—1867 in 1967, and 1868 in 1968, 1869 in 1969, and so on.

Save to a few antiques snobs or to such as may contemplate an ill-advised attempt to defraud the United States Customs Service, the definition is in any case meaningless. Everyone else knows right well what an antique is in the view of the vast majority of people, collectors or not, and everyone uses the word in a popular and readily understood manner. Furthermore, as the pace of life, innovation, and even obsolescence speeds up, the interval it takes for an article or an entire category to be looked upon and sought as an antique lessens. Every man, for instance, understands that an antique radio is today regarded as one manufactured in the 1920s or 1930s, and that an antique television set—and there already are a number of collectors of antique television sets—is recognized as one made in the 1930s or 1940s. Furthermore, they are aware that these dates will inevitably progress rapidly; even in the late 1960s there were collectors of radios who were starting to set aside and retain sets made in the 1940s.

It goes without saying that there must be some, especially among those who have in one way or another possessed a long-standing connection with antiques, who grimace even to hear an expression such as "antique radio." On the other hand, many of these same people find nothing grotesque in using the term "antique lamp" even when applied to an art-glass lamp of the 1920s that is actually contemporary with the "antique radio." A lamp can be of variable age; the word when used in antiques circles itself suffices to imply a background of whale oil, hence to term a lamp from the early 1920s, even though an electric one, an "antique lamp" is to such thinkers not at all an act of impropriety, while "antique radio" seems a self-revealing abomination.

PRICES AND TRENDS

Many of what might be termed "old-line" or "conventional" antiques commentators and dealers are also disturbed that many of the things whose collecting stature has been developed wholly or at least in the main through masculine enthusiasm are today among the most sought, prized, and costly of antiques. They are in the view of such thinkers insultingly priced and prized out of all proportion to what they may select to call "real antiques." In short, they can accept a price in five figures for a fine highboy made shortly before the Burr-Hamilton duel, but not the fact that certain automobiles manufactured about the time Princip potted the Archduke Franz Ferdinand may readily command a similar figure. If such prices strike a reader as high, as indeed they most certainly are, it can be said that the same duality of outlook and acceptance obtains right down the line, through articles that customarily sell in four figures, in three, in two, and even in one. To those who reason thus, five dollars, say, for some oddment made in the 1830s seems logical; five dollars for something

Cardboard advertising display pieces. Left, a 20-inch-high Winners cigar sign of 1898. Right, Coca-Cola window display cut-outs of 1909–1910.

Ward Kimball *(left)*
The Archives, The Coca-Cola Company,
Atlanta, Georgia *(right)*

made in the 1930s must perforce appear irrational. The whole situation of relatively high prices for late, mass-produced artifacts strikes them as shockingly irreverent, vulgar, ridiculous, and completely opposed to the accepted order of things. This shock, it must be pointed out, is often compounded by the starkly fiscal fact that, when such comparatively recent antiques lay as fields wide open before them, they did not deign to descend from Olympus to enter into what was going on below, and often treated those who did cavalierly and with a scarcely concealed contempt.

They missed the boat and, even long after it was obviously sailing on a successful voyage, all they could do was to profess to believe it was all a fluke that would inevitably end up on abiding reefs. In short, they had been schooled in the old basically feminine-oriented antiques world and simply could not conceive of what a masculine-oriented antiques world would be like should it emerge. Furthermore, they had to a considerable extent come to look upon trends in antiques as something to be artificially launched and nurtured when the occasion was ripe and appeared to call for popularizing new groups of collectables; that trends actually could launch and nurture themselves was to many of them simply incomprehensible.

It should hastily be emphasized that any talk of high prices, even in so loosely and indefinite terms as three figures, four figures, and so on, is highly dangerous. There are always far too many who are willing to take the exception in any category for the standard or even the commonplace. Far from every automobile manufactured around 1914 is valued as highly as noted here; the majority certainly are not, nor anywhere near such a figure. The eager collector still can secure at considerably lower prices examples of articles similar to those that command the top prices. This is true throughout every category of antiques and it must always be borne in mind that, because one piece sells for a startlingly high sum, every closely or distantly related piece does not necessarily have a similar value. It is the awareness of the informed collector as regards his specialty that creates these great price differentials whereby one item in, say, a particular original color avidly is sought and sells for ten or twenty or more times the figure that the same thing but in a different original color, or even a different shade, will bring if, indeed, as in many cases, the latter can find a ready market at all. The highly scientific and logical manner in which most categories of masculine antiques have been studied and arranged in a relatively short span of time still proves a great wonder and puzzlement to those who for one reason or another have failed to initiate themselves into their intricacies.

This basic point about specific items, models, or minor variations often commanding prices greatly in excess of others or most of their general type cannot be emphasized too strongly. The failure fully to appreciate this is the cause of endless disappointments, misunderstandings, and bad feelings on the part of both collectors and dealers.

In all fairness insofar as concerns the perception of the validity and permanence of trends in antiques popularity in their early stages, it must be admitted that it is an extremely difficult thing about which to make successful predictions. This is especially true with those trends that commence and grow substantially of their own accord. There have been few successful prophets in the antiques game, whether from a positive or a negative standpoint. As regards the latter, there is almost always considerable diversion to be obtained through reading in books and magazines of only a few decades ago the various reasoned explanations as to why this or that collecting trend was only a regrettable departure from good sense and why the articles in question could never be accepted as valid collectables by persons of intelligence and taste. Sometimes these trends do fizzle out, although almost never for the reasons adduced. In any event, it should be underlined that as a general rule it is an extremely dangerous thing to speculate in antiques in the expectation of making a quick killing on the basis of prophecies, supposed trends, or just plain intuition. Theoretically, in an idealized context, it is not considered desirable for anyone to attempt thus to commercialize a hobby. Such niceties apart, from a purely practical standpoint experience has shown that almost invariably those who attempt such manipulations get their fingers burned, often badly.

On the other hand—although it is by no means certain if this thought is truly opposed to the foregoing—it is possible that in this last third of the twentieth century the age of innocence as concerns antiques has largely passed. Too many people now are more or less aware of the fact that if you keep anything old, or even merely obsolete, long enough it will eventually take on some interest and value

Planes are particular favorites among collectors of old tools. Shown here are a smoothing plane of American or British origin, dated 1727 (top), and an elaborately incised Dutch smoothing plane of 1756.

Old Sturbridge Village Photo *(top)*
The Smithsonian Institution *(bottom)*

as a collector's item. How important and desirable it will become still, of course, is a moot question, but the general concept is now fairly well known and accepted. All too often, of course, the hopeful owner of some such artifact finds that it by no means possesses the value he anticipated it held, an awakening which, human nature being what it is, is often accompanied by a feeling akin to that likely to come over a man who has actually engaged in an unsuccessful speculation.

ORIGINALITY AND RESTORATION

The novice antique collector is almost certain to hear a great deal concerning the relative desirability of original condition, and the propriety and desirability of so-called restoration. The latter really is a word that can cover a multitude of things, some sinful and some not, and sometimes varying with the particular category of antique that is involved. "Restoration" might, for example, be employed to refer merely to the act of completing an incomplete specimen, using authentic original parts in original condition, a perfectly proper and in all cases acceptable act. Or "restoration" may be used to refer to what might much more accurately be described as repairing something or putting a specimen into working order once more. This, too, is legitimate, although just how important it may actually be in the eyes of an experienced collector and how far an active collector might want to go in this direction are open to question. Actually, in the case of many categories of antiques, working order is of relatively little importance and adds little to the actual cash value of an item. Very often someone with something to sell, or a novice collector, will expend a sum on repair work that actually is substantially in excess of the value the work adds to the specimen. In fact, repair work when clumsily done by someone who feels workability is more important than authenticity actually will materially reduce the value of a specimen. In the process the item may be improperly cleaned, a desirable patina of age polished out forever, the paint retouched or completely done over or other unwitting vandalisms committed. There are numerous instances of such bungling in which a fairly desirable and readily salable item has been reduced to virtually no value at all.

The best advice to anyone possessing anything old that he desires to sell is under no circumstances to do anything whatsoever to it. Ninety-nine times out of a hundred he will not make it more valuable and salable, certainly not in proportion to what he spends on it, and in many cases he will substantially reduce the value. There are innumerable cases of antiques that had their original paint, lettering, and decorations completely ruined or greatly reduced in value through ill-advised attempts to clean them using various common cleansing preparations ranging from commercial detergents to plain and seemingly harmless good old soap and water! Leave the piece strictly alone. Offer it to a collector or a dealer exactly as is and allow him to do whatever he deems proper or necessary after he owns it. You will not be the loser by adhering to this advice.

Unfortunately, there still exist too many antique dealers who are as yet not fully aware of the generally rigid requirements for original state among men who collect. To a woman, appearance often is the greatest factor in determining the purchase of an antique. To a man, originality is almost always the matter of greatest importance. Nat-

Old amusement machines. Left to right, "The Elk" slot machine, 1920s; Unique Gum Machine, early 1900s; a coin-operated fortune-telling machine, "Future Partner and Family," ca. 1920; a stereopticon photograph viewer, not coin-actuated, and a Liberty Bell slot machine, ca. 1920.

Mr. and Mrs. Charles A. Penn, Bumble Bee Trading
Post, Bumble Bee, Arizona, Hogan Smith Photograph

urally, a specimen is desired in as near the original condition as possible, but originality is the prime requisite. Bear in mind that minor differences in finish, paint, lettering, and so on can be of enormous importance in determining the value and desirability of a specimen, and this is most particularly true for men collectors, who usually engage in very serious studies of the articles they collect and of their history and background.

The accepted outlook on originality and restoration can be summed up as follows:

1. Any item is considered far more desirable in its original condition than if wholly or partially refinished or otherwise tampered with.

2. If an antique that originally had some working function is desired for use, such as a clock or a music box, then repair and restoration is permissible.

3. Antiques whose actual use obviously involves factors of human safety, such as old automobiles, airplanes, and the like, must of necessity be reconditioned and restored in order both to assure that safety and to inhibit further deterioration while in use. Obviously, this also applies to such things as, for instance, an old chair on which you plan to sit yourself or to offer to a guest.

There are, as suggested, those who will deny the correctness of the three foregoing points and inform you they are unrealizable dogma of dreamy perfectionists. More frequently, however, they will cite the admitted need to restore such things as old automobiles as proof that restoration is universally desirable and acceptable. You can believe them if you will, but the unalterable fact is that articles in original condition are considered infinitely more desirable by knowledgeable collectors than repaints or restorations, no matter how carefully they may be done and how closely they adhere to the original. There are, of course, individuals who make a business out of repainting and so-called restoring, and of furnishing reproduction parts. Not surprisingly, they will insist that the desire for originality is a snare and a delusion. They will offer to make your old typewriter, toy, vending machine, cigar cutter, or what have you look just like new; so much like new, in fact, that it will deceive a specialist. As a matter of fact, although some of these worthies are capable of turning out some rather nice-looking work, it is almost impossible to fake a finish that cannot be detected, and in their boasting they seemingly fail to appreciate or care about the truly awesome danger that would be presented to all collectors were this possible. As a matter of fact, reputable restorers are proud of their work and, far from making an effort to conceal it, mark it as such.

FAKES AND REPRODUCTIONS

Few people would attempt to deny that there is considerable faking in antiques, but most people think of it in terms of the proverbial unscrupulous cabinetmaker creating artificial worm holes in spurious antique furniture. It is to be hoped that the statement will not dissuade any potential hobbyist, but most men collectors bask in an erroneous belief that they are relatively safe from the attention of fakers because it does not pay to fake most of the types of articles they collect, or because it simply is technically impractical. In many cases neither assumption is correct. Many fakes start out as innocent reproduction items mass-produced for the decorator trade or for some other legitimate purpose. But it is not at all difficult for a skilled workman to set out cold and produce many types of fakes directly for sale to antique collectors, fakes that in many cases will pass fair muster under the inspection the average collector is equipped to give them.

Again let it be emphasized that this is not intended to be alarmist, and admittedly it is just as easy to overemphasize the potentiality and prevalence of fakes as it would be to play down or completely ignore the subject. The point is that spurious items are not to be feared only by those who collect articles that generally carry very substantial price tags. The first thing a collector in almost any category should do is to endeavor to acquire a fair idea at least of the types of things within his particular category that are being fabricated for the decorator trade. Today there are regularly produced a literal mass of reproductions and pseudo-reproductions. A pseudo-reproduction might be defined as an article in simulation of the styles and materials of another day but actually an out-and-out new design, a reproduction in spirit and "feel" as opposed to a line-for-line reproduction of an original of years gone by.

On Fifth Avenue in New York City, there is a large building that

Fake old photographs may be produced by rephotographing motion-picture stills. This is the genuine Brady photograph of Abraham Lincoln and General McClellan seated in the latter's tent. Compare the details carefully to avoid spurious prints made from photographs of reenactments of the scene.

George S. Indig Photograph

occupies an entire block; here in numerous showrooms and in those in adjacent buildings that make up a sort of specialized district, you can find, freely offered for sale for exactly what they are, reproductions and pseudo-reproductions in an almost endless array of seemingly old artifacts: Hessian andirons, oil lamps, cast-iron toys, Civil War recruiting posters, trade signs, decoys, brasswork, and so on. You will not find everything you can think of here simply because there are still categories whose popularity has not yet reached a point where it is profitable to reproduce them, but you would probably be in for some surprises were the opportunity to present itself to make the tour. Old telephones, for example, now are being widely reproduced.

It is hardly within the province of this book to attempt to read the thoughts and motives of men. Reproductions are manufactured and initially sold for exactly what they are and supposedly go to decorators, house-furnishing stores, novelty and souvenir shops, and the like. If a portion of the output, perhaps even a relatively small portion, ends up at antique shops and shows, who can say? Such items may readily give themselves away to all but the least alert by their bright new appearance. Sometimes items have been deliberately artificially aged. Dealers themselves may have been deceived by those who have offered them this material, although it seems improbable in many instances. It is not necessary to assert categorically that an item is old; often it is sufficient simply to place a price tag upon it and let it sit silently until it is noticed and purchased by an overeager collector.

There also are fakes that are deliberately made up to deceive antique collectors, of course, but in the main the prevalent danger to the average collector is in buying something as an antique that would have—although some collectors who have been thus bitten would strenuously debate this possibility—a legitimate existence under a more accurate designation and use. Every category of antiques where fakes exist has its own problems and its own guideposts for detection and protection. It is impossible to generalize, save perhaps to warn that extreme caution should be exercised in securing anything that is cast of aluminum or incorporates aluminum components, a metal that was not widely used until comparatively recent date. Because of its relatively low melting point of 1,220 degrees Fahrenheit, aluminum was at one time widely favored for casting reproductions and fakes of articles originally cast of brass and iron. It was an ideal medium for do-it-yourself fakers, some of whom maintained small melting pots and casting operations in their barns or basements. This practice has, however, lessened considerably in recent years both because the prices fakes could in many instances command when sold as genuine or the

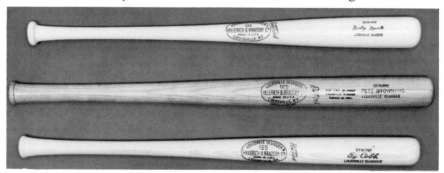

The lower two bats are reproductions made especially for this book to illustrate changes in baseball-bat styles. Top, a modern Mickey Mantle model; center, reproduction of the first Louisville Slugger bat turned in 1884; bottom, a reproduction of a Ty Cobb model Louisville Slugger showing the type of bat used by Ty Cobb in the early 1900s.

Hillerich and Bradsby Company,
G. William Holland Photograph

quantities that could be merchandised in one manner or another increased to the point where it became practical to have the spurious articles cast in a regular foundry where brass or iron readily could be handled. Also, of course, too many people were becoming conscious of the ready giveaway inherent in the employment of aluminum.

Any sand-cast item can be dismantled and the castings themselves used as patterns for the molding of any number of reproductions. There is invariably shrinkage in such instances, which can be revealing to trained eyes but which usually is insufficient to arouse suspicion in overavid beginners. The ease with which sand-cast objects—produced in nonpermanent molds of sand—can be reproduced has to a considerable extent created an impression that only such artifacts customarily are reproduced. This is no longer the case. Rubber-mold casting processes have enabled the reproduction of die-cast artifacts and components with substantial success, and there even now are craftsmen who manage to achieve considerable success in imitating stamped metal articles either entirely by means of handwork or even through the use of temporary dies. Furthermore, it is not merely items of fairly ancient age that have been reproduced. Toy trolley cars originally made around 1910 and toy locomotives manufactured as recently as 1930 have already been reproduced and, old toy trains being among the most popular of all masculine collectables, other and even later such items in all probability will follow. Naturally, the ostensible purpose of such reproduction is legitimate—for the use of model railroaders. What happens when they fall into the hands of less than honorable individuals and are offered as originals is, of course, another story; *caveat emptor*, which may be cold comfort indeed. The fact is that men can be extremely gullible and quite willingly, almost deliberately, shut their eyes and eagerly rush to allow themselves to be deceived.

Paper antiques are among the easiest things in the world to reproduce and for which to find acceptance. The advent of motion pictures and the accompanying wide distribution of still shots from pictures (the collecting of such stills is itself a popular avocation) have made possible many easy and inexpensive-to-produce fakes, both in the form of allegedly old photographic prints and historical documents. There is, for example, the famous Matthew Brady photograph of Lincoln and McClellan seated in the latter's tent at Antietam in 1862, the original negative of which was claimed in *Portrait Life of Lincoln*, by Francis Trevelyan Miller, published in 1910, to be valued at ten thousand dollars. A photograph made from a printed reproduction reveals the giveaway halftone screen; this is not the case when a movie still reproducing the scene is rephotographed and prints finished in sepia to simulate photographs of the 1860s. In the original movie still there also appears a third figure, that of a photographer at the right in a rather dramatic pose. This figure, which would provide a dead giveaway, is, of course, cropped out of the reproductions, which can then be detected only by a careful comparison with a known original, a copy of which will be found on these pages.[1] In point of fact, it is impossible to estimate how many "original" prints of cabinet or *carte-de-visite*–size photographs of Abraham Lincoln prized in collections do not actually portray the visage of John Carradine, Frank McGlynn, Sr., or one of the many other actors in full makeup who have essayed the role!

Then, too, there is the famous—or infamous—Jesse James reward poster including the name of the "St. Louis Midland Railway." No such common carrier ever existed; the name was coined for the 1939 motion picture starring Tyrone Power as Jesse to provide a libel-free cover for the machinations of the villains whose unkindness to the youth was supposedly responsible for his seeking vengeance by robbing their trains. Within less than twenty years' time not only were copies of this document being widely sold to collectors but it even had been reproduced in at least one elaborate pictorial history of the West as a supposedly authentic Jesse James reward poster! Since 1939 there have been a half dozen or more motion pictures dealing with Jesse James. An almost invariable "prop" has been a made-to-order reward poster, usually for a scene where it is observed by Bob Ford and sets the wheels going in his head, and sometimes with fantastic amounts being advertised. Almost every one of these has been reproduced and offered to collectors, sometimes initially as acknowledged reproductions

[1] Robert Weinstein, an authority on Civil War photography, believes that the fake Lincoln-McClellan photographs are not copied from a motion-picture still but, rather, from a photograph of a diorama built for advertising purposes by a film manufacturer during the Civil War Centennial, 1961–1965.

A Jenny Lind pipe, a hand-painted eyeglass case, and an original letter dated May 28, 1852—"Sir, You must kindly excuse me if I send your money in return without the Daguerreotype as I never gived [sic] my likeness to a person I never knew. Yours respectfully, Jenny Goldschmidt born Lind." She sailed from America the following day.

W. Porter Ware

of supposedly authentic originals, sometimes artificially aged and worn as originals themselves. James gang reward posters are particularly popular with men collectors.

So, too, evidently, are the original and authentic firearms supposedly carried by Frank and Jesse James, Billy the Kid, Wyatt Earp, Bat Masterson, Wild Bill Hickok, Pat Garrett, and other remembered worthies of the Old West. It has been estimated that something like an average of one hundred "authentic" weapons belonging to each of them repose as prizes in various collections, as well' as a like number of the derringer allegedly used by John Wilkes Booth to shoot Abraham Lincoln. It would appear that, along the outer peripheries of antiquing where such things carry weight, such firearms have replaced the eminence once undisputably held by "genuine" cases of razors originally owned by Napoleon I, who apparently was the shavingest man ever. The writer, in fact, does not recall seeing a first-class set of Napoleon's razors, once a standby, offered for nearly twenty years now. In his later years, when sports editor on a New York newspaper, Bat Masterson found pleasure and profit in purchasing old Colt .45 revolvers in pawnshops and distributing them to the zealous collectors who were always pestering him for his old gun. According to Bat, on such occasions he did not exactly say that he had used the weapon in the West, neither did he specifically deny it.

Valid Uses for Reproductions

When reproductions are deliberately offered as originals, or when originals are proffered with spurious attributions whether direct or implied, even when the latter come from Bat Masterson, the facts should unquestionably be revealed. However, it must also be said that on certain occasions denunciation of reproductions has been carried too far; there are instances when reproductions, recognized as such, can play a valid role.

At times there have been specimens identified and denounced as fakes or recent reproductions that were neither. This is particularly true in the field of glass, as explained in Chapter V, but it has occurred at times in other areas of antiques as well. Sometimes this has merely been due to ignorance or lack of ability correctly to interpret readily

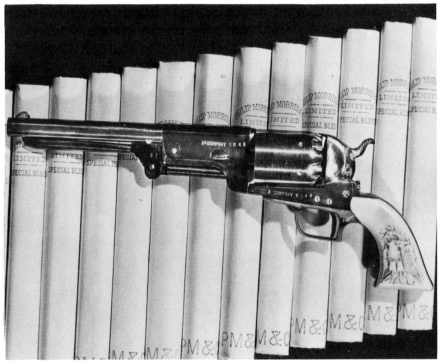

*Top, a Colt "Whitneyville Walker" .44 caliber Army revolver, one of 2,000 manu-
factured on contract by the Whitney Arms Company, Whitneyville, Connecticut,
starting in 1847. Below, a model of an antique, a one-inch scale replica of the
"Whitneyville Walker."*

Colt Industries, Colt's Firearms Division *(top)*
Milwaukee Public Museum *(bottom)*

available source material. At times, however, it has suited the arcane purposes of certain individuals in the antiques field to erect smoke-screens of supposed fakes for one reason or another, sometimes to divert attention from fakes that they themselves were fabricating or at least purveying. There are indeed many curious things to be encountered at times in the world of antiques. All this naturally makes things just so much the more difficult for the legitimate collectors, dealers, and commentators.

Reproductions, denoted as such, frequently are quite properly used for demonstrations and displays in museums, restorations, craft classes, and similar legitimate instances. It is far more desirable to make and employ a reproduction on many occasions than to subject an original to continual handling, much less to cut away a portion to reveal the internal design or to chop up a series of specimens to demonstrate step-by-step fabrication. Modern-day museum display techniques frequently call for the use of various reproductions in the creating of more vivid and educational exhibits. The reproduction baseball bats on page 68 were especially made up for use in this book to illustrate progressive points in the development of the bat by the Hillerich and Bradsby Company, Inc. The makers of the famed "Louisville Slugger" bats wish it to be emphasized that they have no old bats available, cannot undertake to make up similar reproductions for sale, and are unable to engage in correspondence on these matters.

Reproductions certainly serve a valid end when used for purposes of decoration, or even for a functional purpose, as in the case of a reproduction clock. Very often it is preferable to employ a reproduction for such a purpose than to subject an original specimen to exposure, handling, and use. The latter is a point concerning which many probably will disagree, citing the old saw concerning the exposure of large diamonds, "Where I come from, those as has 'em wears 'em." Not at all surprisingly, of course, many who knowingly make decorative use of reproductions of collectables find little difficulty in forgetting they are not originals when showing them off and discussing them. Probably some of the emulators of Diamond Jim Brady were beset with a similar memory gap.

There is one other point in connection with originals and reproductions which does not seem ever to be discussed, and that concerns

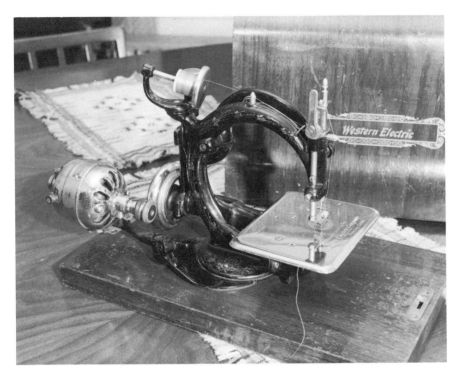

As both a mechanism and an example of production manufacture, the sewing machine has always held considerable interest for men collectors. This is a Western Electric model of about 1915, brought into being by adding their motor to a Wilcox & Gibbs sewing machine.

Western Electric

their employment in the restoration of old stores or rooms. A number of men who are fortunate enough to possess the space and the means enjoy undertaking the creation of such scenes. When the purpose at hand is the simulation of, say, an old office or railroad-station waiting room, not only are originals desirable but there is no objection to their showing, as they almost inevitably will, signs of age and wear. In the case of re-creations of an old store, however, it may definitely be more desirable to employ reproductions insofar as possible, and they may well, curious as it may seem at first thought, provide a greater measure of the authenticity that is desired than will originals, assuming the purpose is to take the viewer into a store as it was fifty or a hundred years ago. If the hobbyist is in a position to stock the store entirely or at least substantially with fresh, brand-new merchandise of the bygone era, originals are obviously to be desired. This, however, seldom is possible, and efforts are made to re-create a scene as it once was employing obviously aged, soiled, or worn originals. Infinitely more desirable as such originals are per se as individual collector's items, they usually fall down badly when employed in this manner. It should be remembered that at the time the store supposedly was in operation the fixtures were relatively new and well kept up, and the stock was sparklingly factory-fresh. Many visitors to the usual sort of store re-creation find it curiously if inexplicably depressing and unauthentic. The reason is that the store is furnished and stocked with old things that inevitably carry with them an intimation of their age. Those considering the re-creation of old store scenes should consider these facts carefully and see if it would not be the case that what they desire to achieve actually would not be far better accomplished by employing reproduction fixtures and stock. This suggestion, strange and even startling as it may seem, has not been made without considerable thought and consideration.

TRACING LINES OF DESCENT

Although many men are notoriously uninterested in family trees as such, male collectors have developed a rather remarkable and complex historical and collecting interest in the lines of descent of products, companies, and even of individuals and families in connection with their inventiveness and commercial productivity. As early as 1916, in *English and American Tool Builders,* Joseph Wickham Roe literally traced out with genealogical charts—which he designated by that name—various lines of descent, travel, and mutation of factories, individual inventors, executives, superintendents, and foremen. There are, for example, more than thirty major entries—ranging from the Sharps Rifle Works, of Hartford, Connecticut, to the White Sewing Machine Company, of Cleveland, Ohio—on Roe's "Genealogy of the Robbins & Lawrence Shop," of Windsor, Vermont.

Collectors have not as yet developed every such possible sequence as the basis of a collecting activity, but there have been a number of interesting collections formed along such lines, and in any event the general impact of the implications inherent in such thinking has been most important to the antiques field. It was men collectors, for example, who first noticed and then annotated the mechanical and productive achievements to be credited to one remarkable Connecticut family from approximately 1830 onward, that of Ives. A most extraordinary strain of inventive, artistic, and creative genius revealed itself in the

A combination working store and old-store restoration in the now revitalized old Western ghost town of Bumble Bee, Arizona. Among the collectables preserved in this corner are a slot machine, coffee grinder, scales, typewriter, guns, bottles, steins, and a coin-operated Polyphon disc music box.

Mr. and Mrs. Charles A. Penn, Bumble Bee
Trading Post, Bumble Bee, Arizona
Dick Carter Photograph

nineteenth century in a surprising number of descendants of William Ives, who settled in New Haven in 1638. The Iveses would appear to represent an unusual inborn impulse to creativity and practical commercialization, somewhat in the same manner as the Adams family may be said to represent a hereditary political strain and the Huxleys, a scientific one.

It was Edward R. Ives and his son, Harry C. Ives, who first attracted major attention of men collectors to the family. They were America's most notable toy manufacturers, and toys are, of course, one of the most popular of all collector's categories among men. It has always surprised antique dealers that when the name Ives is mentioned to men collectors, their immediate primary association almost invariably is with the toy manufacturers, not with the James Merritt Ives of Currier and Ives lithographic fame. Nevertheless, James Merritt Ives was a cousin of Edward and Harry. So, too, related in one way or another, were Chauncey Ives and his brother, Lawson, the noted clockmakers; William A. Ives, the tool manufacturer; Frederick E. Ives, the color-photography pioneer and camera manufacturer; and a half dozen or so more proprietors of perhaps only slightly lesser known manufacturing enterprises. It will be observed that each of the specialties enumerated above—toys, lithographs, clocks, tools, and cameras —are categories of rather substantial importance and popularity among men collectors. Indeed, virtually anything that can be identified as made by a company including Ives in its name has more or less automatically come to be regarded as a collector's item and to be snapped up, if the price appears right; almost certainly if the artifact was made in Connecticut, it will be found there exists an actual and fairly close blood relationship with *the* Ives family. Connecticut provenance is not absolutely requisite; Currier and Ives were, of course, located in New York City, and the Hess-Ives Corporation, which manufactured the cameras, was based in Philadelphia, Pennsylvania. It might even accurately be said that Ives products comprise a collector's category of their own, based on no more connection than the family itself.

The Ives family was probably the leading one in this respect, for no other family's activities appear to have been quite so widespread or to have embraced so many really popular collectables. There are a number of other, somewhat similar instances, however; for example, the North family, also of Connecticut, who were active in clocks, firearms, and tools among other things.

Somewhat similarly, men collectors will sometimes settle upon one individual who was noteworthy in several important if seemingly unrelated areas and attempt to base a collection upon his work. Such an individual was Jerome Burgess Secor (1839–1923), whom many regard as one of America's most adept mechanicians. Secor was involved importantly in the creation and production of three categories of artifacts: toys, typewriters, and sewing machines. His typewriter connections started in the 1870s, although it was not until early in the twentieth century that a typewriter was marketed bearing his name; many typewriter aficionados regard it as the finest typewriter ever made. This opinion may be in part at least a prejudiced one, but the machine unquestionably was extremely highly esteemed by contemporaries. Of Secor's major fields of effort, the first two, toys and typewriters, are important categories of men's collectables, and the third, sewing machines, gives portents of being of no mean status itself,

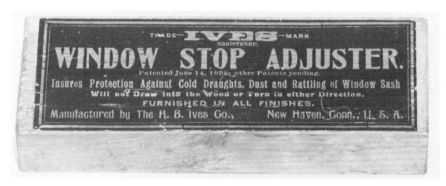

Product segments used for promotional use are of much interest to men collectors. This is a sample of the Ives patent window stop adjuster, manufactured by the H. B. Ives Company of New Haven, Connecticut, in the 1890s.

George S. Indig Photograph

if only perhaps to some extent because of Secor's participation therein. Electrically powered sewing machines, which he did not produce, have of late attained a fair measure of interest as electric antiques.

Disposing of Your Collection

Saddening as the thought may be, almost certainly sooner or later your collection is going to be disposed of and, in all probability, dispersed. You can only content yourself in regard to this thought by the fact that other collectors in time will derive much the same enjoyment from your possessions as you have yourself, but, frankly, this is usually small comfort to the average and, it must be admitted, somewhat gluttonous collector who, if anything, would by far prefer to take it with him. You can, of course, give or will your collection to a museum or other public institution, but if you do you had better make absolutely certain that you are indeed setting up the permanent memorial to yourself and permanent benefit to mankind that such a procedure usually implies to those who contemplate it. That is, you had better make certain in advance that the fortunate recipient can and will retain it on public display, that it will not be packed away forever out of sight, or even that it may not be sold off to add to the general fund. You may, in fact, find it more difficult to give away a collection than you imagine and at the same time be assured of having your wishes carried out, for a surprising number of institutions simply no longer will accept such gifts if there are strings attached, unless perhaps they are accompanied by a substantial bequest.

If you are in a position to do this, you can also consider setting up your own museum, with its attendant income for upkeep, or endowing a new library or town hall in your community with the provision that your collection be ever housed therein on public display. There are quite a few pretty little nineteenth-century libraries scattered over the United States these days wherein the founder's collection of stuffed birds, armor, or what have you are silent witnesses as the board of directors scrutinize the original documents in the hope of finding a loophole whereby they can sell off the dust-gathering junk and purchase a new heating plant or sound projector with part of the proceeds.

If you are realistic, you will face up to the fact that in all probability your cherished collection is going to pass into other hands and the best thing for you to do is to arrange for the inevitable dispersal to be as orderly and beneficial to your survivors as it is possible to make it. Nor does the disposal of a collection always necessarily or even ideally wait upon the death of its owner. There may be good and sufficient reasons for its sale during your lifetime. It may be that an enthusiast will tire of collecting one particular category or feel he has carried the accompanying research as far as is practical and wish to switch to something else. A collector may even find that he has in effect been priced out of continuing activity as more and more people enter the same field and values grow increasingly higher, and determine upon a change of course for this reason. Almost all collectors are incurable; they must collect and, if they cannot collect one thing, they will collect something else with equal fervor.

The important thing to bear in mind in disposing of a collection—and it should be impressed upon everyone who may in time have anything to do with handling the dispersal of your collection if you are not around to superintend it yourself—is that it is always better to sell a collection as a unit if possible, either to another collector or a dealer or a group of collectors or dealers, or to have it auctioned off in toto. You, or your heirs, will almost certainly secure more this way than if attempts are made to sell it off piecemeal, or in groups. When a collection is broken up for sale, the result almost invariably is that the most desirable pieces are quickly disposed of, leaving the lesser

Examples of one man's inventiveness and productivity. Anything made by the noted American manufacturer Jerome B. Secor is highly prized. Shown here are a Secor sewing machine, the one pictured being a special mother-of-pearl inlaid specimen displayed at the 1876 Centennial Exposition, and a Secor typewriter of the early 1900s.

George S. Indig Photographs

and commoner specimens, which usually comprise the greater bulk, to be sold with more difficulty and usually for less than might otherwise be the case. In short, when sold as a unit, the better items carry the lesser ones. It is better to leave the piecemeal sale of the latter to someone who has purchased the collection as a whole.

All too often a collector dies and friends request the privilege of each purchasing an item for remembrance before the collection as a whole is displayed or offered. The widow agrees, and five friends buy one piece each at, say, one hundred dollars apiece. These prices may well be fair ones for the specimens involved; the less said about the possibility of good friends cheating their dear old buddy's widow under such circumstances the better. However, granting the validity of the prices, assume the collection comprises a hundred pieces. In most cases, by the law of averages, there may be five or ten prime pieces, ten or twenty middling specimens, and the remainder of the collection will be made up of quite common items. The widow—the presumption here being that she has been kept totally uninformed concerning the value nuances of the collection (perhaps for, in the deceased's view, good and sufficient reasons)—assumes that because she has sold five pieces at one hundred dollars each the remaining ninety-five also will command an average of a hundred dollars apiece for a total sale price of $10,000 for the collection. This not only is extremely faulty thinking that inevitably results in a great disappointment, but in any event the remainder of the collection will bring far less than otherwise would have been the case had it not been gutted of a substantial proportion of its greatest attractions before it was offered for sale as a unit.

It may be that in such a sale in toto an amount will not be realized that corresponds to the total of the individual theoretical values placed on each and every piece, but the fact is that, from a practical standpoint, the better items always help carry the lesser ones and that you actually will realize more, especially when the time and effort involved in a long-drawn-out piece-by-piece sale are taken into account, by selling everything together. Naturally, a dealer must purchase a collection for a price that will permit him a profit, just as an auctioneer will require a commission for his services, but there are advantages in selling everything as a unit to a dealer. Most dealers will not be too inter-

A wall clock of about 1777, with engraved moon dial and moon hand, and displaying the double case typical of early shelf clocks and fully-cased wall clocks. This example was made by Simon Willard, of Grafton, Massachusetts.

Old Sturbridge Village Photo

ested in buying the remaining commoner specimens, save possibly at an extremely low price, once the prime pieces have been sold off privately. Also, it should be remembered that, if a collection has been in existence for a fair length of time, it is likely that today's "wholesale" price offered by a reputable dealer usually will, by the simple general increment in values, equal or exceed the "retail" cost at which the collection was assembled.

As to auction selling, there is much to be said for it *if* the auction can be carried out by an established auctioneer at a public auction gallery and is properly advertised generally as well as publicized directly to a fair group of known collectors. There is, however, little to be gained and much to be lost simply by throwing a collection into a general local auction. If a collection is of a category or categories in which there presently exists substantial interest and recognition, a sale in an established auction gallery may well produce the best results with a minimum of bother, the increased prices a good auctioneer can bring forth from an enthusiastic crowd more than making up for his commission. An established and reputable gallery will not accept a category of antiques for sale unless it feels it is sufficiently established to warrant dispersal at such an auction. In short, if you happen to collect something that up to now perhaps only a dozen others also collect, an auction sale would be fruitless, and as a matter of fact, it is extremely dubious if any first-rate gallery would even accept the project. As with so many things in antiques, all this is progressive. Not too many years ago the conception that a well-known antiques auctioneer would undertake the sale of a collection of, say, old automobiles or old toys or old advertising materials would be ludicrous; today some of the world's best-known galleries gladly and successfully accept such sales. As interest increases and enhances, this will prove true of many other categories of men's antiques.

Certainly those who may have to handle the sale of your collection should be impressed with the idea that it is a collection and does have value; if you can furnish an idea of the total and individual value, so much the better. Be careful, however, not to overestimate, for this may inhibit the acceptance of what actually may be quite fair offers. At the same time stress the fact that collectors' values are variable and may well increase. But, above all, emphasize the idea that what you have is a collection, not an eccentricity, and does have value. Even today, with all the awareness of antiques and collecting that assuredly does exist, there are intelligent and otherwise well-informed individuals who are unaware of what may in many instances constitute a valuable and important collection. "Yes, of course, I knew to have a dealer in to look at the books and china. Naturally, the first thing I did though was to throw out all the old junk he had accumulated; you'd never believe what he saved—boxes of old tools, toys, theater programs, McKinley buttons, and what have you!"

CHAPTER III

A Case History: The Typewriter

The antiques of commerce are divided into two major classifications, the actual machines and equipment employed in carrying on a business, and what is now considered the background material, mainly of paper. The latter, no matter how important it may have been to a business at the time it was current or how important it is for its present-day display or nostalgic value, is now almost always of even greater interest and value as the source material for vital research by the collector and historian in tracing the development of a business or a product. In the first group are found such things as office and store equipment, either of types common to most businesses, such as typewriters, or relics of a more particularized nature, such as trade signs. In the second group are found such collectables as catalogs and other advertising and promotional materials generally looked upon originally as of a rather ephemeral nature but now of extreme importance both in themselves and as sources of information.

It is hardly possible to overestimate the importance of this second group, both as a collecting category in itself and as material of extraordinary relevance not only to the more substantial artifacts of business discussed in the first part of this chapter but equally to almost every other category of collectable covered in this book.

Leaving aside the paper material for the moment, however, much of importance regarding collecting practices and patterns pertaining to almost every category can be demonstrated at this point by taking a single article and examining it in a little detail. Inasmuch as the typewriter probably is the primary business antique, it will serve as an ideal example for this purpose, bearing in mind that most of the factors of collecting and research involved with the typewriter will be equally applicable to telephones, shaving mugs, tools, clocks, or any other category of collecting items. It just happens that the typewriter provides an ideal example because it happens to have just about everything that makes an antique interesting for a man to collect and study; it is a manufactured product of considerable mechanical complexity with an extensive and interesting commercial background of its own and is of substantial historical importance. Furthermore, its own history has to this date by no means been completely or adequately revealed; it is a field that still presents an enormous area for continuing research. Almost every basic principle of collecting and research—and particularly research on an industrial product—can ideally be demonstrated with the typewriter. Lastly, if only incidentally to the main issue at hand, it is a collectable of sufficient size and heft to satisfy most men's inclinations toward such attributes, yet not so large that a fairly extensive collection cannot be handled and housed without too much difficulty, although as with every collectable, no matter how small, there can eventually develop problems of space.

The history of the writing machine as a conception has been traced back as far as 1714. During the first two-thirds of the nineteenth century dozens of men "invented" and built such machines. A few were sold, and there even are several definite—and tantalizing—possibilities of actual commercial production prior to 1871 that still require further investigation. A production run of over one hundred of John M. Jones' "Typographer" was destroyed in a factory fire in upstate New York in 1853 and a quantity of what was called by its inventor and manufacturer, Giuseppe Ravizza, the "Cembalo-scrivano" appear to have been sold in Italy later in the 1850s, to name two examples. The point is that it seldom is difficult to find an early primogenitor in any given field; histories of invention and manufacture, particularly those written by or under the auspices of interested sources, are likely to be filled with hedging references to the "first practical" this or that. At times even more involved elisions or downright omissions are resorted to. The intelligent collector or student—and the two words should be more or less interchangeable; at least every collector should also be a student of his subject—always is most careful in examining and accepting such claims, particularly when they appear in advertising material promoting a specific product. Also, by setting up their own determinations and interpretations of what is to be regarded as "practical" or whatever term is employed, anyone can step in at any point in the progression of development of any product and justify whatever they desire as the "first." For example, if the definition of heavier-than-air manned flight is set at a minimum of one thousand feet, it can be established that the Wright brothers did not fly at Kitty Hawk in 1903! This is by no means the bizarre thought it may seem at first reading; many industrial historical claims are based on precisely this sort of made-to-order definition.

For now, however, for purposes of demonstration, let us simply accept as valid the supposition that the first commercial and practical typewriter was the machine developed in Milwaukee, Wisconsin, in the late 1860s and early 1870s by Christopher Latham Sholes, who is generally recognized as the primary inventor, and his associates. The commercial history of the typewriter usually is recognized as having started with the introduction of the machine evolved from these experiments and which was to become the Remington. Many typewriter histories have referred to it directly or obliquely as the "Remington," although, as virtually all typewriter collectors are aware, it originally was known as the "Sholes & Glidden." Up to now, however, very few are cognizant of the fact that there are at least five and possibly more distinct production models of the Sholes & Glidden.

Apropos of the contemporary nomenclature, W. O. Wyckoff, of Ithaca, New York, who held the selling agency for the machine in the central part of that state and operated a pioneer typewriting school, delighted in circulating the following bit of promotional poetry during his salad days in the mid-1870s, before the famous firm of Wyckoff, Seamans & Benedict was dreamed of:

> Tell me not in mournful numbers,
> "Life is but an empty dream!"
> Rouse yourself and go and purchase
> A Sholes & Glidden writing machine.[1]

The last two lines certainly provide an excellent injunction for the typewriter collector of today—providing, of course, he knows just

[1] This is quoted from a hand-typed book owned by the noted typewriter collector, David Golden, that was prepared in 1875 by Wyckoff's "amateur operators in the type-writer school."

where to journey in order to make the desired acquisition without delay.

Many categories of antiques have their comparatively well-established but actually totally mythical items. So it is with typewriters. Thanks to the general garbling of typewriter history and illustrations, many collectors continue fruitlessly to seek a machine they have been led to anticipate will be marked "Remington No. 1," a machine mounted on a table with a treadle for returning the carriage at the end of each line. There is no such Remington typewriter or machine bearing such a designation, regardless of illustrations so captioned. The typewriter thus shown and designated is, at the very best, the third type of Sholes & Glidden Type Writer (it is spelled as "Type Writer" on the actual machines, but frequently was hyphenated in advertisements and catalogs) and the first type of Sholes & Glidden actually manufactured in the Remington factory. As a matter of fact, the name of this earliest style of machine remained the "Sholes & Glidden Type Writer" for a number of years, and it seems quite probable that no machine of this general form was ever turned out bearing any other marking. In any event, it should have been apparent to all who attempted to comment upon the matter that until such time as at least one further model was introduced—the Nos. 2, 3, 4, and 5 machines were announced in 1877—there was neither necessity for nor logic in designating the basic original version by a model number; it was simply *the* Type-Writer.

In numerous categories of antiques there exist such often widely publicized and avidly sought but totally nonexistent "rarities" as the treadle-operated "Remington No. 1." Needless to say, such mythical items often provide a field day for fakers. In the case of the "Remington No. 1," the writer is not aware of the existence as yet of any completely newly fabricated faked treadle machines, but there is reason to believe that at times later-model Sholes & Glidden typewriters have been doctored so as to pass muster as examples of the so-called Remington No. 1.

Dual Tales of Typewriter Birth

The reason for much of this seeming confusion is that there have long been two basically different stories in circulation concerning the birth of the typewriter. Neither is, in fact, accurate, but together they provide an ideal example of how industrial history may be edited to suit the needs of those who submit it, and of the necessity of the collector's being prepared to approach such matters with an open mind that is ready to examine things in a manner different from that in which he has traditionally been schooled.

Both versions start out substantially the same; that in the late 1860s Christopher Latham Sholes and a varying group of associates began to develop the writing machine that they initially named simply *the* "Type Writer" or "Type-Writer." The most important among the group next to Sholes were Carlos Glidden and Samuel W. Soulé. The first patents were secured in 1868. Shortly after the work was initiated, an interest was acquired by James Densmore, an interest that gradually increased to a controlling one as Densmore invested ever more money in the development work. In typewriter history Densmore stands, depending on where you wish to sit, as either the vitally necessary promoter and financier or the schemer who swindled the poor naïve inventors out of the bulk of their birthrights for the proverbial mess of pottage. Subsequently Densmore sold part of his interest to a gentleman bearing the sonorous name of George Washington Newton Yost, reputed to be a most persuasive talker. Both Densmore and Yost were to remain active typewriter men all their lives and to see their names appear as the brands of two makes of typewriters, the Densmore and the Yost. It was, however, James Densmore's brothers, not James himself, as most assume, who initiated the Densmore typewriter enterprise; and the first Densmore typewriter did not appear on the market until 1891.

The cast of major characters thus being assembled and in possession of a workable but supposedly very crude writing machine, the two basic stories diverge. In version No. 1, which was put about by the various interests controlling the Remington typewriter from the 1880s to the 1920s, Densmore and Yost went to Ilion, New York, the site of the well-known gun and sewing-machine manufacturers, E. Remington & Sons, in 1873 and sold them on buying the machine. The Remington mechanics took the crude idea, refined and redesigned it, and it emerged in 1874 as the Remington typewriter, the "Remington No. 1." Most of these accounts even specify William K. Jenne of Rem-

Two typewriter classics of the 1890s. The Densmore No. 3 (top), in common with all Densmores, employed ball bearings on its typebars and carriage. The Williams No. 1, with curved keyboard, was one of the first machines successfully to approach visible writing.

Milwaukee Public Museum

ington as having added the treadle because of his previous experience in producing the Remington sewing machines.

Version No. 2 was instituted and circulated by competitors of Remington who not unnaturally did not desire to provide Remington with any more credit than was necessary. It was in fact much more accurate than the old Remington version, although based on a number of false assumptions and in no sense complete or fully correct. In this version, Densmore and Yost went to Ilion and arranged to have the typewriters manufactured for them on contract by Remington, the resulting machine appearing on the market in 1874 as the "Sholes & Glidden Type Writer," and so marked, Soulé by this time no longer holding any interest in the invention. Subsequently—the inference usually is very shortly thereafter—Remington bought the machine and rechristened it the "Remington Type-Writer." In short, in this version, the first typewriter was not the Remington but, correctly enough albeit rather incompletely because of the acceptance of many already established traditions, the Sholes & Glidden.

In his historical account of the typewriter (still spelled "type-writer") in 1895, Clarence Seamans of the firm of Wyckoff, Seamans & Benedict, which then owned the Remington typewriter, very neatly got rid of the embarrassing problem of the Sholes & Glidden; he simply did not mention it, and spoke of "the first machine, the Remington." In fact, he did not find it necessary even to mention the names of Glidden or Soulé. They were mentioned in *The Story of the Typewriter* put out by the Herkimer County (New York) Historical Society under the obvious auspices of the Remington Typewriter Company in 1923, supposedly marking the fiftieth anniversary of the birth of the typewriter, and there is even a rather oblique and disarming reference to what is described as "the Sholes and Glidden model of 1873"—that is, an original handmade sample—but the basic question at issue was taken care of in the following, extremely carefully worded sentences:

The machine was then known simply as *"The Type-Writer."* Today it is known as the *"Model 1 Remington,"* and it will aways be known as the *"Ancestor of All Writing Machines."*

It is only proper to observe that in recent years the present manufacturers of the Remington typewriter, the Sperry Rand Corporation,

have recognized the existence of the early machines bearing the Sholes
& Glidden name.

THE THIRD VERSION

As noted, neither of the traditional versions is complete. Both do
a considerable disservice to the actual facts of the history of the typewriter. Collectors have pored over often incorrectly identified pictures
and if anything confusion has begat greater confusion. As so often
happens in any field of production endeavor, handmade models have
been shown for production models—and models therefore conceivably
available to collectors—and production models have been designated
experimental pieces. Unfortunately, there is as yet no adequate history
of the typewriter available.[2] The following facts will briefly relate
the actual story and, together with the accompanying illustrations,
provide a guide to the earliest and most important series of machines.
But it should be remembered that the purpose here is not merely to
provide specific collector's information on the history and variation of
the Sholes & Glidden typewriters but, in a large and more important
sense, to demonstrate the situation and problems that the collector
will find obtaining in almost any category of antiques of the types
likely to be of most interest to men.

It is hardly proper to speak of the "manufacture" of typewriters
by Sholes and his associates prior to 1871. A number of machines were
made by hand, evidently almost every one of them differing in some
way from the others.

However, production of a standardized model to be offered for sale
began in 1871, three years prior to the date usually cited. These first
machines, which were self-contained and required no stand or treadle,
were encased in wood that concealed the inner metal framework. They
differed substantially from later models in that the ribbon ran from

---

[2] The most accurate and detailed account to date is *The Typewriter and the Men Who
Made It* by Richard N. Current, published by the University of Illinois Press in 1954
and now out of print. It does not, however, provide the collector with much detail concerning the various production machines. The Milwaukee Public Museum, 800 West
Wells Street, Milwaukee, Wisconsin 53233, has available for $1.00 a booklet, *The Carl
P. Dietz Collection of Typewriters*, that illustrates and describes almost three hundred
machines and which would appear to be the best guide presently available to collectors.

front to back and the lines were typed *around* rather than *along* the platen. Illustrations of one of these 1871 machines are frequently reproduced as being of the sample that Densmore and Yost took to Ilion in 1873 to show the Remington people. This is obviously incorrect; they naturally took the highly perfected 1872–73 model with them. The 1871 model in the Remington archives undoubtedly was subsequently shipped to Ilion, along with whatever other material that might in any way have been of possible help to the designing staff there, after the 1873 contract was concluded, and in later years, appearing the simplest and crudest, was wrongly taken to represent the 1873 demonstration machine. Probably somewhere between ten and twenty-five of the 1871 machines were manufactured either in Chicago or Milwaukee, or perhaps in both places. This was hardly really quantity production, but it nevertheless was the start of actual mass production of a truly "manufactured" machine. The 1871 machines were largely sold to telegraph companies, their primary use at the time being envisaged as an aid to telegraphers who frequently could send messages faster than the recipient could take them down in longhand.

Although always previously identified as a handmade demonstration sample made in 1873, this is actually an example of the first type of production Sholes & Glidden typewriter, manufactured in Chicago in 1871. It wrote around *rather than* along *the platen.*

Sperry Rand Corporation, Remington Rand
Office Machines Division

The Sholes & Glidden typewriters manufactured in Milwaukee in 1872 and 1873 were considerably improved, although still retaining a wooden casing over their metal frames; the style given in an 1873 advertisement is "Sholes & Glidden's." The ribbons passed from one side to the other and they wrote *along* the platen, the carriage could be raised to examine what had just been typed (all of the early typewriters were, of course, nonvisible writers). Here a point of confusion still exists as to just how many distinctly different models were successively manufactured in 1872 and 1873. Eventually this matter will no doubt be established satisfactorily, but contemporary drawings and photographs and surviving specimens reveal the possibility of important variations. In any event, by 1873 the machine had developed to the point where, mechanically at least, it was substantially the machine to be made at Ilion in 1874 and was mounted on a table or a sewing-machine stand which, with the attendant treadle for returning the carriage, formed an integral part of the machine. (It is manifest that, far from the supposed addition of the sewing-machine base and treadle by the Ilion designers, a principal reason that Remington was approached with the proffer of the contract was that they were already in the sewing-machine business and possessed the patterns for these somewhat minor but supposedly vital components.)

The 1873 model at least was the realized Sholes & Glidden typewriter, although the above-the-table portion was perhaps twenty percent larger than the Ilion machines. The greater size of the 1872–73 machines was, if anything, exaggerated by the artists who prepared the woodcuts showing them, either in sheer exuberance or in a deliberate effort to make them appear even more prepossessing than they actually were, but they certainly were what typewriter collectors justly can term a "giant kugel," although not in the same sense as the designation has been applied to the eighteen-foot-high, fourteen-ton Underwood that was computed to be 1,728 times the size of a production Underwood No. 5. This famed monster (see the postcard illustrating it in Chapter XI), a fully working typewriter in every way, was built for the Panama-Pacific Exposition of 1915, then displayed in Atlantic City for over two decades, moved to the New York World's Fair in 1939, and finally dismantled for scrap during World War II. (The giant was given a new external casing for the Fair to make it resemble a 1939 model.)

Left, a surviving specimen of the second basic type of Sholes & Glidden type-writer, manufactured in 1872–73. Note the absence of the carriage-return mechanism and differences in the top plate when compared to the machine in the photograph at the right. Also shown is an 1872 photograph of the Milwaukee machine shop where Sholes & Glidden typewriters were produced. Note the machines awaiting shipment on the sidewalk.

Sperry Rand Corporation, Remington Rand
Office Machines Division

Advertisements for the Sholes & Glidden typewriter published in 1873, evidencing machines similar to those pictured in the previous illustration being offered for sale in that year. The drawings here evidently show a sample machine differing in details from those pictured in the preceding figure.

Western Electric

How many Sholes & Glidden typewriters were manufactured in 1872 and 1873 is uncertain, but there were undoubtedly more than the 1871 model. In any event, enough were made and sold to convince the then newly founded Western Electric Manufacturing Company of Chicago, which then held the exclusive sales agency, of the potential of the typewriter, sales to telegraphers then still seeming the primary market. It was Western Electric who supplied Densmore with most of the down payment required by Remington in 1873 to begin contract manufacture of what was at least the third model Sholes & Glidden. Western Electric subsequently sold out their interest. According to the recollections in 1913 of Enos M. Barton, one of the founders of Western Electric and at that time the chairman of the board, the $10,000 they received was clear profit. Actually this would appear to be substantially the amount they had advanced Densmore in 1873 so that production could be commenced in Ilion.

There is an interesting corollary to the "loss" or suppression of the fact of the 1871–73 Sholes & Glidden machines. This relates to the precedence of manufacture in Europe of the Hansen Schreibkugel,

THE TYPE WRITER.
A MACHINE TO WRITE WITH TYPES AND SUPERCEDE
THE PEN FOR COMMON WRITING. PRICE $125. FOR
INFORMATION AND CIRCULAR SEND TO

JAMES DENSMORE,
1 HANOVER STREET, NEW YORK.

MILWAUKEE, WIS. JANUARY 21, 1874.
FRIEND DENSMORE :---
MY PAGING MACHINE IS VERY POP-
ULAR WITH THE PROFESSION HERE, SO FAR AS IT HAS
BEEN EXAMINED. THERE SEEMS TO BE NO DISSENT TO
THE OPINION THAT IT IS A MOST DESIRABLE MACHINE.
I THINK I SHALL HAVE TWO TO BUILD---ONE FOR NEI-
DECKER, AND ONE FOR SEIFERT. I MAY HAVE NEITHER
BUT THE INDICATIONS ARE FAVORABLE. SHOULD I SO
GET THEM, I SHALL CLEAR FROM THE PRICE I GET
FOR THOSE, THE ONE I MUST HAVE BUILT FOR MYSELF.
BUT--- BUT THERE IS ALWAYS AN AFRICAN IN THE FE-
NCE OR A SKELETON IN THE CLOSET. I FIND ON EXA-

These are the opening *lines* of a letter from Mr. Sholes
in which he is making use of the firm stationary.
This letter is wholly devoted to his paging machine,
from which the invention of the typewriter was
evolved.

*A letter written by C. Latham Sholes to James Densmore on January 21, 1874,
using one of the Sholes & Glidden typewriters manufactured in Milwaukee. The
letterhead evidently was printed in a typeface that matched the work of the
typewriter, but when the price was raised to $125, the alteration was inserted in
a different type.*

David Golden

already mentioned in Chapter II as the source of the typewriter col-
lectors' term "kugels," and the Sholes & Glidden in the United States.
The date of the introduction of the Schreibkugel is rather uncertain,
the first British patent being 1870 and the United States patent, 1872.
Many have regarded it as the first production typewriter, the Sholes
& Glidden being believed not to have been manufactured before 1874.
A number of American commentators have simply ignored the existence of the Schreibkugel in order to shore up the status of the Sholes
& Glidden as the first machine. Without attempting to comment on
the historical ethics of such a not uncommon procedure or to get
involved in chauvinistic claims, such practices in relation to the
Schreibkugel may have been entirely unnecessary if the actual initia-
tion of Sholes & Glidden production in 1871 is taken into account.

There were at least two models of the Schreibkugel, the more
elaborate version actually having been partially electric in operation.
Not surprisingly, the Schreibkugel itself—as distinguished from the
generic nickname of "kugels" for all typewriters—has become a byword
of extraordinary rarity and desirability among those typewriter collec-

tors who are aware of its existence. Both as specifically concerns the Schreibkugel and as an example of such frequent traditional overratings of storied specimens in many categories, it should be said that the Schreibkugel probably is not by any means so rare as legend has it. In *The History of the Typewriter,* a British book of 1909, George Carl Mares observed that there were then still many Schreibkugels in active use in continental European business offices. These machines, despite their, to modern views, unusual designs and name, evidently were manufactured and sold in fairly large quantities.

THE ILION MACHINES

Only after the third Sholes & Glidden production model did Remington begin manufacturing typewriters at Ilion. Depending on how you choose to count major and minor varieties, there were from three to five distinct types of Sholes & Glidden typewriters made at Ilion from 1874. The writer inclines to regard them as properly ratable as five major types and one minor variation.

All of the Sholes & Glidden typewriters manufactured at Ilion were basically similar in appearance, the wooden exterior of the 1871–73 models being replaced by cast-iron and sheet-metal components, and there were numerous other alterations and refinements which the accompanying illustrations will make obvious. However, there are distinct differences between each major type as set forth below.

The first type of Sholes & Glidden manufactured at the Remington plant is the machine often pictured as the "Remington No. 1." It is mounted on a base that incorporates sewing-machine base castings and employs a treadle to return the carriage and turn the platen. Incidently, similar tables, but without the treadle, were manufactured and offered for sale simply as typewriter tables at least up to 1888.

The second Ilion machine abandoned the base and treadle, and substituted a long hand lever mounted on the right side of the machine to perform the functions previously done by the treadle. It is quite possible that the first Ilion type was continued in production for a while after the second type was introduced. There is also some suggestion that the second type may have been developed originally for the export market. In any event, there appears to have been two dis-

Left, the first type of Sholes & Glidden typewriter manufactured at the Remington factory in Ilion, New York, with treadle carriage return. The first of these machines were delivered in 1874. Right, the second Ilion-made Sholes & Glidden, with hand-lever carriage return mounted on the right side of the machine.

Sperry Rand Corporation, Remington Rand
Office Machines Division *(left)*
Milwaukee Public Museum *(right)*

tinct minor variations of the second Ilion or side-lever type of machine. In the first type (illustrated), the carriage is identical to that used on the first type of Ilion machine, the wheel in front on which it moves showing both above and below its bearing piece. In the second type, the carriage is of the flanged or lipped variety employed on subsequent Sholes & Glidden typewriters and the wheel in front shows only below the portion of the carriage casting that serves as its bearing plate.

In the third type of Sholes & Glidden typewriter manufactured at Ilion, the side-mounted carriage return and platen-indexing method, whether activated by a treadle or a hand lever, is abandoned and the machines provided with a carriage lever hanging down over the right front of the typewriter. The carriage lever is sufficiently similar to that on a modern typewriter instantly to be recognized for what it is, and its form in fact remained basically the same on most of the Remington nonvisible typewriters through the No. 9. The top plate on the third Ilion model at first glance appears identical with that on the first and second. However, the top-plate castings on the first and second models were notched at the right rear to accommodate a pulley over which the cord ran from the carriage to the treadle or side lever. This notch theoretically should not be present on the third Ilion model and generally is not. It is possible, however, and indeed even probable, that there was some carry-over of notched top-plate castings and that the third Ilion model exists in two distinct minor varieties, with and without this notch, and possibly even top plates containing pulleys that were on hand were used up without alteration on some of the earliest of the third Ilion model.

The fourth type of Sholes & Glidden typewriter fabricated at Ilion at first glance appears almost identical to the third Ilion machine. However, whereas in the first, second, and third Ilion types the scalloped edges in the top plate are cast to the entire depth of the plate, in the fourth type the irregular edges are cast only to about one-third of the thickness of the plate, the lower two-thirds of the plate having straight edges.

The fifth type of Sholes & Glidden typewriter made at Ilion is similar to the fourth type and makes use of the same revised top-plate casting. There is, in fact, very little external difference between the fourth and fifth types, and some might incline to regard them as being merely minor variations of the same basic type rather than two distinct and separate types, which they are. In the fourth type the portion of the front cover just below the upper hinged section is secured as in the three previous types by means of two screws, one screw going directly into each of the main side-plate castings of the machine. In the fifth type the upper mounting of the front cover is by means of a single screw on the right side which runs into a threaded hole in a boss cast inside the right-hand side plate.

The first two Ilion models have a high paper shelf. The third, fourth, and fifth Ilion models are customarily fitted with a hinged top cover, as pictured in the illustrations of the third and fourth types. The introduction of this top cover necessitated the employment of a lower paper shelf. The illustration of the fourth type of Sholes & Glidden made at Ilion pictures a specimen whose original paper shelf was replaced with a paper shelf from a substantially later typewriter, probably a Remington No. 2 of the late 1880's or 1890's, bearing the Remington seal and cleaning instructions. This is a good example of how later-day replacements on any sort of manufactured product, even though they may have been made for what was a perfectly legitimate purpose, can confuse and mislead collectors. The paper shelf bearing the seal was not actually introduced until the later 1880's.

Although the hinged top cover was an important feature of the third, fourth, and fifth types of Ilion machines, some of these models were put out without the top covers. If a typewriter was supplied complete in a wooden cabinet case, it evidently was not furnished with the hinged top cover, the rolltop cover of the wooden cabinet case being deemed sufficient protection for the top of the machine. Theoretically there could have been such versions of all three of the later type Sholes & Glidden typewriters. Specimens found today without the top covers could, therefore, represent either units from which the top covers have become detached or, alternately, machines that initially came in wooden cabinet cases. It might well be argued by enthusiasts that such latter specimens can be deemed truly complete only if they are still housed in their original wooden cabinet cases.

It may appear odd that the seemingly slight change in the method by which the front cover is secured should be considered a proper basis for designating an entirely separate type, whereas the much more ap-

Left, the third Ilion model Sholes & Glidden typewriter, with carriage lever in front. Right, the fourth Ilion model. Note differences in top-plate casting. Both machines have the second type of carriage, as readily seen in the mounting of the wheel in front. The machine at the right has a replacement paper shelf with Remington seal from a later machine similar to that in the illustration on page 114.

Milwaukee Public Museum

parent and seemingly much more important difference in the carriage on the second type of Ilion machine is regarded as merely a minor variation of the same basic type. One reason is that the different carriage on the second type of Ilion machine may merely represent a later-day replacement of the original carriage, analogous to the aforementioned replacement of the paper shelf. Regardless of this, however, there is no doubt that the alteration in the method of mounting the front cover on the fifth Ilion type necessitated making a revised pattern for casting the right-hand side plate.

Accurately dating the various Ilion models of the Sholes & Glidden is by no means easy or certain. The first Ilion type, of course, came out in 1874, and the first of the carriage lever machines (the third Ilion type) appeared in 1877. Presumably, therefore, the second type of Ilion machine, the model with the side lever, was introduced in either 1875 or 1876. It is probable that production of the Sholes & Glidden continued well into the 1880's, but it is not possible, given our present state of knowledge, to attempt to assign specific dates to the fourth and fifth types of Ilion machines.

CLASSIFICATION

The foregoing will suffice to suggest some of the problems that are likely to confront any collector of a manufactured product, as well as, in fact, for the first time presenting a proper enunciation of the Sholes & Glidden typewriters. It is not practical to continue a detailed listing of subsequent machines, but there are other important aspects of collecting that can best be illustrated at this time both verbally and by means of actual photographs making further use of our chosen example, the typewriter. These problems confront collectors in almost every possible category. They may be summarized as Classification; Assumption of age, rarity, and desirability; and Variations.

Classification: There are as yet comparatively few established modes of classifying specimens among most of the categories of collecting that are most likely to appeal to men. There are exceptions to this, of course, among the most popular groups, such as clocks, firearms, and toys, and some categories provide virtually automatic self-classifying. Sports antiques, for instance, obviously in the main divide themselves into items associated with each specific activity, baseball, boxing, golf, and so on. Most men's collectables are as yet not assisted by recognized classifications, which makes collecting itself difficult. The collector must proceed more or less on his own, making use as far as possible of his own good sense and plain logic, although it must also be observed that very often existing and accepted technical and trade classifications for a product or group of products are by no means practical or acceptable to collectors.

The novice typewriter collector often tends, for example, erroneously to divide typewriters into office or standard machines, and portables, automatically putting all machines that are small or furnished with cases in the latter division. This is incorrect because many of the smaller nineteenth- and early twentieth-century machines were in their day offered simply as typewriters as such, and also because for many years after their inception virtually every typewriter of any substance came equipped with a wood or metal case or cover furnished with a carrying handle.

More experienced typewriter collectors classify by the mechanics of the machines. This can be carried out to all sorts of divisions and subdivisions, as in the case of the system followed by the Science Museum of South Kensington, London, in their booklet on their collection.[3] It is, however, somewhat too technically complex for the average collector. The average collector will find that—forgetting all about standard and portable typewriters as such—almost all typewriters he encounters will divide themselves into one of three groups. These, with references to examples illustrated herein, are keyboard machines with separate typebars, each typebar carrying one to three characters (Sholes & Glidden, Caligraph, Densmore); keyboard machines with all of the characters mounted on a single segment (Blickensderfer, Hammond); and indicator machines, which have no keyboards but in which a single indicator of some sort is moved to select the character to be printed (Hall, New World, Odell). There are almost endless variations of form in this classification, and they drift down from fairly substantial and widely accepted as practical machines in their day to others which even at the time they were made were acknowledged to be simply toy typewriters.

In any field of collecting, it will usually be found that the simplest

[3] *Handbook of the Collection Illustrating Typewriters*, by G. Tilghman Richards (London, 1938; cover title: *The History and Development of Typewriters*).

Three typewriters of the indicator class, all originating in the late nineteenth century and continuing to be made into the early twentieth. Top to bottom, the Hall, with a rectangular index plate; the New World, with a semicircular index plate; and the Odell, with a straight index plate.

George S. Indig Photographs

and most basic classification will be the best, as exemplified by the foregoing threefold division of typewriters. Dividing a category by present-day trade customs (standard machines and portables) would be fallacious from a historical standpoint. So, too, would be a division by a previous trade custom, such as visible and nonvisible writers, a point of primary importance in the 1890s and early 1900s, a primary reason being that once such a classification is attempted the collector finds himself running into definitions and degrees of visibility. In short, once again applying the example to all types of collectables, classification systems are best when they are obvious, nonoverlapping, and not subject to argument or individual interpretation.

Assumptions

In every area of collecting the hobbyist is all too likely to be misled by assumptions or deductions based on incomplete knowledge or evidence concerning age, rarity, and desirability. In the case of typewriters, the individual accustomed to the more or less standardized typebar machine and motivated by a natural impulse to assume what seems a logical technical progression, often develops a concept that the indicator machines are the earliest; machines with keyboards and with the characters mounted on a single segment are next, and that the typebar machine represents the final step in evolution. Actually, taking the Sholes & Glidden typewriter as a starting point, the typebar machine appeared first. The machines with the characters on a single segment, although for several decades unfamiliar to many, were by no means ever totally obsolete. The present-day Varityper, a type shuttle machine, is the lineal and continuing descendant of the Hammond. The type-wheel machine, probably best represented by the Blickensderfer, made what at the time seemed to many its last stand in the late 1920s as the Rem-Blick, then manufactured by Remington. Less than four decades later, the type-wheel principle was reintroduced, on a modern electric typewriter. Thus, to many collectors in the 1930s, 1940s, and 1950s, any type-wheel machine seemed a rather self-evidently old-fashioned implement; to most novice collectors it appeared an especially rare and desirable machine. Some type-wheel machines, of course, do approach such a description, but as a matter of fact, as

The Blickensderfer typewriter, manufactured in large quantities from 1893 to 1917, was the most successful of the type-wheel machines. Pictured here are the No. 7 (left) and the Home model (right), in their wooden cases, both popular in the early 1900s. Also shown is the last-stand of the Blickensderfer, the Rem-Blick (top), manufactured by Remington in the late 1920s.

George S. Indig Photographs *(left and right)*
Sperry Rand Corporation, Remington Rand
Office Machines Division *(top)*

an overall make, the manually operated[4] Blickensderfer type-wheel machine is undoubtedly one of the commonest—albeit undeniably one of the most interesting and historically important—of all old typewriters, having been manufactured by the tens and tens of thousands.

A somewhat parallel case may be found in the matter of typewriter keyboards. The present-day standard four-bank keyboard is almost identical in its arrangement to the keyboard arrangement on the first Sholes & Glidden machines. When the first machine that could write both capital and small letters was introduced in 1878, the Remington

Two famous double-keyboard typewriters, fathered by the sonorously named George Washington Newton Yost. Left, the Caligraph No. 3, a ribbon machine introduced in 1883, and, right, a Yost direct-inking machine of the 1890s.
Milwaukee Public Museum

No. 2, the same keyboard was retained with the addition of the shifting mechanism. Over the years, however, a great many other keyboards have been employed on other makes of typewriters. There were a few machines with two-bank keyboards, and a great many with three-bank keyboards. In the three-bank keyboard machines, there were separate shift keys for capital letters and for numerals, each regular key being capable of typing one of three characters depending on which, if either,

---

[4] There was also a Blickensderfer electric typewriter in the early 1900s, a scarce machine today, and there were Blickensderfer typebar machines, the Blick-Bar and the Blick Ninety.

Typebar typewriters with three-bank keyboards, all of approximately the World War I era. Top to bottom, an Oliver No. 9, a type and make popular from the 1890s to the late 1920s; a Fox No. 1 folding typewriter; and a Molle No. 3.

George S. Indig Photographs

shift key was depressed. Furthermore, even earlier there were double keyboard machines, with no shifting device and with a separate key for each letter.

New collectors usually regard any typewriter with one of these other-than-standard keyboards as necessarily an extremely early and scarce machine. Some of them are, although, in typewriters and virtually every other category of antiques, earliness—which is always comparative depending on the category, of course—and scarcity are never by any means synonymous. However, the Smith Premier No. 10 was a double keyboard machine that did not appear until 1908 and which was made until 1923, and there were three-bank keyboard typewriters manufactured even in the 1930s.

In short, in all collecting, assumption is all too often the inevitable handmaiden of error and disappointment. The collector paying too high a price for a given item—an easy pitfall for the beginner, especially when in the physical presence of the seemingly highly desirable artifact—is very likely to be in for a sad awakening with the coming of greater knowledge. It may not be in all such cases so much that too high a price has been paid in itself, for collectors almost always manage to average such things out in the long run, as the bad taste that such experiences are likely to leave in the mouth, resulting frequently in a general disgust with and perhaps even the complete abandonment of a hobby that, properly handled, could promise and deliver so much.

Whether, as in the example, a seemingly unusual typewriter, a wooden frame plane, a theatrical poster, a Colt .45 army revolver, or any other collectable, be careful never to jump to assumptions on your own or blandly accept as fact everything a vender may tell you. Throughout this book there are cited instances of various items that potentially may lead to such assumptions, but all of these, too, merely are examples mentioned among countless possible ones. This cautionary note has nothing to do with fakes or reproductions as such; the articles in question usually are quite genuine, but the novice's verve can make them as potentially dangerous and disheartening as out-and-out fakes and reproductions.

VARIATIONS

A substantial clue to the matter of variations and their effect on the pattern of a collection already has been provided in Chapter II, but

The Bennett typewriter, which first reached the market in 1910, was regarded as the ultimate miniaturization of the typewriter. It measured less than eleven inches in length but was a complete type-wheel machine, with keyboard and ribbon inking.

George S. Indig Photograph

something further should be said now, using our selected ideal example, the typewriter. Nobody knows with any certainty how many makes and models of typewriters have been manufactured since the first Sholes & Glidden. A determination of the second point would depend upon an individual's interpretation of a "model" and whether it is to be based primarily on the manufacturers' designations or on the variations actually known to collectors. The late Carl P. Dietz, a pioneer who collected over four hundred typewriters, had, by 1944, managed to compile a personal list of more than six hundred seventy-five "different" pre-World War II typewriters that had actually been on the market, a figure seemingly based on both makes and models, although most of today's collectors probably would find it deficient from the standpoint of actual major collectable variations. An educated guess would probably place the total from today's standpoint somewhere in four figures, but there would still be much debate concerning what constituted a "major" and what, a "minor" variation.

As with many manufactured products, some typewriters differ only in the brand name applied, many having been produced under quite a few different names at various times, for sale in different countries, with a change of ownership, for proprietary sales by mail-order houses and other large accounts, and even, on occasion, merely for one particular sales campaign. The primary typebar model of the American, for instance, was also sold as the Mercantile and the Pullman-A in the United States, and as the Armstrong, Elgin, Europa, Favorit, Fleet, Herald in Europe, and possibly under other names as well. Naturally, the collector considers each of these as representative of a different make or brand of typewriter, although there may be found examples with more mechanical variation between two specimens of, say, the Armstrong than between an Armstrong and any given example sold under one of the other names.

When the basic brand or make is known—in this instance the American—it usually is felt that the proprietary brands or "specials" are somewhat scarcer and more desirable. This usually but not always is correct. The situation and the principle will be found to obtain in a number of categories of collectables of current and increasing interest to men.

This situation should not, however, be confused with contract manufacturing, a practice which frequently is confusing to new collectors and thereby often leading to misunderstandings and errors in classification. In many cases, articles were actually produced in one factory on contract for a manufacturer who did not possess his own factory, or who could at any rate produce certain articles at a better price in this manner than if he undertook actual physical production himself. The manufacturer of record and of classification in such cases is the firm which controlled the product, not the company owning the factory where it was made. Thus, the first typewriters made at Ilion, New York, were Sholes & Glidden typewriters, although physically produced by Remington. Similarly, the Wilcox & Gibbs sewing machines were long made on contract by Brown & Sharpe, but they are classified as a Wilcox & Gibbs product, the Brown & Sharpe connection merely being an interesting historical addition. An interesting example of a double contract connection is represented by a Western Electric sewing machine that is based on the Wilcox & Gibbs. Wilcox & Gibbs contracted to supply the machines to Western Electric, the latter furnishing the motors and related electrical parts. In turn, the actual physical manufacturing was done by Brown & Sharpe on contract for Wilcox & Gibbs. But Western Electric was the manufacturer of record, the machines bear that name, and they are classified by collectors as a Western Electric product. Other styles of Western Electric sewing machines were made on contract by certain other sewing-machine manufacturers; these, too, are properly classified as Western Electric products.

It will be seen that in most cases such a situation was substantially different from that wherein a manufacturer, for one reason or another, put out his own product under various special brand names, as in the example provided of the American typewriter. The increasing interest among men collectors in such mass-produced items makes these expositions, of a sort that previously have not been thought required in general antiques books, desirable if not absolutely essential here. Again, the principles are almost universal throughout manufacturing, and the same manufacturing and selling practices will be found obtaining in countless other categories.

WHAT'S IN A NUMBER?

Manufacturers' model numbers or other designations may or may not reflect important changes, or, equally, the continued use of the same number may, to the unwary, conceal very important modifications. The Remington No. 2 typewriter, for instance, has been well

The Remington No. 2 typewriter, the first machine to write both capital and small letters, introduced in 1878 or shortly thereafter. The specimen illustrated, however, is an example manufactured somewhat later, and has the paper shelf with Remington seal.

Milwaukee Public Museum

publicized as the first machine to write both upper- and lower-case letters and as having been introduced in 1878. It was manufactured for many years, well over 100,000 having been produced under this number. Most typewriter collectors secure a Remington No. 2 (in the perhaps not too distant future this reference to "most" will probably strike hobbyists as somewhat grotesque, for even now a No. 2 is by no means so readily obtainable as in the 1940s), classify it as "1878" and rest satisfied, possibly rejecting offers of other No. 2s without examining them. In by far the majority of cases, the attribution of 1878 is highly incorrect; most of the No. 2s being of considerably later origin and design and of a type not made prior to 1888! Such a later No. 2 is pictured. A basic point that distinguishes it as a later No. 2 is the presence of the carriage-lift handle on the left, as distinct from the models that carry only the carriage return and indexing lever at the right. There are thus two very important basic variations of the No. 2, with and without this handle. But within each of the two types there will be found a number of other variations which the collector will observe according to his acuteness and collect according to the pattern he has set for himself.

Some such manufactured collectables will be found only with definite production variations, variations common to most if not all of a unit being put through the factory at a given time. In the case of other articles, of which typewriters are a prime example, there will be found selective variations that were in the main dependent upon the wishes of the individual purchaser, such as, with typewriters, the length of the carriage or the inclusion of special characters in the typebars or typewheel and in the corresponding keys. These are legitimate and collectable variations, and many typewriter collectors would retain them as such, but for the most part they are not properly classifiable as being in the nature of specific factory production changes. In a few early machines carriage length was concurrent with model numbers and usually were the most noticeable but far from the only changes. (It was not until typewriters had been accepted for some time that the concept of providing interchangeable carriages of different lengths for the same basic machine was evolved.)

As opposed to what may be termed "selective variations," almost any artifact manufactured over a period of time—and even, in many cases, one made but comparatively briefly—there will be found numerous progressive modifications, some minor and often scarcely noticeable, such as a change from one type of screwhead to another, and others of a major and immediately apparent nature. Manufacturing practice has, overall, witnessed a continual speeding up in model-designation changes since the mid-nineteenth century, although annual model-number changes on most products are of comparatively recent date. It is up to the individual collector to determine just how far he wishes to go—and just how far may, indeed, be practical, in collecting variations. The true specialist in any given field usually—and properly—collects every variation that comes within his grasp, for only in this manner can a true and complete picture of industrial progression be ascertained and recorded. Yet it cannot be denied that, in the view of many, such things can be carried too far and take on a measure of the ridiculous or merely provide what amounts to a cover for hoarding. Of course, much depends on just where you sit. If you have no Remington No. 2 and your friend has two slightly different ones and declines to accede to your requests to be permitted to possess one, your outlooks are likely to be quite different if equally justifiable.

There undoubtedly exist what must be classed as hoarders and speculators in many fields of antique collecting, but it usually is difficult justly to draw a line that distinguishes such an individual from the hobbyist who painstakingly has assembled a pertinent series of specimens presenting major and minor variations.

To emphasize once again, most of what has been said in reference to typewriters will be found equally applicable to any other form of production antiques now popular among men collectors. The specifics may change greatly, but the principles will remain basically valid.

CHAPTER IV

Machines, Fixtures, Advertising, and Other Antiques of Commerce

Next to the typewriter, although evidently at least at present some distance behind it in overall popularity, the most popular business-machine collectable would seem to be the cash register. Compartmented cashboxes and cash drawers, often fitted with some sort of secret latch or so-called combination lock—usually five finger pulls on a cash drawer that could be set to open the drawer in any one of twenty-five possible combinations—were long used in stores. The purpose of the cash register, or cash recorder as some of the early units were called, was not so much to provide added security for the cash but to record receipts, and, as time went on, perform other useful functions for both merchants and customers. The pioneer registers, some obviously recognizable to present-day viewers as such, others not so obvious, evidently first gained acceptance in the 1880s. Most collectors appear to prefer the smaller registers of the type used in barber shops and candy stores because of the factors of size and weight, although naturally the greater number of features, such as a receipting device, usually are found only on the bulkier machines. A fair but by no means infallible indication of a relatively early register (the first ones did not have them) is the presence of a metal rod or bar across the front

117

Three National cash registers of the late nineteenth and early twentieth century. The receipt-issuing feature incorporated in the register on the right was first used in 1893. The presence of the metal bar above the drawer is a good but not infallible indication of an early register.

National Cash Register Company

of the machine above the cash drawer. The fairly light weight of many early registers resulted in a great deal of shifting of the register when the drawers were closed against the heavy-tension release springs. Accordingly, the bar was added so that the operator might grip it with his fingers and hold the register steady while pushing the drawer shut against the springs with his thumb. Subsequently, with the evolution of heavier registers, the bar became unnecessary and was abandoned.

Prior to the widespread use of the typewriter and of carbon paper, probably the most important machine—one as simple as the typewriter is complex—in any business office was the copying press. Letters were handwritten in special ink. After drying, the ink would be moistened slightly with a sponge and the letter placed in contact with a sheet of special tissue. Both sheets were laid in the press and pressure exerted by screwing down the press, thereby transferring a duplicate of the letter to the tissue. In some cases, such as for copies of railroad orders, single sheets of tissue were employed. In most business offices, however, letters were thus copied into large books with numbered pages of such tissue, each letter being indexed by means of a hand-

written alphabetical entry in the front of the book. Most modern filing procedures and equipment are also a result of the introduction of the typewriter, letters received previously usually being folded so as to fit in vertical filing drawers about four inches wide and nine inches high, the recipient endorsing the folded letter or other document as to source and date before placing it in one of the wooden drawers.

Copying presses are important and frequently overlooked business antiques (one may be seen on the desk in the photograph of the restored railroad station), in part because they lack the mechanical complexity that makes typewriters, cash registers, and similar machines so appealing to men, but also to a large extent because most people today simply do not recognize them for what they are or understand their function. When they appear, they most often are erroneously called "bookbinders' presses" and consequently are ignored by most collectors of business antiques.

Anything ever used in an office is, of course, properly a business antique, although it is only fairly recently that any interest to speak of has been evinced in old desks, filing cabinets, and similar furnish-

Check protector of the late 1890s and early 1900s, manufactured by Wesley Manufacturing Company of New York. It sequentially punches perforated dollar signs and numbers into the face of checks.

George S. Indig Photograph

ings. However, there has for some time been a certain interest in mechanical business contrivances, although usually as somewhat of a sideline to typewriter collecting. Among such equipment may be found early duplicating machines, such as the office hektograph, the Cyclostyle, and the Rotary Neostyle, check writers and protectors, adding machines, and the like. They are all well worth collecting, preserving, and studying. It will be apparent, however, that in this area collecting popularity is to a considerable extent governed by two things. One is mechanical complexity and the other is more or less rational size, with enough bulk to satisfy a man and yet not so much as to make collecting, handling, and storage unduly arduous. The evident favorites, typewriters and cash registers, manifestly satisfy both requirements better than most other possibilities, with the edge considerably with the typewriters both because of their greater historical importance and because of the fact that the "works" are in most cases highly visible.

STORE FITTINGS

Counter complexes and large fixtures such as iceboxes and showcases are, barring endeavors to re-create an entire store, beyond the space capacity of most hobbyists to collect. Any sort of smaller store fittings and equipment are, however, highly collectable and extremely popular. In a general way, these include such things as scales, cord holders, coffee grinders; thread, seed, and spice cabinets, and the like; water coolers and small iceboxes; bins, and racks, and the like. There are also many collectors who particularize in the fittings of certain types of stores, such as drugstores, and if any of the equipment is in any way mechanical, such as early soda-water dispensers, so much the better in the eyes of most enthusiasts.

Any sort of animated display or advertising piece is therefore naturally of considerable interest. A good number of such pieces were made available to shops in the late nineteenth century, usually clockwork operated. There exists much confusion between the larger and more elaborate clockwork toys and store display pieces as such, the latter often being offered and sold, knowingly or innocently but nevertheless erroneously as toys. Most incorporated dressed miniature figures and as a result frequently are seized upon by ladies who collect dolls, even in many cases when their actual identification is known. In Europe there was a definite distinction between clockwork toys, and store fixtures and display pieces, the latter being especially manufactured and sold for the purpose. In the United States, however, well up toward the close of the nineteenth century, the quality of the better clockwork toys produced by such manufacturers as Ives was such that they readily could be adapted to window display use, and many were so adapted. The best known, perhaps, is the working figure of General Grant seated in a chair and smoking, which provided an ideal window piece for tobacconists of the late 1870s and early 1880s. Inasmuch as such Ives toys were capable of about an hour's operation on one winding, many of the various models were freely used as window attention-compellers. When finally driven off the market around the turn of the century by the cheap European imitations, there remained no inexpensive source of such reliable window pieces for the average storekeeper, although more affluent firms could secure either stock or especially made animated figures from firms specializing in display pieces, and a number of pieces still were available from Europe. In the case of the European animated display pieces, there was never much if any contemporary confusion or overlapping with toys; they were recognized and sold for precisely what they were, and their status is obvious today. With the Ives pieces it usually is impossible to determine if a given specimen was or was not used as an animated window display and, toy collectors being extremely active and enthusiastic, surviving specimens almost always end up in toy collections, no uncertainty being involved as to the correctness of their presence there.

A particularly attractive and enthusiastically collected store-fitting specialty will be found in the elaborate coffee, tea, and spice containers produced in the late nineteenth and early twentieth century. These were often not sold directly to store owners by the manufacturers or intermediaries, but were furnished to the distributors of the products involved, who purchased them in quantity, painted and lettered to their specifications, and who in turn provided them to their retail outlets. Probably no other group of old store fixtures were so colorful and so elaborately finished, many being provided with an Oriental or, at least, an exotic styling evocative of distant and inaccessible lands where the coffee, tea, and spices originated. Some were lithographed, but many were almost equally elaborately painted, on occasion even incorporating beveled plate-glass mirrors. Although many collectors refer to them indiscriminately as "bins," there was a specialized nomenclature widely recognized—a bin properly was only a unit that stood on the floor, an elaborate counter unit was a caddy, less prepossessing ones canisters or even, simply, cans, and any multiple or combination unit, a cabinet. Even in the late 1960s there were still a few old stores where they could be found in use, but these containers were vanishing rapidly and their relative availability to collectors gave little hint of the fact that they were for the most part originally mass-produced in enormous quantities. In the very early 1900s some models were in such demand that they were manufactured in two or, in some cases, even more different factories of the American Can Company, one of the chief suppliers. The foregoing, of course, also makes it implicit that most of the units found today, regardless of how archaic they may appear to modern eyes, are by no means so old as is customarily implied and accepted.

Although today vending machines may be found almost anywhere

Pages from an American Can Company catalog of grocer's tinware of the early 1900s, a doubly interesting catalog as devoted to store fittings and having color plates. Pictured are two spice cabinets.

George S. Indig Photograph

and sell almost anything, purists may object that, from a historical standpoint, they should properly be classified as store fittings, the assumption being that in their earliest period they were mainly competitive with established retail outlets. This is not by any means strictly true; for a considerable period of time, candy and gum machines were regularly chained outside stores for after-hour sales, and stamp-vending machines were so ubiquitous by 1908 that, in that year, the United States Government started issuing coil stamps for use therein. In any event, the question need really concern only the hobbyist who is undertaking a project of recreating an entire old store in toto. There also is a suggestion that some of the earliest vending machines employing animated figures, such as the Pulver Gum machines of the early 1900s, were deliberately designed with the view of extracting additional pennies from youngsters as much for the novelty of seeing the machine in action as to acquire the commodity the machine delivered.

Chewing-gum machines were, in fact, among the first widely used vending machines, among the earliest and most popular among collectors being the Pulver machines which employed a miniature figure such as one of the comic-strip character the Yellow Kid within a glass-fronted box to reach for the gum and drop it into the delivery chute. (There is an obvious connection, collecting and otherwise, between coin-operated vending machines and other types of coin-operated devices, many of which might also easily be considered store fittings.) In the main the gum-, chocolate-, and candy-vending machines appear by far the most popular among collectors, although widespread interest in bottle collecting has directed considerable attention to soft-drink-vending devices. In view of the great popularity of stamp collecting, it is rather surprising that more attention has not been paid to the early postage-stamp machines, which would appear to constitute a virtually untouched field to date.

The matter of selling bottled soft drinks was, if anything, more related to the development of in-store coolers than of vending machines as such, a warm bottle obviously being of no attraction to a thirsty man on a hot day. The average store seeking such trade usually kept a number of bottles in their big icebox along with the butter and cream, or in an ice-filled barrel or other suitable container, often a water cooler or portable icebox. As a result, such devices, when of

Small iceboxes and coolers for home or store use are of considerable interest to men collectors. Pictured here are, top, a portable metal icebox with faucet for draining the ice compartment, of the early 1900s, and an Icy-O bottled soft-drink dispenser of the later 1920s.

George S. Indig Photograph *(top)*
The Archives, The Coca-Cola Company,
Atlanta, Georgia

a commercial nature and identifiable as such, are of considerable interest to collectors; the old ice-filled water cooler is in fact a prime general business antique in any case. Combination soft-drink vending and cooling equipment was available about as early as 1910 but met with rather limited acceptance, and it was not until the early 1930s that satisfactorily refined machines came into widespread use. One major problem was the development of automatic vending machines that could accommodate sufficient bottles not to require frequent reloading.

Unfortunately, most of these machines are too bulky for the average collector to house, although there are a few who specialize in vending machines to such an extent that they seek to acquire as many examples as possible regardless of size. In the main, however, with vending machines as with many other categories of collectables, there seems to be a more or less recognized practical size for home collecting beyond which most enthusiasts will not go.

Closely associated with old vending machines and often sought by the same collectors are what are known as trade stimulators. Their greatest period of use appears to have been the late nineteenth and early twentieth centuries, and in a certain sense the trade stimulators might be said to have pointed the way toward much of the subsequent vending-machine development and widespread use. A trade stimulator usually was coin-actuated, but it did not dispense merchandise itself. It was a sort of gambling device, the customer's coin being inserted to set the machine in motion. If a winning combination of numbers came up, the customer received two, three, or perhaps more times the amount of merchandise for which he paid—usually candy, cigarettes, gum, and the like. If there was no win, the customer merely received what he had initially purchased. Trade stimulators were made in a variety of forms and degrees of elaboration. On occasion they have not been recognized for what they are, for the category is not too widely known today, so they have either remained rather mysterious unidentified devices or classified as something entirely different.

Any sort of store poster or broadside, counter display, or anything else employed in promoting the sale of merchandise is collected by innumerable enthusiasts, the matter of housing and storage being far simpler than in the case of most of the things generally considered

Two coin-operated store fittings of the early 1900s. Top, a trade stimulator in the form of a miniature bicycle. If the wheels stopped on a winning combination of numbers, the customer received double or triple the price of the merchandise for which he had paid. Bottom, a Pulver gum-vending machine with an animated figure of the Yellow Kid dispensing gum.

The Vendo Company

Nineteenth- and early twentieth-century trade signs: the giant mortar and pestle of the druggist, scissors of the tailor, hat of the hatter, and key of the locksmith. Also shown are a sextant, decorative wooden signs, weathervanes, and toys.

G. William Holland Collection

store fittings. Collected, too, are store signs and, now, even the pre-fabricated raised letters of wood and other materials that were used to create storefront signs. The latter are naturally related to the trade signs discussed immediately below, while the posters and other paper material usually are regarded as more closely connected with other paper advertising and promotional material than to store fittings as such.

Trade Signs and Wooden Indians

The trade sign as such still exists in use to a certain extent, and examples will be familiar to most readers who pass them almost without thinking. The giant spectacles of the optician, the barber pole, and a few other types have enjoyed such traditional vitality still to continue in widespread use, although it is obvious that they, too, gradually are fading out in the face of modern store-design practices, and possibly in time even the barber pole will vanish and become to a new generation of collectors what the wooden Indian is to today's. At one time, countless stores displayed trade signs either above their doors or on the sidewalks before them: the mortar and pestle of the pharmacist, the steer of the butcher, the shoe of the shoemaker or shoe dealer, the dummy clock of the jeweler and clock store, and so on. Concerning the giant dummy watches of the latter, with their hands fixed at 8:20, an enshrined American legend has arisen, retold in hushed tones from father to son; the hands are supposedly always set at 8:20 because that was the exact hour and minute when Abraham Lincoln died. Actually Lincoln died at 7:22 A.M., and the design of dumb horologes had long previously been set at 8:20 in order to provide the optimum space for the display of the jeweler's name and other advertising messages.

It will be seen that a trade sign is not a sign in the sense that it delivers its message primarily by means of words, but is essentially a symbolic figure recognizable as relating to the business in question. Any actual lettering that appears on a trade sign, such as the jeweler's name on a giant clock or watch, or that of a brand of cigars on the base of a wooden Indian, is entirely of secondary import; the sight of the giant watch or the wooden Indian alone was sufficient to inform anyone that here was a jeweler or a tobacconist. There also exist a number of closely related signs of this type, or more properly, perhaps, carvings and decorations, that do not in this manner immediately relate to any specific business, such as American eagles and patriotic shields and the like. They usually are collected along with trade signs but, in many cases, were purely ornamental and often employed indoors to decorate engine houses, meeting halls, etc. Initially, perhaps, most trade signs were individually and often locally carved, although it probably is possible to overestimate this point in the interests of that good old standby, folk art. By the Civil War a considerable proportion of trade signs were as standardized and mass-produced as anything else, specially designed and carved versions being the exception. In most cases, a merchant simply ordered the desired trade sign from the catalog of his wholesale supplier or manufacturer, who carried them in stock for the requirements of his customers; the optical-supply manufacturer the giant eyeglasses, the hat manufacturer the big hat, and so on, or from firms specializing in nothing but the production of trade signs.

The historical importance of trade signs as business antiques has

Coca-Cola store signs of the early 1900s. The "Betty" sign, showing the calendar girl of 1914, was introduced at the close of that year for the 1915 season. It is thirty-two by forty-four inches and a magnificent example of the art of metal lithography, fourteen colors being employed.

The Archives, The Coca-Cola Company,
Atlanta, Georgia

A forty-inch-high wooden Indian of the late nineteenth and early twentieth century.

G. William Holland Collection

been growing in recent years, and they often are collected as a category in themselves or as a segment of a broader collection.

The wooden Indian or the cigar-store Indian perhaps is the trade sign *par excellence*, although neither name is embracingly correct, as not all of them were Indians and not all of them were of wood. On the other hand, it is common to exaggerate the prevalence of figures other than Indians on the basis of a few well-known surviving specimens which have been widely publicized simply because they were not the traditional Indian and whose appearance at cigar stores is, in some cases at least, rather questionable. If a figure does not proffer a bundle of cigars or otherwise carry a specific indication of an association with tobacco, it is almost certainly not a cigar-store figure. Such figures were also on occasion used in connection with other businesses, but even well into the 1930s, when a number still remained in active use, the man in the street usually was correct in his assumption that the store he spotted with a figure in front of it was that of a tobacconist. (Next to the Indians, but a poor second, Mr. Punch seems to have been the most frequently employed cigar-store figure.) The figures themselves might be used indoors as well as out, the smaller figures usually being window-display or counter pieces, the latter often fitted with a small lamp with which a purchaser might conveniently light his cigar. A number of figures were made not of wood but of metal, usually stamped sheet zinc, or of other materials. Metal ones were, of course, stock mass-production items, as were, at least to some extent, those made of wood. Disillusioning as it may be, there were catalogs of standard designs put out by at least some of the makers.

The use of the figure of an Indian to identify a seller of tobacco appears to date back to the seventeenth century in Great Britain and the Netherlands, the connotation being the amiable Indian offering the European the consolation and delights of tobacco. Many have repeatedly expressed wonder as to the seeming paradox of the Indian's being employed as the popular symbol of the tobacconist in America in the late nineteenth century at the very time when most smokers would hardly have cared about, if they would not actually have applauded, the destruction of the Indians. The answer is that the cigar-store Indians were of a more or less similar prototype, a revealingly nubile female often referred to as "the Indian Queen," who in now almost completely forgotten American and British memory was Pocahontas or was specifically identified as Pocahontas by name. When the floodtides of Victorian prudery were at their heights, these figures were the subject of much criticism and found publicly unacceptable. As a result, thousands and perhaps tens of thousands of the old Indian Queens were unceremoniously scrapped, but to continue the tradition of the Indian in front of the cigar store, they were replaced with braves. The comparatively few female cigar-store Indians made and used in the late nineteenth and early twentieth century are evidently of a considerably more modest and abundantly clothed pattern than the original tribe, the few surviving members of which reputedly spent some decades of time in safely isolated fancy houses and men's bars.

The day now is long past when a collector of wooden Indians as a specialty can gather them in by the dozens. It goes almost without saying that they are presently being faked, there evidently currently being several "humble, pious workmen" making a good thing out of carving reproductions of wooden Indians. The genuine article is growing scarcer but still occasionally is obtainable. They represent a particularly interesting type of business antique and, as already suggested, are the epitome of the trade sign. In addition, they comprise an enduringly important memento of the bygone American scene although, even though it may seem somewhat of a contradiction, also as previously indicated, their origin probably is British.

TRADE CARDS

The contemporary paper material relating to collectables of various kinds forms an enormous field. In a sense, all of it comprises business antiques, for its original purpose was to promote the sale of merchandise and services. However, its influence and value as background and research material for specific categories of antiques is in many ways its most important attribute. Thus, in brief, the collecting of such material may be approached in three ways: as a broad group of business and advertising antiques, some and perhaps a substantial portion not without artistic or at least pictorial value; simply as substantially interesting, nostalgic historical and pictorial material in itself, and, lastly and perhaps most important, in selected categories relating to similar categories of actual artifacts and as a vital adjunct to the collecting of these specimens themselves. In any case, the newcomer generally is at first surprised at the attention paid such material and at the seemingly high prices that desirable examples command. In time, however, he is likely to appreciate what at first seems quite strange, the now almost axiomatic situation wherein the experienced collector, presented with a real or imaginary choice whereby he may retain either his actual specimens or his collection of catalogs and other paper material relating to them would almost invariably prefer to keep the paper.

"Paper" is indeed a thin-sounding word for the boundless world of interest and knowledge that the experienced collector continually derives from a thoughtfully gathered assemblage of trade cards, catalogs, posters, instruction manuals, advertisements, and similar material that relate to and shed knowledge on his category or categories. That such material possesses a certain nostalgic and historical value probably no one would deny; it is usually only with the passage of con-

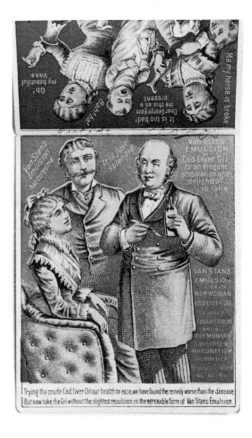

A transformation trade card of the late nineteenth century advertising Van Stan's Emulsion. Flip the upper part of the card away and see the happy change that transpires when you take the right cod liver oil. The other side of the card provided a similar transformation promoting glue.

G. William Holland Photographs

siderable time and the gaining of experience that the novice even begins to appreciate the fascination that such material holds and the inordinate value which, when properly used and interpreted, it provides the serious collector and student from an informative standpoint.

Of the groups mentioned, probably the least important from a historical and informative standpoint, but possibly the easiest to collect as a form in itself and for its own sake, are the trade cards. Trade-card collecting, unfortunately, got off to a bad start with all sorts of overtones of misinterpretation and snobbery, and attempts to erect all sorts of airy edifices concerning them in which might be found profound sociological meanings. Perhaps the less said about all this the better, but older collectors still remember the famed Paul Revere gambit wherein two supposed trade cards both bearing the name of Paul Revere & Son were intricately dissected and expounded upon to demonstrate—one presumably being pre-Revolutionary and the other post-Revolutionary—by means of their styles and wording the whole scope and swirl of the American Revolution and the founding of the new nation, although the most elementary basic research would quickly have demonstrated that the styling of the firm name, Paul Revere & Son, did not come into use until well after the Revolution, and that in fact the son, Joseph Warren Revere, who supposedly participated in the alleged 1775 card, was not born until 1777!

The term "trade card" itself, although well established and generally recognized, is in itself a misnomer, save insofar as that in the late nineteenth century certain groups of stock cards were designed for the use of specific trades. Some believe "trade card" is a contraction of "tradesman's card"; others, that it is of much later origin and is a corruption of the boys' term "trading cards," for the cards were often extensively swapped. In any event, the name is not sufficiently embracing, and "advertising cards" would be a better designation. The cards are of various sizes, some roughly as small as a calling card and others quite large, but the greater number run about two or three inches by four or five inches. Most, but not necessarily all, are highly colored; they are in effect a representation of the flowering of the lithographer's art in the late nineteenth century, and many were produced by the famous lithographers of the day and sometimes bear their imprints, including that of Currier & Ives. While the great era of these cards was the late nineteenth and early twentieth century, the issuing of various forms, particularly of those packed in chewing gum, continues, and many fairly recent items are assiduously collected.

Due to the numbers, variety, and overlappings of cards, classification has always been extremely complex and difficult. For simplification here, it might be suggested that most cards, regardless of other possible divisions, might be divided into those that came packed within a product, such as cigarettes, candy, and gum, and those which were distributed free of charge simply as a form of advertising. This no doubt will appear to many as a gross oversimplification, yet it seems the most practical way of summing up a most complex and extensive subject. The insert cards generally were issued as long sets which might run to twenty-five, fifty, or over a hundred cards, the prospect of completing the set presumably being an incentive to continued purchases. The advertising cards might promote a specific product or a store or some service. At times they run to sets, usually four cards to a set, but sometimes more, as in the case of the Budweiser Beer opera cards, of which three examples are illustrated, or the Singer Sewing Machine set, which portrayed the Singer in use in seemingly almost every country of the known world.

No intent is present to play down the insert cards, which are collected by an extremely extensive and enthusiastic following, but the advertising cards are likely to have more historical and research value in themselves and to merit more specific comment here. It should be understood that the possible designs in each group run into the tens of thousands. The advertising cards may further be classified as follows:

1. Cards designed and issued to advertise a specific product, as exemplified by the aforementioned Budweiser and Singer cards, or a store or a service.

2. Stock cards designed for the imprint of a related product or store or service. Sometimes such stock designs were designed so as to be adaptable to almost anything. The "Ye Head of Ye Heap" card illustrated, which depicts William K. Vanderbilt (not, as generally is thought, his father, the Commodore) astride a locomotive, is a good example of a card of this type. The reverse of the specimen pictured is imprinted for Hughes Witch Hazel, but it could serve equally well for any of a dozen other products.

Late nineteenth-century American trade cards. Top, three cards from the Anheuser Busch opera series, wherein each card parodied an opera or operetta to advise the purchase of their beer. Below, the famous Chocolat Menier card with the design considered an advertising classic at the time.

G. William Holland Photographs *(top)*
George S. Indig Photograph *(bottom)*

"Ye Head of Ye Heap" depicting William K. Vanderbilt, one of the better stock-design trade cards of the late nineteenth century, on which manufacturers or merchants could imprint their own name and advertisement.

G. William Holland Photograph

3. Stock cards that merely presented attractive or humorous designs, and for which no relationship was sought between the card design and the store or service making use of and imprinting the card. Cards of this type often were used by local merchants, sometimes merely rubber-stamped with their name and address, and sometimes merely distributed without bothering to identify their source.

The local stores were in fact the chief means of distributing all of these cards, merchants being supplied with them by manufacturers or securing their own, and slipping one or several into shopping bags or the hands of youngsters. It is obvious that a widespread collecting hobby existed for these cards at the time they were current, and innumerable enthusiasts filled countless albums with them. Today's collector, therefore, is likely to secure a good proportion of his cards from albums, necessitating careful soaking, peeling, and cleaning to remove the card in good condition and most particularly without damaging the reverse side, which, in many cases, is of equal interest and importance to the face.

A particularly interesting, attractive, early, and widely publicized group of cards comprise those mid-nineteenth-century cards advertising clipper ships and soliciting passengers, having elicited the interest of more collectors than did cards in general. Approximately one thousand different designs are known, but in most cases at best only a few specimens of a given type. In the main, they are somewhat larger than most cards. They provide a specialty of considerable interest but one comparatively difficult to pursue at this late date, although specimens do come to light from time to time.

As the term implies, the vast majority of trade cards are printed on lightweight card stock. A few items that properly qualify for this designation, however, were printed on relatively thin paper. On the other hand, many larger pieces, usually on paper, some on card, that properly should be classified as flyers, dodgers, throwaways, broadsides, or posters have erroneously been designated "trade cards." The collecting of all of these is at once a separate hobby in itself, or at least a distinct category of advertising antiques, and also an essential segment of catalog collecting, many early manufacturers issuing only a single sheet describing and promoting their lines. Many of the advertising posters are extremely colorful and attractive, although often of more interest from a visual standpoint than as a source of sound research information. This, too, should be noted: as with trade cards, posters divide themselves into special and stock designs. Most of the posters and signs advertising specific products were special designs, but a great many of the old country-fair and race-meet type of posters were stock designs. They were simply imprinted with the name and date of the event to be featured, a point not realized by many collectors, who often are puzzled by finding identical posters advertising events many miles and months apart.

Such posters are not, as some unaware of their stock origins believe, extraordinary flukes and rarities, or, as some have built up the legends, astounding examples of pictorial piracy. In the main, however, in the case of both trade cards and posters, it is impossible to generalize as to the relative rarity and desirability of special and stock designs, each piece having to be assessed as an individual case. It may be said, though, that many of the special trade cards were issued and distributed in such vast quantities that numerous good stock designs usually are considered of greater interest; "Ye Head of Ye Heap," for example, indisputably rates as a much better and more desirable trade card than any of the Budweiser opera series.

Catalogs

In the case of catalogs, "catalogs" alone is sufficient, most knowledgeable collectors finding "trade catalog" an inept and irritating redundancy, although there are other types of catalogs, such as the catalog of an exhibition. To the average individual, whether in the nineteenth century or today, the word "catalog" automatically conjures up a picture of a listing of goods for sale. The reference to the previous century also brings up the matter of dating. There were innumerable catalogs issued in the late eighteenth and early nineteenth century. Often then, as on occasion much later, they bear titles which attempted to make them sound somewhat grander and less overtly commercial. An example of this from 1884 will be found in *The Practical Dog Book for Both the Professional and Amateur Fancier*, pictured here. It is a catalog of particular interest because of both its full-color frontispiece and its content. Despite its title and the inclusion

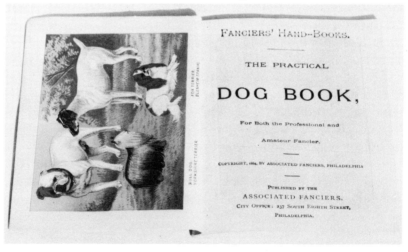

Title page and full-color frontispiece of an interesting 1884 item. Ostensibly a dog book, but actually it is a catalog with prices of dogs and supplies. Over fifty breeds of dogs are illustrated, described, and priced, puppies and adults, males and females.

George S. Indig Photograph

of some general information, it is actually a catalog with prices of dogs and supplies issued by Associated Fanciers, which operated a gigantic dog, poultry, and cage-bird breeding operation near Philadelphia, Pennsylvania. It includes descriptions and offerings of over fifty breeds of dogs, plus ferrets, trained and untrained.

There is nothing more ephemeral than catalogs; at times, they even contain notices advising those who receive them to destroy all previous issues to avoid possible confusion. On the other hand, there evidently always have been people who find catalogs of all sorts fascinating and who regularly retain everything that comes their way. As an overall category, old catalogs are therefore not difficult to come by, although securing catalogs relating to a particular category of antiques or issued by specific companies may well prove quite a different story. Pre-Civil War catalogs as a class are rather difficult to find today, although examples do turn up. Age alone, as with physical artifacts, is never a criterion of the desirability and value of a catalog. Some of the most desirable catalogs have been issued comparatively recently, whereas there exists an abundance of nondescript nineteenth-century catalogs of relatively little importance or value.

While there are as with all things, exceptions (the aforementioned dog catalog, for example), as a general rule it may be taken that the catalogs of greatest interest are those relating to things that are widely collected plus the things in which most men are interested and would like to collect if it were practical. For a list of desirable catalog subjects it would, in fact, be necessary only to run through the topics covered in this book. Thus, catalogs of office machines, electrical goods, cameras, tools, toys, automobiles, fire engines, sporting goods, firearms, and clocks are pieces usually of considerable interest to a great many hobbyists. On the other hand, to give a negative example, catalogs of fireworks—unless they also include such things as toy cannon and pistols, in which case they become of a certain interest to toy collectors—elicit virtually no interest. A few individuals may well make a hobby of studying the history of the fireworks industry or, because of the Fourth of July connotations, they may fit into a few collections of other material, but as far as is known and would appear likely, no one collects old fireworks for very obvious reasons. Hence, fireworks catalogs are generally duds.

Beyond the foregoing thoughts, it is difficult to categorize catalogs

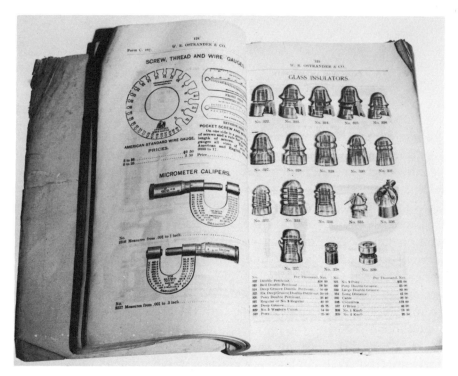

Pages from a W. R. Ostrander & Company wholesale electrical catalog of the early 1900s. The illustrations of the five insulators comprising the top row clearly demonstrate what is meant by the designation "double petticoat" in insulator design.

George S. Indig Photograph

as to desirability. As noted, age alone does not in itself make for desirability and value; a specific catalog of the 1930s may well rate higher than one of the 1880s or even one of the 1830s. Nor is size or elaboration in itself of prime importance, although these are factors that obviously must play some part in determining relative desirability and value, but a simple unillustrated folder can be much more highly esteemed by the collector who knows his field than a large and elaborately colored or bound catalog. It should be borne in mind that, while catalogs do have intrinsic value in themselves, their real value to the collector who is not merely an accumulator but a student of his specialty is in the background information they can impart concerning his specialty.

The alert hobbyist is aware, however, that catalogs are not Holy Writ, and their use in research must be undertaken with intelligence and discrimination. Properly employed, they can be of incalculable value; improperly perused, they can provide an exactly reverse effect. Remember that, when issued, the object of a catalog was to sell merchandise; it was not intended to divert or educate a collector at a much later date. Company and product histories often are written to produce a particular desired impression. Various claims are often, if not intentionally spurious, erroneous. At times, illustrations of handmade samples, differing slightly or in a substantial measure from anything actually produced, are employed. At other times, illustrations of discontinued models are retained long after something quite different is described and is being produced. It may not be remembered, or even thought necessary, to reset standing type when modifications are made in a product and a description may not actually tally with what is being offered. The list could be continued. In short, as the popular collector's expression goes, the enthusiast must know how to read a catalog properly if he is really to derive any benefit from its study.

In the main, catalogs may be divided into several distinct classifications, regardless of format and product, as follows:

1. Manufacturer's catalogs. These are usually looked upon as the most important and helpful as being the closest to the source, and the most comprehensive and authoritative. Presumably they cover everything that was being made at the date they were issued, although this is not always completely true, as there often were various specials which were not included in a regular catalog listing and which often become known only through the location of an actual specimen or by being found listed in other types of catalogs. Many manufacturer's catalogs are found bearing the imprint of a jobber or of a retailer— as jobber's catalogs may at times also be found with the imprint of a dealer, a circumstance that may be momentarily confusing but which does not, of course, alter the actual status of the catalog.

2. Jobber's catalogs. These generally are regarded as being of secondary importance and usefulness to manufacturers' issues, as they often show abridged lines and descriptions or a good deal of merchandise which is not overtly identified as to make or make use of their own rather than the manufacturer's numbers. On the other hand, jobber's catalogs often show much special or proprietary merchandise that is not to be found listed elsewhere and on occasion include important and otherwise unobtainable information concerning contemporary trade conditions which can be of tremendous value at times to the judicious researcher.

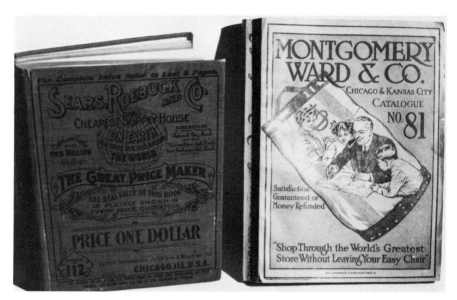

Classics of commerce. Left, a 1901 Sears, Roebuck & Company catalog in the hardcover edition. Right, a 1912 Montgomery Ward & Company catalog.

George S. Indig Photograph

A magnificent hardbound British catalog of the late nineteenth century, with 261 14½-inch-high pages, over 70 of them in full color. It includes china, glass, lamps, statuary, store fittings, and so on, including the curious 38-inch-long coin-operated barroom music box with animated "Sleeping Beauty" and two mechanical serpents, illustrated here.

George S. Indig Photograph *(left)*
G. William Holland Photograph *(right)*

3. Retail catalogs. In this grouping may be included catalogs issued by individual stores, for use either in counter or mail-order sales, and catalogs intended only for mail-order use and often specifically classified as mail-order catalogs. There are many of the latter, but, of course, the largest and best-known are those of Sears, Roebuck & Co. and of Montgomery Ward & Co. For the most part, retail and mail-order catalogs are of considerably lesser value to the researcher than are the manufacturer's and jobber's issues, but, again, information at times appears in them concerning products that are not described elsewhere, and they cannot lightly be dismissed either as sources of information or as collectables in themselves. In recent years, the big mail-order catalogs have become the subject of much attention and collecting them has, in effect, become a sort of subhobby. It should be observed here as a caution to researchers that to some extent their value as documents of overall social and business history is now widely overrated. For many years their contents were largely oriented toward a rural audience, and in any event their listings seldom included the most elaborate and expensive merchandise in any given category. But, properly employed, they can be valuable tools for the researcher and often reveal the existence of proprietary lines that are not to be found cataloged anywhere else.

OTHER PAPER ANTIQUES OF BUSINESS

Old instruction manuals often can be of surprisingly important value to the collector and historian where mechanical artifacts are concerned. The reason is that they frequently make specific reference to the existence of models with progressive constructional changes of whose existence the collector might otherwise be unaware. Thus, instruction manuals for such things as typewriters, cameras, and the like can prove of considerable informative value when carefully scrutinized either by themselves or in comparison with actual specimens. Of necessity, instruction-manual texts and illustrations had to reflect more closely the exact structural and mechanical forms of the articles in question than did many catalogs, although this is not to say that on occasion instruction manuals and sheets will not be found that make use of obsolete drawings or that otherwise do not accurately reflect

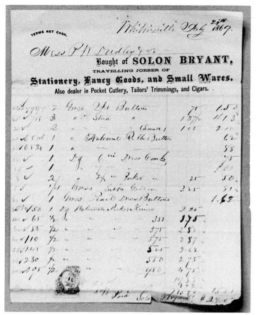

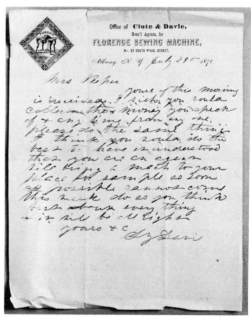

Any old paper material relating to business is of interest to collectors both in itself and as research material. Pictured here is an 1869 bill of Solon Bryant, a New England "Traveling Jobber," mainly for buttons and pocket knives, and an 1870 letter from the Albany, New York, agents for the Florence Sewing Machine.

G. William Holland Photographs

the actual device with which they were furnished. Any item that originally was furnished with an instruction manual is naturally enhanced in value when the original instruction literature still accompanies it. In addition, instruction manuals in themselves are interesting and pertinent collectables in connection with any category of antiques to which they apply and comprise in themselves another and distinct group of the paper antiques of business, although one closely allied to catalogs and usually regarded as a part or at least an adjunct of a collection of catalogs.

Any paper material relating to business, whether business in general or to a specific firm or product category, is of potential interest and value both in itself and as research material for the study of actual specimens. This includes correspondence—often the most interesting and informative—which also is collectable from the standpoint of the letterheads as well as the content, bills, invoices, office and factory records, ship manifests, and so on. The illustrations provide a suggestion of the possibilities inherent in this sort of material. Anyone fortunate enough to come into the possession of a large quantity of consecutive business paper material of a past era has before him, if he has the time, inclination, and ability, the opportunity to undertake a substantial research project that will reveal an interesting and often important picture of bygone commerce and industry. It is only now that substantial interest is being taken in the possibilities of this sort of thing, and by now, of course, a great deal of the possible source material for such studies has long since been pulped. From time to time, however, opportunities turn up for a collector to acquire such groups of material and at least to preserve it, if not actually to analyze its contents in depth.

Lastly come advertisements themselves, again a type of material of value and interest both in itself and as a source for research, with which might also be grouped trade magazines. Most of the old trade publications had relatively small print runs, and copies seldom were preserved, although there are exceptions to both limitations. If you are not interested in the subject covered, there is probably nothing less interesting than an old trade magazine. If, however, it relates to a subject you are collecting and researching, it can be an aid of tremendous interest and value. As with other types of material, the collecting of old trade magazines also can be a hobby in itself. Toward the close of the nineteenth century there were over one thousand different trade papers and magazines published in the United States alone.

Much that has been said for previous groupings can be said for old advertisements; they can be collected in connection with a specialty or as an end in themselves, and they can provide important sources of information. Furthermore, a great number are highly decorative, and the display possibilities of a group of framed old advertisements should never be overlooked, although a great many enthusiasts prefer, when possible, to collect old magazines intact and to leave them unclipped and thereby, of course, of greater collector value in themselves. In this connection, the following cautionary note is most important. At one time, almost all magazines grouped their advertisements at the front and back with no adjacent carry-over reading matter. When the magazines were bound, it was the almost invariable custom to remove and discard the advertising pages, which were regarded as worthless matter. Consequently, the collector who orders bound volumes of old periodicals in order to secure the advertising pages without first ascertaining if they are present is likely to be in for a sad disappointment. The paradox is that today, in the case of most old magazines, it is the advertisements and not the text that are the material of interest and value. Single unbound copies usually have the advertising pages remaining and are the most promising source of old advertisements for the collector.

There probably exists no collector who would not exult in the possession of one or more original drawings, paintings, or other art work prepared for advertisements. Such material seldom is met with in collections, not so much because it does not exist, although it certainly is far from common, but because, when observed, it is not recognized for what it is. A certain percentage of such art work does survive and may turn up on occasion in portfolios of assorted matter offered in antiques and book shops. It may not shriek out its original purpose by such devices as including a can of baking powder in a scene, but if the collector is familiar with the general run of past advertisements relating to his specialty, he may immediately recognize it for what it is or at least possess sufficient intuitive ability to suspect what he has run across. As a broad although by no means comprehensive hint, artists did not customarily draw or paint kitchen or bathroom scenes for other than advertising purposes. If a collector comes across such drawings or paintings, the chances are that he has stumbled upon some original advertising art work.

CHAPTER V

Electrical and Scientific Antiques

Mention scientific antiques and the traditionalist antiquarian, admitting such things can indeed exist, is likely to turn in thought immediately to something on the order of the surveyor's compass in the Smithsonian Institution made by David Rittenhouse, the eighteenth-century Pennsylvania savant and clockmaker. Such an article is, beyond question, an admirable and desirable piece. The fact is, however, that practically collectable scientific antiques may be no farther away than the electric-light fixture your neighbor replaced last week in his fifty-year-old house.

Interestingly enough, the glass collectors are well aware of this, but in collecting the beautiful shades used in the late nineteenth and early twentieth century, they have completely neglected the fixtures which called the shades into being. Anything made of glass, of course, has a unique and virtually immediate collector following. The lure of glass in practically any form seems almost irresistible, a point to which there will be occasion to allude again shortly. But enthusiasts for glass itself find it rather curious that for the most part an increasing array of men collectors are interested first in the fixtures and only second in the shades. The collector of electrical antiques is not exactly a new breed; some men have been quiet collectors for decades, but it is only comparatively recently that most people have become aware of the existence of the category, which now bids fair to become one of the most popular among what can broadly be classified as scientific antiques.

From a standpoint of age alone, the electrical artifact that most frequently reveals itself to the novice collector is the medical battery. The collecting of old medical and dental materials is, of course, a hobby in itself, although a related interest more frequently manifests itself in the collecting of old drugstore fixtures and most especially druggist's jars and bottles, which it need hardly be pointed out are also of interest to glass collectors. Inasmuch as electricity manifestly is recognized as having therapeutic values, it is difficult for the layman to attempt to comment on medical batteries and the onetime craze for the do-it-yourself home treatments that employed them. Suffice it to say that in the late nineteenth and early twentieth century there evidently existed a widespread belief in their properties and, quite apart from the apparatus made for professional use—obviously also collectable—there existed a considerable trade in home medical-battery outfits consisting usually of a battery and a few electrodes and sponges, although at times they seem to have been used more as shocking coils to startle unsuspecting visitors than anything else.

A medical battery does not, in fact, literally have to include a battery. The little water motor illustrated is from a widely sold, inexpensively cased outfit of approximately World War I vintage. A water motor is really a little turbine which attaches to a faucet either directly or via a length of rubber tubing and drives a dynamo, which may be either integral, as in the case of the unit pictured, or a separate unit. A prepossessing water motor and dynamo setup of the 1890s or early 1900s was capable of delivering about one ampere of twenty-volt current at fifty pounds to the square inch of water pressure, and any water motor is today an interesting and desirable electrical antique.

But then, too, much more frequently met with is any sort of early electrical device, complete apparatus, or even individual component, whether a small motor or dynamo, a telegraph instrument or telephone, or something really large and unwieldy such as a horse-operated farm generating plant—there were such things manufactured and sold at the dawn of the universal electric age. There was, indeed, a time when anything electrical was a novelty in itself, and a small motor, dynamo, battery, or single electric-light bulb and suitable equipment to illuminate it was a modern wonder to be cherished and gasped at. As a natural result, a great deal of the early electrical devices of this type that the collector is likely to run across may be borderline cases between actual electrical apparatus and toys, and consequently properly of interest to collectors of both categories.

THE BYGONE ELECTRICAL WORLD

This should be neither surprising nor inhibitive to the collector, for in many cases the same companies produced what might be termed both toy and actual apparatus, and at times the distinction was one more of use than of the design of the equipment itself, although there were many articles that obviously proclaimed themselves for exactly what they were. The Porter No. 1 motor of the 1890s and early 1900s was pretty much manifestly a toy—also widely used in classrooms as an educational aid in teaching physics. The biggest motor in the series, the Porter No. 6, however, was a substantial machine intended and sold for practical workaday use in such applications as driving sewing machines or even light lathes. The Voltamp Electric Manufacturing Company of Baltimore, Maryland, turned out a line of motors starting with toy sizes and working up to substantial machines; they also pro-

Three interesting electrical antiques. Left to right, a late nineteenth-century dry cell, a World War I belt flashlight, and a water motor from the same era. The latter is a miniature turbine generator designed to be affixed to a household faucet, the mouth of the faucet passing into the rubber fixture shown facing the camera.

George S. Indig Photograph

duced beautifully wood-encased annunciators and meters of which examples are pictured. The Carlisle & Finch Company of Cincinnati, Ohio, manufactured toy electric trains—and also a full line of practical power motors and dynamos, as well as searchlights of a quality acceptable for use on United States battleships. While the toy collector can select the electrical articles that manifestly fall within his province, the electrical collector will find it difficult and probaby fruitless to attempt to draw any line; his collection of motors, dynamos, and such other equipment will be limited only by what he can find and house. Generally speaking, the larger the apparatus, the more difficult it will be to locate today, but it can truly be said that even today an amazing amount of material still awaits the seeker.

The telegraph provides the collector with literally thousands of potential items; no one yet seems even to have attempted to count up the number of models of sounders and receivers, not to mention the many related articles that were produced over a period now well exceeding one hundred years. The telephone industry provides less variety, but generally larger and, to some viewpoints at least, more prepossessing instruments. In any case, telephone collecting appears to be much more extensive and developed than does telegraph collecting.

The telegraph and the telephone combined have given rise to a particularized and now widely popular type of collecting—insulators. In the light of what already has been said in this chapter, it will not be surprising to learn that, in most of its aspects to date, this has been a glass-collecting rather than an electrical-collecting hobby. An article in the October 1968 issue of *The National Bottle Gazette*[1] went into considerable detail as to how to distinguish from the ground a certain milk-glass insulator from one of white porcelain, the latter presumably not being worth the collector's climbing the pole on an abandoned line to recover. The difference was that on the milk-glass insulator the inner petticoat does not extend below the outer one, while on the porcelain insulator the inner petticoat is longer than the outer one. Presumably a pair of binoculars would be of considerable assistance in this somewhat peeping-Tom-sounding investigation.

Some insulator collectors refer to the lower outer surface of a

[1] Published by John C. Fountain, Amador City, California 95601, $3.75 a year, $.50 per copy.

Grey's printing telegraph of the early 1870s. Instruments of this type were employed for police and other municipal telegraph lines, as well as, prior to the advent of the telephone, for private telegraph lines.

Western Electric

Lewis legless telegraph key of the late 1870s and early 1880s. This was an innovation in telegraphy at the time, the feature being that the connections were made to binding posts on top, and it could be fastened to a table without having to remove the key itself from the unit.

Western Electric

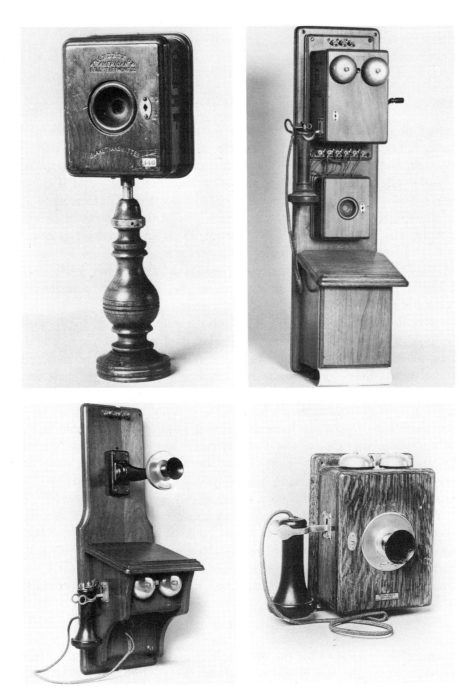

Early production telephones: (top left) the Blake transmitter of the 1880s mounted on a desk stand (the receiver is not shown); (top right) a magneto wall set of the 1880s using the Blake transmitter; (bottom left) a common battery wall set of about 1900; and (bottom right) a compact wall set of about 1913.

Bell Telephone Laboratories

telegraph or telephone pole insulator as the "skirt" and the separated inner lower circle, if present, as the "petticoat." This is perhaps logical enough, but is not in accord with the proper contemporary nomenclature. The outer surface was known as the "petticoat," and if there was a distinct second and inner circle, the insulator was referred to as a "double petticoat insulator," or, particularly in the presence of ladies, simply as a "D.P." (in the same lexicon, "D.G." meant "deep groove," not double groove). The page of insulators reproduced from a catalog of W. R. Ostrander & Company of New York of the early 1900s (see Chapter IV) will make graphically clear precisely what is meant by a double petticoat insulator.

Needless to say, the electrical collector is not in the least spellbound by glass itself and eagerly collects insulators of all types, glass, porcelain, wood, or what have you. Augury is dangerous and to be resorted to only with due respect for the embarrassment that so often overtakes those who place in print what turn out to be false prophecies. Nevertheless, interest in glass in any form being seemingly irrepressible, here is a prediction whose results seem likely to parallel closely those of insulator collecting: One of the next categories of glass to attract interest will be old glass battery jars! It may be argued that there really is very little danger in making such a prediction because old battery jars seem to be about the only thing of any age made of glass that is not yet widely collected. The electrical collector is, of course, already active in this area, but it seems probable that we can look forward soon to hearing much of the relative beauty of color and form, and of rarity and desirability, of the jars once widely fabricated for the Bunsen, the Fuller, the Grenet, and the other types of early wet cells!

LIGHTING DEVICES

Another possibility for the glass collector to borrow from the electrical collector also lies in the field of old electric-light bulbs. As with most forms of antiques, what is surprising, once collectors become busy, is not how much has been destroyed and lost forever, but just how much does remain obtainable. So it is with old light bulbs, although they obviously are fairly fragile things and must be treated with considerable respect.

Tipped electric light bulbs of the early 1900s. Also shown are two wood-base battery rheostats with their original boxes, a Voltamp and a Kendrick & Davis, and three types of switches including, lower right, a foot-operated switch for use under a rug.

Mark Haber, Andrew B. Haber Photograph *(top)*
George S. Indig Photograph *(bottom)*

As seems pretty well known, the sign of what generally is considered an "old" bulb is that it is "tipped." The tip occurs at the point where an opening was left through which to draw out the air and create the vacuum, and then sealed off. The tip usually is found at the top of an old bulb, although a few side-tipped examples have been found; in a modern bulb the air is drawn off at a point which subsequently is concealed in the base. It seems reasonably safe to say that, today, any old tipped bulb is a collector's item, the qualification as to age being necessary because in fairly recent years tipped bulbs have been made again for special purposes, usually reproductions of Edison's first incandescent light and from time to time these replica bulbs turn up now at antique shops and shows as supposedly something very early and rare.

Anything to do with early electric lighting is, in fact, a meritorious collector's item, although a great deal of material still is relatively common, being represented by substantial stores of old light fixtures, switches and switch plates, fuse boards, and the like that have been stripped from old houses. Apropos of this, many city-bred collectors invariably overestimate the age of gas illumination and are particularly puzzled by the appearance at times of combination electric and gas lighting fixtures. Up to World War I and perhaps even later, a number of houses were equipped with alternate gas lighting for emergency use if there was a failure of electricity; if every fixture was not of this type, then at least sufficient were provided to serve as an adequate standby. But it should also be remembered by collectors in general that even in the 1920s and 1930s many homes not located near electric power lines were built for gas illumination and that, in any event as recently as the late 1920s, the gas companies were still promoting gas lighting as a form of illumination much superior to electricity.

The earliest incandescent bulbs present many kinds of interesting base types for the collector, there being considerable variety before a measure of standardization was achieved, and there are, of course, sockets of correspondingly varied design and, in many cases, fabricated of wood. In the field of electrical antiques a great many materials are found used—and used well—that now virtually have vanished from electrical components manufacture. It is always somewhat invidious to attempt to argue—as many collectors often like to do—as to real or imagined superiorities in materials and constructional methods employed in past products as compared to those of contemporary make. Be that as it may, there is no denying that in the electrical collectables, with their often heavy use of wood, solid brass, japanned iron, vulcanite, and similar materials, there is coupled with their electrical interest a certain cumulative character that adds up to a large group of articles that possess extraordinary attraction for the male collector.

To a certain extent, this extends also household appliances, even those of comparatively recent date and now including almost anything manufactured prior to World War II, although interest still centers somewhat on slightly earlier items. If it is electrical, whether a toaster, iron, hot plate, sewing machine, or a relatively large article such as a washing machine or refrigerator, it now is eminently collectable. However, as in most categories, the largest items are impractical for the average enthusiast to house, which means that a great deal of electrical history will be, if not lost, then at least somewhat screened or diluted as far as representation by the widespread retention of actual specimens is concerned. This is unfortunate, for electricity has become a major power in our lives, and within a few decades at the most, the larger appliances of the first quarter or third of the twentieth century will be found to have become almost as scarce as they will be historically important.

WIRELESS, RADIO, AND TELEVISION

To a certain and commendable extent at least, this should not prove true in the case of one important subdivision of electrical antiques, that covering wireless, radio, and television. For some years now this has been a fairly widespread if "quiet" field of collecting, seeking and receiving comparatively little publicity, but perhaps more than any other group of electrical antiques this equipment has been appreciated and preserved, possibly because many of the collectors, although by no means all or even a majority, are themselves amateur radio operators possessed of a historical and practical appreciation of their avocation. But it must also be remembered that there exists a tremendous nostalgic interest in broadcasting as a whole, both in terms of its being one of the modern wonders of the first quarter of the twentieth century, first with wireless and then, in the 1920s, with what originally was known as "radio telephony," and also in the programs themselves that went out over the air waves in the 1920s and 1930s. This latter interest manifests itself in the collecting of everything to do with the now so-called Golden Age of Radio Broadcasting, from the souvenirs and premiums offered over the air to copies of such of the original program recordings that survive—and a surprising number of the oiginal "electrical transcriptions," as the contemporary phrase went, have been dug out of hiding.

For practical collecting purposes, the radio age may be considered to have begun shortly after the culmination of Marconi's experiments in the mid-1890s, although the fairly widespread manufacture and distribution of equipment did not begin until a few years later. The boom in radio telephony started in 1921, and the first commercial television sets were available in 1937. These are all dates comparatively recent as many collectables go but are typical of the age range of many things that men enthusiastically collect. As observed previously in this volume, any radio set made in the 1920s and even in the 1930s is now an antique radio; any television set manufactured in the late 1940s, much less one dating from the 1930s, is rated an antique television set. It is dangerous to make such statements regarding dating in a book that is hoped to have some permanence; it may not be long before the foregoing outlook on dating such things will appear most unduly conservative, as time and collector interest spans continually move forward.

As is true of much electrical collecting, wireless, radio, and television collecting covers not only complete units, but all the separate components as well, whether the larger units such as amplifiers, earphones, and loudspeakers, or the smaller components such as sockets, dials, tuning units, crystal detectors, and so forth that went into the building of either homemade or commercial transmitters and receivers and other equipment. Particularly and most meticulously collected are the early tubes, each of which possesses its own identity in the eyes of the old radio enthusiast.

OPTICAL ANTIQUES

From the collector's standpoint, the definition of "practical" scientific antiques will be well understood and obviously can embrace

Optical antiques: a Bausch & Lomb microscope of the 1870s, and a pair of French field glasses of the 1890s or early 1900s, with case. During World War I the United States requested citizens to lend binoculars to the Navy and this pair was so lent and returned after the war, the left barrel carrying the Navy identification and number applied at that time.

Bausch & Lomb *(top)*
George S. Indig Photograph *(bottom)*

a considerable variety of articles and instruments of more or less varying importance and interest. The collecting of barometers, although
more as individual decorative pieces than simply as barometers, has
long been well established, yet there obviously exists a rather unplumbed area here for the collecting of the less prepossessing but widely
used barometers of both the mercurial and aneroid types. The beautiful and extremely delicate pocket aneroids, often elaborately gold-
or silver-mounted, designed for nineteenth-century travelers seem a
strangely, almost totally neglected category. The collecting of antique
nautical instruments is a fairly popular category and includes articles
usually classified as optical, such as telescopes, of course, although
the primary nautical antique undoubtedly is the sextant. Old sextants
are by no means uncommon and it is worth mentioning in passing
that the invention and use of the instrument dates back only to about
1730. This is old enough for most collectors, and the average enthusiast
would be well satisfied with a good series of nineteenth-century examples. Obviously, the collector will look with more than a merely suspicious eye upon the sextants not infrequently offered as those used
by such noted explorers as John and Sebastian Cabot, Christopher
Columbus, Vasco da Gama, and the like. In recent years, the sextant
has replaced the well-discredited telescope as the main object of nautical antique tomfoolery.

Telescopes, properly dated, are naturally important optical antiques, as are binoculars—more properly "field glasses," for "binocular"
may refer to any two-eyepiece optical instrument—and microscopes,
although somehow all of these are more the sort of thing of which the
average enthusiast collects only one or a few examples but does not
go into in depth for some reason. So, too, are magic lanterns and slides,
a considerably more popular category and one closely allied both to
photographic materials and to toys. The prepossessing magic lanterns
were in the main professional showmen's implements and accordingly
are discussed in Chapter IX; they and their slides are of considerable
collector's interest. On the other hand, there has never been manifested
any particularly strong enthusiasm among toy collectors for the toy
magic lanterns, which are legion, and they cannot be said to constitute
a secondary, much less a major, position as a category of collected
toys. Most collectors of toys in general possess a representative assortment and let it go at that.

Optical amusements of the late nineteenth century. Top, a kaleidoscope for view-
ing changing geometric patterns of small pieces of colored glass, and, bottom, a
Zoetrope with a number of animation strips. The Zoetrope was a persistence-of-
vision device and a forerunner of the motion picture.

Stereoscope viewers and pictures. Left to right, Underwood & Underwood "Sun Sculpture" viewer of the early 1900s; Keystone viewer of the early 1900s; and Keystone telebinocular stereoscope manufactured up to the mid-1920s. Note that the first and third fold into containers made to resemble books.

W. van Roosbroeck

Stereoscope viewers and pictures are a fairly popular category of optical antiques and again one closely allied to photography. Also popular and always interesting in themselves are any optical devices that may be considered precursors of the motion picture and which depend upon the principle of the persistence of vision for their operation, the best-known probably being the Zoetrope, which overall may be considered to be a sort of cross between a toy and a Victorian parlor attraction. So too, although far more universally known and used, is the kaleidoscope, a viewing instrument, which by means of internal mirrors transforms small pieces of colored glass into endlessly changing beautiful geometric patterns. The kaleidoscope, too, however, is mainly looked upon by collectors as the type of thing of which, if you own one, you own them all. In a way, this is unfortunate because it is a device whose ingenuity and long-time popularity justly merit a more extensive investigation into the history of its manufacture than, at the moment at least, seems likely to be accorded it. One trouble with tracing the history of many optical and scientific antiques is that many of the instruments themselves were marked with the name of the importer or dealer, and it is often difficult or, in some cases, almost impossible to ascertain the identity of the actual manufacturer. This is true of a certain number of clocks as well.

Photographic Antiques

When you have passed on from any of the aforementioned optical antiques, you come to what unquestionably is the most popular category of scientific relics, photographic antiques. Their collecting may embrace either or both the instruments and equipment of photography, or the photographs themselves. Many enthusiasts refer to it simply as "camera collecting," which is acceptable enough as a broad description and pinpoints what probably must be considered the major facet by many hobbyists, although by no means should the collecting of old photographs themselves—which also includes stereoscope views, and motion pictures, and many magic-lantern slides—be sold short. In any event, the collecting of photographic antiques is a field that, while perhaps only now perceptibly starting to make noticeable ripples, has

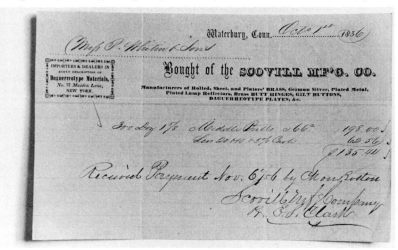

An interesting photographic-business antique of 1856, a billhead of the Scoville Manufacturing Company of Waterbury, Connecticut, making special reference in the box at the upper left as well as in the main heading to their daguerreotype materials.

G. William Holland Photograph

long been pursued by a considerable body of active enthusiasts. It has its own basic guidebook, *A Collector's Guide to American Photography*,[2] by Louis Walton Sipley.

Photography may be dated from 1839, when Daguerre's findings were published. For some three decades photography remained almost literally a profession. It was not until the 1870s that, with the gradual perfection of dry plates, photography could be promoted widely as a popular amateur pastime with the resulting vast proliferation of small cameras and other equipment. As a result, while every photographic collector would delight in securing a number of examples of earlier cameras, or indeed professional cameras of almost any past era, it is to a large extent the smaller amateur cameras of the 1870s onward that are the mainstay of most collections. A further consequence of this situation is that, insofar as the earlier period is concerned, collecting interest is especially strong in the photographs themselves whereas, from the 1870s on, the photographs largely give way to the cameras as the major collectables.

The original common type of photograph, the daguerreotype, largely gave way after the mid-1850s to the ambrotype. Before 1860 both the ferrotype or tintype, a still cheaper process, and the paper print from a glass negative also were in use. The daguerreotype, ambrotype, and ferrotype all produce reverse images and there is much confusion concerning them although the ferrotype is naturally readily identifiable as being on sheet metal. There is, however, an all too common tendency among many novice collectors as well as an almost universal one among antiques dealers to refer to any framed picture of this sort as a "daguerreotype." When held in the hand and moved into different positions, portions of a daguerreotype will reflect light instead of showing the image; an ambrotype or ferrotype will look the same regardless of the position in which it is held. Early photographs are collected simply because they are early, because of their subject because of having been made by a particularly noted photographer, or because of their cases. Or, to put the last in another way, daguerreotype cases and frames—but most especially the cases—are a popular collectable in themselves. Many materials were used for these cases;

[2] Published in 1957 by the American Museum of Photography, 338 South 15th Street, Philadelphia, Pennsylvania; $3.00 cloth, $1.50 paper.

some are beautifully molded of gutta-percha, which, as frequently has been pointed out, was in effect a pioneer plastic. Often the cases, particularly the large ones decorated with historical scenes in relief, such as Washington crossing the Delaware, are of fairly substantial collector's interest and desirability.

On the other hand, as concerns the general run of small daguerreotypes and ambrotypes themselves, it should be remembered that great quantities were made and that an old family portrait was not something likely to be readily discarded over the years. As a result, there is nothing particularly rare or desirable about most of the surviving specimens.

In the case of cameras themselves, the enthusiast has a group of masculine collectables that are of great interest for their scientific, optical, structural, and mechanical elements, as well as their historical importance both in themselves and as recorders of people and places. In addition, cameras are still fairly readily obtainable as an overall group and, for the most part, of a size that makes extensive collecting and housing practical for most individuals. The reasons for the ever-increasing popularity of camera collecting are therefore manifest. The illustrations herein provide but a suggestion of the range of things available. Early motion-picture cameras and projectors naturally also are collectable as a segment of this category.

Two types of cameras deserve special comment both by means of their photographic interest—their identities often are confused—and as a matter of general interest:

One is the so-called—properly—"detective camera." This was a great promotional gimmick for snapshot cameras in the late 1880s and 1890s. The idea that you could sneak up on someone with a camera that did not look like a camera or was concealed inside your coat or in a paper bag and snap their pictures without their knowing it was appealing to jokesters of all ages, and the detective connotations held added interest for youngsters. A boy could secure a Scoville & Adams "Waterbury Detective," a simple little box camera or some similar instrument and hopefully hang around the local livery stable waiting for horse thieves to appear so that he could snap them in the act.

A twin-lens stereo or stereoscopic camera, however, is not a "detective camera" in this sense, although a number of people believe it is

Left, the actual type of camera designated the "Waterbury Detective" camera in the late 1880s, designed for roll-film holders. Right, a stereo camera of 1890 of the type often erroneously called a "detective camera" by later collectors because of its association with the novel The Camera Fiend. *Both cameras were manufactured by Scovill & Adams.*

American Museum of Photography

A type of camera actually manufactured in the 1880s for use concealed under the coat with the lens projecting through a buttonhole. Made by Western Electric, it took a 2¼-inch-diameter circular picture, using a four-exposure 6½-inch-diameter special circular plate.

Western Electric

Early twentieth-century roll-film folding cameras. Top left, Anthony & Scoville four-by-five pocket Ansco; lower left, Eastman Kodak autographic postcard-size camera; right, large Eastman Kodak with wooden lens board and track.

American Museum of Photography *(top left)*
George S. Indig Photographs *(lower left and right)*

and refer to all stereo cameras by this name. The stereo camera was, of course, employed for making dual photographs for use in stereoscope viewers, for some time a fairly popular amateur as well as professional camera usage. E. W. Hornung is best remembered for his Raffles books, but authored a number of others, including *The Camera Fiend*, published in 1911. Hornung was the brother-in-law of Sir Arthur Conan Doyle, the creator of Sherlock Holmes, and a man much interested in psychic phenomenon. Hornung wrote *The Camera Fiend* partially at least to chivy Doyle on this matter. In *The Camera Fiend*, mad Dr. Baumgartner goes about London shooting people, literally and photographically, with his stereo camera, one lens of which has been removed to make way for an automatic pistol which fires simultaneously with the shutter of the other lens, Dr. Baumgartner's purpose being to secure photographs of the soul leaving the body at the moment of death. Hence will be seen the popular chain of association of ideas—Hornung, Raffles, Doyle, Holmes, detective—that has led so many erroneously to term any stereo camera a "detective camera."

Understandably, after reading *The Camera Fiend,* a number of people felt a little queasy the next time someone pointed a stereo camera at them. The story that the book was the prime cause of the phasing out of stereoscope popularity may, however, simply be classed as another Friend William Smith-type legend.

EDUCATIONAL MATERIALS

It seems improbable that many men collect specifically under this heading, yet there is collected a considerable body of material that can perhaps best be classified herein, although some of it might well qualify for inclusion in other categories. Some old-line and rather stodgy collectors attempt to provide a greater dignity they evidently feel is required by some of this material by referring to it as "philosophical antiques." This supposedly makes them sound more imposing; it also sounds like an affectation to most men and can almost be guaranteed to scare them away from the subject.

In this grouping will be found globes—both terrestrial and celestial —orreries or models of the solar system, mathematical and drawing instruments, art and home-craft outfits, art instruction books, coloring

A celestial globe, manufactured by Gilman Joslin of Boston, Massachusetts, and bearing a notation that it is "Corrected" to 1870. This may originally have been one of a pair, the other unit being a terrestrial globe.

Ward Kimball

books, question-and-answer wheels, sets and "cabinets" of specimens of minerals, chemicals, woods, fabrics, and the like, progressive demonstration displays such as those showing what can happen to a flax seed or a castor bean after it reaches the hands of commerce, and a host of other collectables of varying but often surprising interest not readily classifiable elsewhere. Some originally were made specifically for schools; others were intended for edification at home; and yet others have no real connection with education as such but are, directly or indirectly, educational—painlessly, it is to be hoped. Some represent even today still virtually wide-open fields for the collector who is interested and is able to see the not inconsiderable if not obvious possibilities that lie within this grouping.

Old schoolbooks are obvious educational antiques. Some men have confessed that they have heard it iterated so often that old schoolbooks are of absolutely no collector's interest or value that it set them out in a simple reflex to the active and enjoyable collecting of nineteenth- and early twentieth-century school texts.

CHAPTER VI

Collecting Glassware and Other Containers

As every businessman knows, the package can be all important. Thereby at this point we must come face to face with glass, the material in which so many things were and are packaged. As already hinted, this can be a difficult confrontation, and not only because old glass and glass collecting can be a veritable landslide in itself. The fact is that the average man, not long after first dipping his feet into almost any aspect of glass collecting as it now is widely accepted and practiced, is very likely to feel that he has unwittingly passed the frontiers of Never-Never Land or taken a journey through the looking glass, whether in company with Alice or with an older and more enchanting companion.

In glass collecting they say such things and they do such things, all straight-faced and seemingly with no appreciation of the elements of the downright grotesque that enter into the maneuverings, as simply to boggle the ordinary rational mind that still retains a belief that two and two equal four and that there exist certain logical standards that apply to all forms of collecting. This is not to say that everyone who collects and studies glass believes these things or practices them, but enough do and even often enough proclaim them as erudite findings as to make many wonder whether the glass-collecting ship really is seaworthy after all.

Take as a prime example the matter of purple bottles. In glass collecting, as in other categories of manufactured collectables, color variations very correctly form an important consideration, and it is only proper that a piece of glassware as originally manufactured in one color may often be regarded as a much rarer and more desirable specimen than the same article in another color or colors. Thus, an excess of iron in the sand resulted in a greenish glass, or cobalt was added to the mix in an effort deliberately to produce a blue glass, a blue stronger than the intermediary range of green-blues that results from the natural iron content in almost any sand. However, although deliberately colored glass often was sought for, a great desideratum of nineteenth-century glassmakers was to be able to manufacture an inexpensive clear glass and for this manganese was added to the mix. Well and good.

However, a property of such glass is that it will turn amethyst or purple when exposed to the direct rays of the sun, which is precisely what happened when discarded bottles were left exposed on desert dumps for years. Now anyone would suppose that such sun-purpled specimens of what originally was clear glass would be collectable enough, but only as defective or secondary specimens to be retained until they could be replaced with examples of the same ware in the original clear glass. Not at all! The purpleized glass is figured by many collectors as worth about twice what the same thing in the original clear glass is worth! But this is far from all—collectors actually frequently are instructed how to turn their clear specimens purple by placing them in direct sunlight (no window panes to filter out the ultraviolet waves intervening) and even urged to do this! They can even purchase chemical preparations that are claimed to speed up this process of turning good original specimens into what, in any candid consideration, amounts to defective ones!

No further comment seems necessary, save that, in spite of such things, there would seem to be enough of interest and importance in glass and its collecting to make it worthwhile for a strong-willed man to investigate further and make his own way in the field by clinging stoutly to somewhat more logical concepts.

A CAPSULE HISTORY OF GLASS

Here is a capsule history, or perhaps nonhistory, to illustrate some of the problems involved: Most of the earliest American glass was

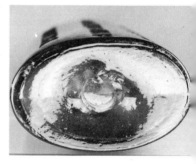

Left, a free-blown snuff bottle, ca. 1840, and a mold-blown medicine bottle, circa 1850. Center, a "MORSE'S CELEBRATED SYRUP" bottle, ca. 1852. At the right is pictured the base of the Morse's bottle showing the open pontil scar found on some specimens of this bottle.

Bill Wilson

free-blown, the ancient method using a blowpipe and the lungs and skill of the glassblower. In the course of free-blowing a bottle or similar article, a pontil or pontil rod which had a little hot glass at the end was fused to the bottom, thereby allowing for holding the article when the blowpipe was freed. When the bottle was finished, the pontil rod was broken off, leaving the so-called pontil mark on the bottom. Thus, the collector will be told and often asked to accept that anything with a pontil mark is necessarily very old and very desirable —including presumably even President John F. Kennedy Memorial Flasks, which were produced complete with artificial pontil marks, presumably because glass collectors have been brought up to regard anything with a pontil mark as "good," or any of the considerable free-blown glassware produced in large quantities even to this day in many parts of the world.

Next, theoretically, came the mold-blown bottles and other wares. Blowing the glass to fill the interior of a mold made it possible to achieve a uniformity of external size and design as well as, in most cases, increased productivity. Perhaps equally important, it permitted any desired designs, pictures, and lettering to be placed on the exterior surfaces wherever desired. The impression usually given novices is that the mold-blown ware replaced free-blown in the early 1800s and lasted up to dates variously given as anywhere from the 1840s to well into the 1900s. The only trouble with this seeming aid to ready dating is that the process of mold-blowing glassware has been known and practiced for something like 1,500 years at least and is still employed today, sometimes especially for the benefit of unwary collectors. Of course, anyone familiar with glass to any extent at all can readily distinguish between a genuine ancient Roman or Syrian mold-blown specimen and something mold-blown in the United States in the nineteenth century, but the point is that many of the set dates and periods so often rattled off to beginners are meaningless.

Pressed glass came along in the 1820s, made by an ingenious mechanical process that rapidly gained popularity and in which the molten glass was forced into a mold by means of a ram. This method produced extremely beautiful glassware, but it took several decades to perfect the process and it by no means replaced mold-blowing for many wares. However, pressed glass made table and decorative glassware so inexpensive that pressed glass was not surprisingly denounced as unworthy of the attention of any self-respecting collector for years, and as recently as the 1920s there are statements on record on the part of then old-line antique collectors to the effect, although they did not phrase it quite so inelegantly, that they would sooner be found dead than with a piece of pressed glass in their collections.

Finally, there came mass-production machine manufacture, which was a further great boon to commerce and to mankind in general at the time and to collectors today, but this seems to be a rather confused issue with all sorts of qualifications and counterclaims as to when it originated, which was the first "practical" (again) operation, and when it was put into widespread use. The date of 1903 frequently is cited for its introduction, but it would appear that at best this date marked the coming of one particular type of machine. The 1880s would seem a more reasonable date for what can properly be considered machine-made mass production of glassware, but obviously this is a matter that requires considerably further careful investigation.

HISTORICAL FLASKS

Perhaps not surprisingly to some, the forms of glassware that seem to attract the greatest interest among men collectors are those that originally contained spiritous liquids or were used to package and sell commercial products; in short, as a general thing, flasks and bottles.[1] Even a teetotaler, however, can appreciate the appearance and history of what are generally termed historical flasks.

American historical flasks have long been a prime collector's item, probably the first category of glass to attract extensive attention on the

---

[1] Of books on bottles and on glass in general there are legion. Possibly the best introduction to the subject is *The Antique Bottle Collector* by Grace Kendrick, $2.50, obtainable from the author, 485 West 4th Street, Fallon, Nevada 89406. The same author has also written a book on the bottle-making process, largely illustrated with photographs taken in present-day Mexican glassworks, *The Mouth-Blown Bottle*, $6.95. For liquor bottles alone, *Spirits Bottles of the Old West* by Bill and Betty Wilson, $10.00, Hennington Publishing Company, Wolf City, Texas, is recommended. The most comprehensive work on early American glass in general probably remains *American Glass* by George and Helen McKearin, originally published in 1941, $12.95, Crown Publishers, Inc., 419 Park Avenue South, New York, New York 10016.

An example of an early American historical flask. This particular flask is a Masonic flask of the crossed-keys type. Masonic flasks were very popular in the early nineteenth century and a number of Masonic designs were produced by various glassworks.

G. R. Bouck, The Bitters
Bottle, Newton, Connecticut

part of men collectors, and this some years ago. It is therefore all the more curious that little has ever been presented concerning their exact provenance and history; they simply exist, mold-blown, allegedly half-pint, pint, and quart flasks bearing a contemporary or commemorative design or portrait, and, in their original incarnation, dating roughly from the early 1800s to shortly after the Civil War. The subjects vary widely and rather without perceptible pattern or scheme, a fairly limited number of subjects often appearing on a number of slightly or substantially different flasks. These subjects include such diverse things as "Success to the Railroad," "Liberty and Union," Masonic emblems, American eagles, cornucopia designs, and portraits of such notables as Washington, Franklin, William Henry Harrison, Zachary Taylor, and Jenny Lind. The identities of the glasshouses making some of the models have been established, but seemingly the flasks themselves have never properly been set in their exact context in the commercial scheme of things save in terms of certain romantic and inconsistent legends.

Distillery bottled liquor was almost unknown in the eighteenth century, and barring a few dealers in the big cities who imported French cordials and the like, there was nothing approaching a package store. The chief source of liquor was the local tavern, where it was dispensed from the barrel. If you wanted to drink at home or enroute, you had the tavernkeeper fill one or more bottles or flasks for you, "pocket bottles" being then the most popular designation for what later were called "flasks." It is scarcely sufficient to say that the historical flasks of the nineteenth century were simply a newer form of the plain pocket bottle. To some extent, the historical flask that was made possible by the use of the mold-blowing method was a sales device and, to some extent, a political-campaign aid—although this latter aspect has been greatly overemphasized, and the known range of flasks simply does not square with this often-cited explanation at all.

When the popular romantic explanations have been discarded as really insufficient, there remains only one possible explanation for the pushing of the commemorative flasks. Reason tells us that they must have been, to a good extent at least, a clever device to enable bartenders and tavern owners to provide undermeasure! Some time ago a prominent antiquarian related that he had had occasion to test the actual capacities of a number of historical flasks and had found a startling variation in the actual liquid content of so-called quarts, but he hesitated to follow this through to the seemingly inevitable conclusion, at least publicly. It is to be suspected that he had hit the nail on the head. The prudent man did not trust the tavernkeeper's free-blown "quart," but all of a type of mold-blown flask looked pretty much alike. If his La Fayette or Jackson flask held a true quart, it was logical to presume that the seemingly identical La Fayette or Jackson flasks his tavernkeeper could furnish would hold an identical amount, for were they not one of the latest marvels of American industry and production know-how? Externally, flasks blown in the same mold were identical, but the thickness of the walls and bottoms could be varied by the amount of glass that was gathered at the end of the blowpipe and blown into the mold. Glass and freight were cheaper than liquor. The obvious method of shortchanging a liquor buyer was to water the rye, a process carefully watched for by suspicious customers, and a publican caught in the act was likely to be threatened with a rope necktie. But, even if discovered, who could blame the man for something a supposedly inept workman had done at a glasshouse perhaps hundreds of miles away? It would not even have been necessary to spell any of this out in catalogs and orders. A tavernkeeper could simply tell the flask drummer with a knowing wink that he'd take three barrels of General Jackson quarts in the "heavier glass" in his next shipment and the deed was done.

The decline in popularity of the historical flask after the Civil War was not caused by any diminution of patriotic or commemorative zeal. There were two reasons. One was the increasing popularity of bottles filled with an exact liquid measure and sealed at the distillery. This in turn had to a large extent been brought about by the second cause, the fact that the manipulations in flask measures must have become pretty well known by this date.

ENDLESS STREAMS OF BOTTLES

Probably no one will ever be able accurately to compute how many bottles have been manufactured in the United States. It must at once be obvious that, for every one that survives today, dozens or hundreds must have been made and broken, and equally obvious from the numbers that do survive and are available for collectors that the overall quantities made must have run into billions. Bottles may be classified according to method of manufacture, shape, and original contents, the last usually is the primary method among collectors, although not always entirely satisfactory. There are, of course, bottles for spiritous liquids and, closely allied to them in content and in collector popularity, bitters bottles. Bitters, to be blunt, although theoretically for medicinal purposes, were a less obvious but equally potent road to alcoholic consumption than the open intake of whiskey. Many a Victorian, male or female, who was known "never to touch a drop" kept himself (some times even quite unknowingly) in an almost perpetual state of semi-drunkenness via the bitters route. The alcoholic content of most bitters and other patent medicines was usually greatly in excess of that of most acknowledged spirits. Many were virtually pure alcohol, with a few bitter herbs—hence the name—for that noble medicinal taste, and a little coloring matter added.

Making and selling bitters and patent medicines was an enormously

Three interesting nineteenth-century bottles. Left to right, a "TRICOPHEROUS FOR THE SKIN AND HAIR" bottle, ca. 1865; an "OLD SACHEM BITTERS AND WIGWAM TONIC" bottle of the 1870s, a so-called barrel type of bitters bottle; and a figural bottle, "BROWN'S CELEBRATED INDIAN HERB BITTERS," also of the 1870s.

Bill Wilson

profitable business in the years before the federal government began to get testy about labeling claims, whether conducted in an extensive manufactory or in hotel rooms and on the tailgates of wagons. Such bottles are often also very important advertising antiques, because it was to a very large extent for the benefit of the manufacturers of these nostrums that the advertising-agency business was established in the United States following the Civil War. Any man with an extensive listing of the innumerable small newspapers then published throughout the country who could find a patent-medicine manufacturer with whom to work could find himself set up in the new and potentially highly profitable business known as advertising. Some patent-medicine manufacturers found advertising anywhere so profitable that they simply ran a notice at the bottom of their ads authorizing any country editor who saw it to pick it up and run it in his newspaper and bill them.

Other types of bottles of especial interest to men collectors are those in which any food or personal or household product was packaged, medicine bottles, ink bottles (an obvious business antique), soft

Stages in the development of the Coca-Cola bottle. Left to right, a Hutchinson-stopped bottle of the late 1890s; a paper-labeled bottle ca. 1904; two straight-sided bottles with the trademark molded in, ca. 1906; and examples of the standardized bulge bottle, ca. 1916 and 1920. Early bottles varied considerably at times among individual bottling plants.

The Archives, The Coca-Cola Company,
Atlanta, Georgia

Another display of old apothecary jars, bottles, and other early drugstore equipment in the collection of Mr. and Mrs. Warren Blair.

Mr. and Mrs. Warren Blair,
G. William Holland Photograph

drink and mineral-water bottles, the soft-drink bottles in particular providing a widely and enthusiastically followed category, and druggist's bottles, both the bottles, jars, urns, and vials used for storing and dispensing drugs and also what were known as "show globes," the elaborate bottles which, filled with colored liquids, were used as window displays and counter ornaments and which constitute a sort of druggist's trade sign that was universally recognized as such. Most collectors prefer bottles of any kind that are identifiably branded by means of paper labels or lettering molded in the glass itself. Bottles of the latter type are not, however, necessarily rare or so universally desirable as many believe. In the late nineteenth century anyone could have such bottles made up merely by paying the cost of a matrix or plate that fitted into a standard mold at a cost ranging from about five to fifteen dollars. Once the plate was made and paid for, there were no additional charges for its use over the regular cost of plain bottles. The writer is of the opinion, although it is contrary to a belief held by many, that as a general thing old bottles with paper labels are scarcer and more desirable than those with molded lettering. The latter type retains its lettering as long as the bottle itself survives, whereas many bottles that originally were paper-labeled have survived as bottles but with the labels long since vanished. Incidentally, bottles with molded lettering originally were properly known as "labeled ware," not, as many collectors incorrectly refer to them, as "embossed bottles."

There are also enthusiasts who collect old paper labels themselves or any type of labeling or bottling equipment and supplies. In passing, it might also be pointed out that this is much akin to the popular hobby of collecting old cigar bands, labels, and boxes. Many of the bottles employed for stock in old drugstores were completed with glass labels, often extremely colorful and decorative, which can hardly be collected without collecting the entire bottle. But there also were glass drawer labels in use in such establishments, and these can be collected simply by retaining the drawer pulls alone, assuming that the collector is not in a position to reassemble and preserve a complete old drugstore. There also were lettered porcelain drawer pulls.

The lure of glass has seemed so compelling, however, as to shove into the background collecting containers molded of materials other than glass, and, of course, the glass units were almost always in the overwhelming majority. However, there are antique porcelain and various types of pottery and china to be considered and collected. Certain products traditionally came in pottery containers or bottles. We are told that Falstaff's sack would in his day invariably have been supplied in a pottery bottle. At any rate, there are numerous heirs from the nineteenth century available for the collector in the form of pottery jugs and bottles that originally contained stout and other mainly imported beverages. In the United States, however, home-brewed liquors traditionally were delivered and served up in pottery jugs, not glass, and the collector who seeks to diversify his packaging interests may well pay honor to our own tradition of the little brown jug. Then, again, ink was a product long traditionally supplied in a pottery, not a glass, bottle. A fair amount of what was known as apothecary shop fixtures—jars, urns, and bottles—was made of china and not of glass, although some of these articles that appear at first glance to be of china actually are of opaque white glass. In the main, for really interesting and collectable masculine china, the collector must look to the barber bowls and shaving mugs discussed below.

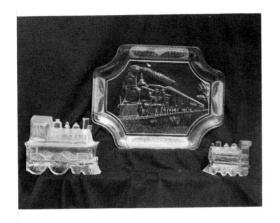

Glass and porcelain railroadiana. On the left, late nineteenth-century train platter of glass manufactured by the Canton Glass Company, Canton, Ohio, with (left) two-piece glass locomotive dish, manufacturer unidentified, and (right) glass candy container, probably West Brothers Company, Grapeville, Pennsylvania, both early 1900s. On the right, the porcelain locomotive Eros, nineteenth-century European, with a late nineteenth-century railroad souvenir spoon.

Ward Kimball

An early soda-fountain counter dispensing urn for Coca-Cola, introduced in the late 1890s. Old soda-fountain equipment of all types is of considerable interest to men collectors.

The Archives, The Coca-Cola Company,
Atlanta, Georgia

Besides bottles and related packaging materials, a field of glass of interest to a number of men is historical glassware, that is to say, plates, platters, and other pieces marking or commemorating a historical event or a scientific achievement, and this same theme of collecting can be carried over into chinaware. Steins and drinking glasses of all kinds usually are considered masculine antiques, and there are other things in either glass or china that proclaim themselves as classifiable under this heading, such as glass or porcelain miniature automobiles or locomotives, or theatrical figures. A very popular glass-collecting category for men is glass candy containers. Glass candy containers represent one of those groups that almost automatically are popular because of their multifaceted nature; they are at once glass, toys, packaging antiques, and also classifiable according to subject as a segment of many another collecting category, such as sports or automobiliana. They do not appear to have originated much before 1901 and many are of very recent date; their greatest period of popularity seems to have been around 1910 to 1930, although there was a revival during and following World War II when many other materials were in more critical demand than glass. Glass candy containers exist in many forms, such as airplanes, automobiles, locomotives, animals, telephones, humorous figures, lanterns, pistols, and so on. Approximately four hundred different types of American-made glass candy containers are known and recorded, and undoubtedly some others still remain unknown to collectors.

Any glass or china object that can authentically be tied up to a specific promotional use by a manufactured product thereby automatically becomes a business antique. Undoubtedly, a great many specimens exist that were employed for this purpose or even specifically designed and manufactured for such use, but identification unfortunately is in most cases extremely difficult unless the piece itself is so marked. Almost invariably this was not the case, for those making use of the glassware or china naturally did not want it to proclaim to their guests that the table service had been secured courtesy of such-and-such a soap or cereal. Some years ago a lady commentator wrote quite chillingly of certain patterns of glass that she recognized as having been distributed with household products; the tone was that of denunciation both of the glass and those who might be so gullible as to collect it. Most unfortunately, she did not specify either the products or the glassware in question; had she done so, she would unknowingly have supplied the basis for some very interesting and important modern-day collecting of business antiques. As it is, most such wares regrettably probably will forever go unrecognized.

OLD AND NEW MOLDS

Earlier in this book reference was made to the confusing situation in glassware concerning so-called fakes, reproductions, "old" molds, "new" molds, and so on. Everyone has tried to find some suitable interpretation of their own for this situation, both in the cases of those who say and write, and those who listen and read. What will be said applies to some extent to the types of glassware that have been discussed here, but even more pertinently perhaps, in fact to many other types of collected glass in general. It will explain the seemingly incomprehensible fact as to how there could be "old" molds that were seemingly different or sharper or "better" than the supposed original molds, and how there could be allegedly "new" molds that were reportedly—and correctly—found in old glasshouses. If all this sounds a little confusing, admittedly it is, for it represented a situation that seemingly no one could figure out, with the result that a lot of perfectly legitimate old glass was stigmatized as being fake or a modern reproduction, which often was the impression the facts were marshaled to convey, for reasons less than commendable. This is the story:

In the late nineteenth century there existed a powerful "combination" among the leading glass manufacturers in the United States, and there was a similarly potent combination among the chief British manufacturers. The combinations were able to set and enforce their rules, and one rule was that glass was sold only in the original packages—crates, casks, and barrels—according to the way it pleased the glassmakers to put it up. Thus, in a particular pattern, a dealer might get a dozen tumblers and a dozen sugar dishes in one barrel, which meant that his stock was badly out of balance. Or he could order a barrel of nothing but the one tumbler, which would give him more tumblers of that pattern than he might ever hope to use. But there was no middle course. If a jobber opened a barrel to fill in a dealer with a dozen needed pieces, then the jobber was stuck with the rest of the barrel. It was an ideal production and inventory system for the big glasshouses, but hard on everyone else.

Accordingly, the leading jobbers, such as Butler Brothers, calculated the individual pieces most likely to be called for separately, gave samples to the smaller glass manufacturers, paid for new molds, and had quantities made up for their use which they cataloged and sold by the dozen. This was the origin of the expression "open stock"; the dealers thought that the jobbers actually were breaking open the original packages and barrels to supply them with their particularized wants. They were not. They were supplying duplicates made especially for them in other factories and using other molds. In many cases, it is impossible to determine which is the original and which is the duplicate. Sometimes the duplicate molds were not cut so finely and so sharply as the originals; sometimes the duplicate molds were sharper. Hence, in the case of many patterns and pieces, there may have been two or even more versions in production at the same time. Much so-called reproduction glass supposedly made years after the originals was in fact produced contemporaneously with them. Many of the old molds were never used again. Some were found in later years and reused, but they were not "new" molds especially cut to deceive collectors. Some new molds may, of course, have been cut, but this only adds to the confusion. By far the majority of the so-called fakes—because they show slight differences from the assumed originals—were contemporary old glass, and in most cases there was and is no accurate means of ascertaining which mold may have been used by the original manufacturer and which by a manufacturer duplicating a piece for a jobber.

All of which means, among other things, that as far as much old glass and established collector's assumptions concerning it goes, it is all pretty much of a new ball game!

BARBERS' ANTIQUES

Yesterday's barber shops provide some of the most interesting and widely collected of masculine antiques. Anything to do with the furnishings and equipment of a barber shop is, of course, collectable, but primary interest hinges on certain wares made largely of glass and china, specifically barber bottles and shaving bowls and mugs, most particularly upon the latter. Glass barber bottles provide an interesting and colorful group of collectables. They were always used in pairs, one containing water and the other, witch hazel, and preferably collected in pairs, odd singles having comparatively little interest and value, although conceivably there always is a chance that one can eventually be matched up with another of the same pattern and color. In practice, however, this is easier said than done, although conceivably at this date, it might be logical procedure to collect them as singles when available, with any pairs that turn up an added dividend.

The shaving bowl and shaving mug do not, fortunately, present this problem of pairs, although in the case of shaving mugs that were merely numbered rather than identified individually by the owner's name, there can foreseeably be a problem of far greater magnitude than exists in the case of merely matching one barber bottle to another. The shaving mug, and especially the occupational shaving mug, have been the subject of a considerable amount of research on the part of that indefatigable collector, student, and pioneer in various categories of masculine antiques, W. Porter Ware. Mr. Ware's book *Occupational*

A portion of the shaving-mug collection assembled by W. Porter Ware. Most of the mugs pictured here are occupational and other types of personalized mugs of the late nineteenth and early twentieth century. A number of numbered mugs also can be seen.

W. Porter Ware

A group of old barber bowls dating from the fifteenth century to about 1830. The faïence bowl at the upper left was made for the use of an eighteenth-century French bishop.

W. Porter Ware

Shaving Mugs, published in 1949, is unfortunately out of print, a situation somewhat compensated for by the appearance of a considerably more detailed text on the subject that Mr. Ware has contributed to the current *Encyclopedia Britannica.*

Briefly, an occupational shaving mug is one that bears not only its owner's name, but a picture symbolic of his trade or profession, such as a printing press for a printer, a telegraph key for a telegrapher, a fire engine for a fireman, an oil derrick for an oil driller, and so on. Closely related also are photographic mugs, which bear a photograph of their owner, and lodge or fraternal mugs, which carry the insignia of an order to which the owner belonged. These latter as a general rule are not considered so desirable as the true occupational shaving mugs. There also are a number of stock designs that were purely decorative and carried patriotic emblems, scenes, designs, and even humorous figures. Most mugs were stock designs and ordered from catalogs which every barber once kept on hand. The mugs were then finished and fired in the factory and returned to the barber to deliver to the customer. A man's own shaving mug bearing his name and a decoration symbolic of his occupation, standing in the mug rack of his regular barber shop, was once a status symbol of considerable weight. Evidently there was one still higher status symbol among shaving mugs, that used by men who had arrived at a position where their mug needed neither occupational insignia nor identifying initials, as represented by the simple "Whitman" of the mug of Charles S. Whitman, Governor of New York from 1915 to 1919, illustrated here.

Late nineteenth- and early twentieth-century shaving mugs, including a number of occupational mugs. Left to right in the top row are a barber's numerical mug, a society-emblem mug, an unfinished mug, and an early mug with glass label. The mug on the right of the second row down belonged to former Governor of New York Charles S. Whitman.

W. Porter Ware

While even in straight-razor days many men shaved themselves at home, and wealthy men usually had themselves shaved there, most men of substance in their communities had themselves shaved daily, seven days a week, in a sort of ritual at their favorite barber shop. This seven-day-a-week shaving was a chief factor in the downfall of the occupational shaving mug and of the barber shop as a social center. Toward the turn of the century and in the early 1900s many communities suddenly discovered that it was sinful that a barber shop should be permitted to operate on the Sabbath, and Sunday closing laws started widely to appear on the books. This meant that on the most important day of the week and the one on which he wanted to look his best, a man could not secure a professional shave in his favorite barber shop. This and the gradual acceptance of the safety razor spelled the general decline of the personal shaving mug, although the custom still lingered in some communities or individual barber shops even well into the 1930s. However, the Golden Age of the occupational shaving mug probably must be dated from the 1880s to World War I.

Today any old shaving mug is a good collectable; any occupational one, a highly desirable item. In many ways, the occupational shaving mug may well be considered the atypical masculine antique.

OTHER CONTAINERS

Although glass has held a center-stage position in antique collecting for so long that it tends to dominate any field in which it appears, glass and ceramic containers and packaging are far from the whole story or even perhaps its most important segment as far as these types of antiques are concerned. Packages of metal, paper, and cardboard are equally sought and equally or—by their specialist enthusiasts— even more eagerly collected. Furthermore, it is obvious that herein lies a vast and largely untrampled field for serious collecting and research, for the development of the package as well as the step-by-step modifications over the years of the packaging of specific products obviously is a very important part of the history of commerce as represented by business antiques.

If you choose, you can select almost any specific product that has been on the market for a length of time and trace out the mutations of its packaging and labeling. One of the first things to be widely packaged and sold in small cans was gunpowder, and its packaging is guns themselves, yet surprisingly few gun and cartridge collectors just as important a part of firearms history as the development of the attempt to include powder and cap packages in their collections. You can approach packaging in this manner, from the standpoint of a specific collectable, or from the standpoint of the material of the packages—wood, sheet metal with paper labels, lithographed sheet metal, cardboard, and so on—or from that of packaging as a whole. Wherever and however you approach it, you will find it a field that still lies comparatively wide open for the collector and one in which many specimens are still fairly easy to find and acquire, yet one which by its very nature and potential historical importance is almost universally regarded as a comer.

Compared to the voluminous material in print on glass containers, scarcely anything is available on metal and other containers, although there is one extremely interesting book of full-color illustrations, *The*

Early Dupont sporting gunpowder containers, including four types of tin powder flasks and cannisters and a powder keg, all nineteenth century.

E. I. Du Pont de Nemours & Company

Tracing the progressive development of the packaging of a particular product is a popular and interesting phase of package collecting. Pictured here are Jello-O packages of 1925 and 1937, and, running right to left, a series of eight Minute Tapioca packages from 1908 to 1942.

General Foods Corporation

Book of Collectable Tin Containers with Price Guide,[2] by Ernest L. Pettit, from which one plate is reproduced herein in black and white. It is, in fact, the high color values of most of these old containers that makes them so attractive to all, although the styling and use of color may not seem quite so eye-catching as modern packaging designs. However, as most men are aware, once the process of metal lithography enters any picture, the results usually are of extraordinary interest and visual appeal. Many old containers have naturally become

A group of cut plug-tobacco tins from the collection of Ernest L. Pettit, dating from the early 1900s, and averaging about 7½ inches in length.

Plate No. 3 from *The Book of Collectable Tin Containers with Price Guide,* by Ernest L. Pettit

dulled or faded with age and, as Mr. Pettit notes in the introduction to his book, it is best not to try to be too particular about condition when searching for these containers. Take superb condition with gratitude when you are fortunate enough to come across it, but, as with so many other collectables, be prepared and pleased to accept them as they come. As with every category, too many collectors who set their sights too high or who are inveterate cranks on condition end up with comparatively little in the way of either specimens or enjoyment.

[2] $1.50, obtainable from the author, P.O. Box 361, Wynantskill, New York 12198.

Not without a foresighted if still somewhat unusual encouragement from the company itself, which perceives the promotional advantages therein, Coca-Cola relics have become a favorite among collectors of business antiques. This is a serving tray of 1909.

The Archives, The Coca-Cola Company,
Atlanta, Georgia

Any container that takes a special form is of particular interest to package collectors. The Towle's Log Cabin Syrup tins, although used until World War II, are already considered classics of this type. This is a version used in the 1930s.

General Foods Corporation

Packaging collecting is still so new—although there are a few hobbyists who have been active for many years—that there is as yet hardly any realization of the potential magnitude of the subject. Early collectors were usually more interested in acquiring old packages to make up the stocks of restored old stores than in the history and impact of the packages themselves, one notable exception being I. Warshaw of the Warshaw Collection of Business Americana, who was almost a lone voice crying in the wilderness when, in the early 1940s and even earlier, he urged the purposeful collecting and preservation of "the romance of business in the form of ledgers, sample books, posters and tin cans."

Even today there are relatively few accepted standards relating to the collecting of old packages but three points seem fairly well established: first, as with so many other categories, age alone is not the sole criterion of value and desirability; two, a package is worth substantially more if it still contains the original contents; and, third, in the main a considerable measure of desirability attaches automatically to an old package in more or less direct ratio to the extent its form departs from the more or less conventional square, round, and oval forms. The non-tippable Mayo Tobacco Company cans in the form of "Rolly Dollies" are a good example of this, and the various types of the Towle's Log Cabin Syrup tins, made in the form of a miniature log cabin, although some were produced through the 1930s, already are accepted as package collector's classics.

CHAPTER VII

Tools, Machinery, and Transportation

It is not necessary, in order to present the theme of masculine antiques adequately, to attempt to maintain that every man automatically will be interested in every possible category. Admittedly there may be men who do not find such things as empty whiskey bottles and coffee cans particularly interesting, but it seems probable that there hardly can be a man who would remain unmoved by the sight of most of the categories of collectables covered in this chapter.

Show a man an old wood plane—that is, a plane with a wooden body; no hand plane is a metal-working tool—or a brace with a short sweep, or any other woodworking tool whose appearance is perceptibly different from that which he knows he can buy new in his local hardware store today, and watch his eyes light up. He almost certainly wants to own the old-timer, just why he probably cannot logically inform you, and he certainly knows he does not really need it and that, if he acquired it, he would not actually use it. Tool fever has long been noted in men—it applies to modern tools as well as to old ones, but the man who probably will resist the impulse to purchase an extra modern plane in a modern hardware store usually will have little resistance to an old plane in an antique shop. Whereupon, whether he realizes it or not, and whether he carries the matter still further, he has in effect joined the very extensive ranks of old tool collectors.

Old-tool collecting is in fact a relatively widespread and long-established category of antiques, a category often participated in, at

A display tracing some aspects of plane development. A number of types are shown here dating from the eighteenth century, as in the case of the European compass plane at the left of the front row, to comparatively modern types (extreme right of both rows). The third plane from the left in upper row is a Bailey "Liberty Bell" smooth plane introduced by Stanley in 1876.

Stanley Tools Division of
the Stanley Works

An eighteenth-century American wood-turning lathe, operated by foot power and, right, early nineteenth-century wood-turner's calipers. The latter permitted a wood-turner to take readings of two different diameters of work without having to readjust the tool.

Old Sturbridge Village Photo *(left)*
The Smithsonian Institution *(right)*

least at first, by retention as by acquisition. It is almost axiomatic that no man ever willingly discards an old tool, no matter how worn or obsolete it has become. Countless men are tool collectors without knowing it, carefully retaining any hand-me-down from a forebear and even cherishing tools whose purpose they have forgotten; the latter being particularly true in the case of specialized wrenches which came with some long-unrecalled piece of machinery.

Hand tools, particularly woodworking tools, are the most widespread object of tool collecting, naturally having been the most widely made and the most readily obtainable by enthusiasts, although some of the commonest household tools, such as wrenches, which do not precisely fall into such a category also are widely collected as well as, recently, early automobile tools, of which there is an amazing variety. Old tools can be approached from several viewpoints, the tool itself and its history, to which may be added the manufacturing history in the case of tools made for sale, in terms of the use of the tools as assists to a craft or industry as such, and also in the light of the relationship of tools to particular jobs or products. The definition of tools easily and properly can be extended to many farming and household implements as well, although it is probably in the more narrow and basic concept that tools are most widely collected today, and most of the tools that the average collector is likely to run across were in themselves manufactured and even mass-produced products.

It has been said that, if a present-day carpenter were presented with a set of the tools of a Roman carpenter of two thousand years ago, he would instantly recognize and be able to use virtually all of them. This is probably true enough, but it does not mean that the Roman carpenter's hammer, for example, would bear much detailed resemblance to a hammer of today or even one of two hundred years ago. Tool designs, once a collector begins to familiarize himself with them, reveal as many distinct and continual changes as does anything else. Yet, to a certain extent, basic designs change slowly; long-standard tools are not dropped lightly nor are new tools introduced easily; there is an enormous amount of resistance to radically different concepts among tool users. When the iron-bodied bench plane was first widely introduced by nineteenth-century tool manufacturers, it met with so much resistance on the part of carpenters that for many years it was

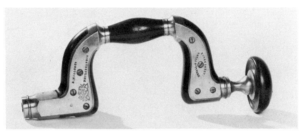

Old braces are another favorite among collectors of antique tools. Pictured here are a Dutch eighteenth-century wooden brace with chuck and bit, and a beautiful metal-reinforced brace exhibited at the 1876 Centennial Exposition by E. Mills and Company of Philadelphia, Pennsylvania.

The Smithsonian Institution

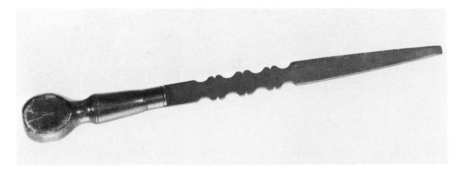

A nineteenth-century screwdriver, American or British, the blade and shank forming one continuous flat piece, with scalloped decorations.

The Smithsonian Institution

Two early nineteenth-century American planes. The plow plane, made by G. White of Philadelphia, Pennsylvania, top, was employed to create narrow channels on the edge of stock. The jack plane, which is marked "A. KLOCK 1818," is not substantially different from planes manufactured a hundred years later.

The Smithsonian Institution

necessary to incorporate the improved blade-adjustment parts that were a concomitant of the iron-bodied plane into wooden-bodied planes in order to find acceptability for them among what was, for a considerable period of time at least, the major portion of the market. Even now the blade of a hand plane is not correctly designated as the "blade"; it remains the "iron" because for centuries it was the only metal component in a hand plane, any adjustments being effected by means of a wooden wedge.

There are still today many old-time carpenters who will insist that a wooden-bodied plane is superior to a metal one, if only because it allegedly produces less friction when being used. Inasmuch as the wooden-bodied plane, usually referred to simply as a "wood plane," is by way of being the traditional symbol of old tools and especially so in the view of most novice tool collectors, and easily the subject of many false assumptions as to age and desirability, it should be noted that the last wood planes manufactured in the United States were a series of six models made by Stanley up to 1942. These had metal fittings, but wood planes of styles substantially similar to those of a hundred years earlier with wedge-controlled irons were still produced by other American manufacturers in the 1920s. Furthermore, such planes are still being manufactured today in Europe!

TOOL COLLECTING PATTERNS

As with all categories and subcategories of antiques, precisely how tools will be collected is largely a matter of personal choice. They may be collected over a broad general spectrum, or one or several kinds of tools made into a specialty, or tools of a particular period or geographic origin, or produced by a specific manufacturer or manufacturers may be collected, or a collection may be based on the tools of one or more particular crafts or trades. In connection with the last, it should be observed that cobbler's tools were long a particularly favored category and may still be so, although in recent years the takeover of old cobbler's benches as a somewhat commonplace decorative item seems to have taken something of the edge off cobbler's tool collecting. In any event, many, probably most, of the "old" cobbler's tools met with today, not excluding the iron stands and lasts, are not very ancient even from a comparative standpoint, being part of home shoe-repair outfits widely manufactured and distributed through the 1930s.

Of farming tools and implements, an interesting specialty, much the same can be said as for woodworking tools; many seemingly old items are in fact comparatively recent, forms often changing very slowly. The open, one-piece wooden handle on spades and forks, for example, which now seems to many so archaic, remained in production until the 1930s. As with all groups of tools, the major task of the new collector is to try to familiarize himself with the subject and, most particularly, with the often subtle changes in progressive design, although there is a great deal of overlapping of designs in almost every type of tool; as noted, resistance to changes in tool design is almost always strong and of sustained endurance. Larger and heavier types of farm tools and old farm machinery also are interesting to collect and are extensively collected, but are the type of thing for which the collector must have something on the order of a small barn in which to house them.

A frequent and interesting starting place for the collector of old hand tools, particularly for one who retains memories of the once-traditional big household or farm chest of tools of former days, is to reassemble the contents of such a tool chest of a selected era. It is only seldom that such chests complete with their original contents become available, and the usual method is to secure a chest itself, and then gradually gather the many tools that might once have been included in it originally. This is not always so easy as it may seem, although most collectors make no effort to secure the tools of the exact make that may have come with a given chest originally, if only because in most cases it is almost impossible to establish what was included. As a matter of fact, the tools included in such chests often were gathered from the lines of several manufacturers, although in some instances a tool company would be in a position to put out a chest containing only tools produced by them or at least with all the tools carrying their brand although some might actually be of outside manufacture. However, while permitting himself some elbow room as to brands of tools if only as a practical matter, the collector should bear in mind that it is virtually certain that all tools of a particular type originally furnished in any such outfit would have been of the same brand—all the saws, all the chisels, all the augur bits, and all the planes. The collector who is striving for a fair measure of authenticity certainly should keep this in mind.

Yet, on the other hand, as some collectors point out, many individuals did not acquire a chest containing an outfit of tools as a unit, but purchased the chests separately and placed within them such tools as they already possessed—very likely a somewhat heterogeneous assortment—and subsequently added tools of various make. Therefore, they reason, any more or less logical assemblage of tools is authentic, and there is nothing to prove one way or another that the half-inch and one-inch chisels of the original owner even were of the same type or make.

In any event, the only difficulty with such a project is that once it is completed—it is completed, period. While the collector might endeavor to upgrade or make the contents of the chest more consistent, the project is one that usually does come to a rather clearly marked ending. The collector is then faced with finding new fields of interest in tool collecting, unless, of course, he wishes to do nothing else than to keep on gathering together the presumptive contents of various old tool chests. A first-class tool chest of around the turn of the century contained about ninety pieces. You could buy one such an outfit, chest and tools, from Sears, Roebuck in 1901 for $23.84, and they were good tools too, including such things as Stanley Bailey planes.

Tools of Manufacture

Or, similarly, a collector might assemble a representative and contemporary set of tools belonging to a particular craft or trade or line of manufacture, for example, a set of tinner's tools. Now, if you go by many of the lists that are printed, you are likely to be considerably misled, because in almost every case what was cataloged as a "set" of tools was a more or less minimal listing of specialized articles only. For example, a list of a set of tinner's tools of the 1870s specifies:

Beakhorn stake
Blowhorn stake

Creasing stake
Square stake
Candle-mould stake
Needle-case stake
Set of five hollow punches
Set of solid punches, four punches and two chisels
Pair of bench shears
Large raising hammer
Small raising hammer
1-inch setting hammer
¾-inch setting hammer
⅝-inch riveting hammer
Creasing swedge
Cullender swedge
Square pan swedge

However, if this were all he had, the tinner was in a bad way for sure and could not attempt to operate. For one thing, he needed an iron bench plate fitted with various-sized openings to receive his stakes and swedges when in use, a soldering iron and a charcoal furnace, and certain hand tools such as nippers, drills, and dividers which, although they were not specifically tinner's tools as such, were absolutely necessary to the carrying on of his work. Furthermore, this is where so much of our traditional business about so-called handicrafts falls down so shabbily with such supposedly complete lists of trade tools. The tin shop where he worked, if not the individual tinner, had to have a certain amount of machinery in order to function. Some was relatively simple hand-operated bench machinery such as folding machines, forming machines, burring machines, and crimping machines. But the fact is that any tin shop that hoped to stand a ghost of a chance of turning out tinware at a price that could compete with the big-city factories also had to have and did have certain production machinery and dies. The fact is that these shops did have such equipment and also that such dies were mass-produced and sold to tinners as stock items as readily obtainable as a pair of pliers. The little old tinner of folklore almost certainly had at least a foot press, and his tinware was made using such dies which were arranged to cut various-

Early nineteenth-century tinner's tool. Supposedly individually made by a black-smith, it closely resembles and appears to perform the same functions as the mass-produced commercial tinner's tools known as a creasing swedge and a square pan swedge.

Old Sturbridge Village Photo

sized and -shaped pieces from the standard ten-by-fourteen-inch sheets of tinplate. Thus, one die would cut three pieces from a sheet of metal, the resulting stampings being used three for the sides of a four-quart pan, four for the sides of a six-quart pan, or five for the sides of a ten-quart pan. There was never anything arcane or difficult in the art of the tinner's combining two or more pieces of metal into a single product, as some have represented. This was always quite standard procedure from the earliest days of tinware manufacture on, given the long constant limitations of the available tinplate stock in ten-by-fourteen-inch sheets.

While assembling the hand tools of a craft or trade is interesting enough, far more difficult, interesting, and certainly required in a true and complete picture is the collecting of the early molds, patterns, and dies made for early production. Such materials are very important relics of early manufacture; examples still survive and can be collected, but by and large the bulk of such things has vanished forever. There is no question but that, to put it bluntly, many early collectors either did not recognize such materials or their function, or deliberately

Original brass patterns from the J. & E. Stevens Company foundry at Cromwell, Connecticut, founded in 1843. The ornamental piece is the pattern for casting the front of a "Book Rack for Churches" of the 1860s. The other pattern, dating from the 1870s, is for casting four coat hooks at a single pouring.

Mark Haber, Andrew B. Haber Photographs

ignored them in an effort to make their collections represent a cherished and often totally nonexistent tradition of individual handcraftsmanship. A very considerable number of stock tinner's stamping dies must have been made, for example, yet few survive. However, it must be said that old stamping dies as a general thing are difficult to find, much more so, it would appear, than old patterns, the wood or metal images of objects that were to be cast in temporary sand molds, and from which repeated molds were formed for the pouring of metal to make the actual production castings. Old patterns are scarce enough, but a number have been found by collectors and preserved. The reasons for this seeming difference in the relative survival rate of dies and patterns is not clear and certainly unaccountable legions of old patterns, too, have been scrapped. A partial explanation may lie in the fact that obsolete patterns had no value in themselves other than possibly as scrap, whereas stamping dies usually were mounted in more or less standard holders, known as die sets. When dies themselves became obsolete or worn out, they usually were removed from the die sets and discarded, and the die sets used for other appropriate dies.

In any case, any old stamping die, permanent mold, or pattern for sand casting constitutes a relatively important relic of early manufacture and commerce, and any survivor, regardless of what it originally made, is well worth collecting either as a specialty in itself or as part of a general tool collection. They also are valuable as a part of any collection of a particular category to which they may pertain and wherein they provide an especially interesting part of the overall picture.

OLD PRECISION TOOLS AND MACHINES

For the most part, tool collecting has been concentrated on woodworking tools and on the tools of the supposedly highly individualized, personally artistic, and nonproduction crafts, all as a part of the general picture of the suspension of disbelief concerning nineteenth-century factory productivity with which the reader will by now be familiar. There thus still lies before a great number of collectors and potential collectors the gathering and preservation of the hand and precision tools employed in production—rules, straight edges, micrometers, vernier calipers, gauges, and so on—and of actual machine tools themselves—lathes, drill presses, milling machines, screw-cutting machines, and the like. At the time of writing, this field would appear still to present substantial opportunities for purposeful collecting, as well as a rather surprising availability of material.

Manufacturing plants being traditionally noted for the rapidity

Early precision measuring tools manufactured by the Brown & Sharpe Manufacturing Company. Left, the first American micrometer caliper, introduced in 1868. Right, the original screw-thread micrometer caliper of 1882.

Brown & Sharpe Manufacturing Company

with which they discard and replace the old, it is surprising that there still appears a fair opportunity for collecting old machine tools, or even old precision hand tools. Certainly the great majority of these artifacts have long since been scrapped. Nevertheless, much does remain available for the searching collector. There in fact seems to be something like an average of a sixty-five- to one-hundred-year longevity for many of these things, and as far as hand tools are concerned, it should be remembered that one mark of a good mechanic always is the care he traditionally takes of his tools. Writing in *English and American Tool Builders* in 1916, Joseph Wickham Roe related that there were then still mechanics using scales marked "D. & S., Bangor, Me." This was the marking of Darling & Schwartz, a styling that disappeared from commerce after 1866. In turn, in 1967, the Brown & Sharpe Manufacturing Company reported still receiving reports of precision tools in regular use that bore the name of Darling, Brown & Sharpe, a form not used since 1892. In the course of a somewhat cursory survey made in connection with the writing of the present volume, the writer found a rather surprising number of old machine

The first type of universal milling machine, manufactured by Brown & Sharpe. It was placed on the market in 1862, its creation and introduction being directly connected with the need for machine-producing twist drills employed in boring the passage in the nipples for Civil War muskets.

Brown & Sharpe Manufacturing Company

A turn-of-the-century twenty-six-inch-high zinc cigar-lighter figure of Punch.
Mrs. L. C. Hegerty, G. William Holland Photograph

Everything connected with business history is highly collectable, as in the case of this interesting example of an advertising antique, a turn-of-the-century hang-up point-of-sale Coca-Cola sign.

The Archives, The Coca-Cola Company, Atlanta, Georgia

*Three early bottles. Left to right, a "*CASSIN'S GRAPE BRANDY BITTERS*" bottle, ca. 1870; a "*LACOURS BITTERS SARSAPARAPHERE*" bottle, ca. 1807, and an ammonia bottle, ca. 1880.*

Bill Wilson

There is probably nothing to equal owning your own railroad if you can realize the dream, as has Ward Kimball with his three-foot-gauge line. The 0-4-2 Chloe, shown with harp switch stand, was originally a Hawaiian plantation locomotive.
Ward Kimball

A 1910 Stanley Steamer Model 60, a ten-horsepower touring car that could be converted to a roadster by removing the top and the rear seat.

Norman F. Schaut

A Silsby rotary-pump hand-drawn steam fire engine built in 1888 and originally used in Cedarville, Ohio. It was the smallest of three standard sizes built by Silsby and had a capacity of 250–300 gallons per minute.

Ward Kimball

The toy electric train, ever a collectors' favorite, probably reached its highest stage of perfection in the 1920s. This is an Ives 2⅛-inch-gauge model of 1928.
George S. Indig Collection

Initially, the Currier print of the burning of the steamboat Lexington *in Long Island Sound, New York, on January 13, 1840, was issued under the title "The Extra Sun" and carried seven columns of descriptive matter. This is the subsequent regular version, with four columns of description.*

G. William Holland Collection

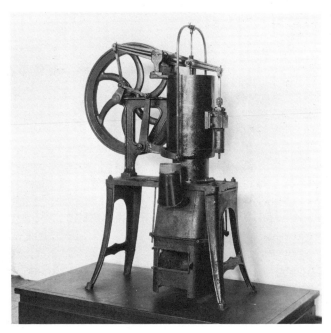

A one-half-horsepower Ericsson hot-air pumping engine, manufactured by the Rider-Ericsson Engine Company in 1906. These wood-burning engines, invented by the builder of the Monitor, *were once widely used for pumping water from wells. It stands about five and a half feet high.*

The Smithsonian Institution

tools and precision hand tools still in regular use in machine and repair shops in the metropolitan New York area. In one suburban shop noted throughout the area for its high-class work, there was found to be in regular operation not only a W. F. & J. Barnes metal lathe built in 1904, but also a C. L. Cady lathe that had started life as a foot-power lathe and later was motorized. The pedigree of this latter machine could be definitely traced back at least ninety years, and it was believed by the owner, whose father it had originally belonged to, to be, if not actually a full hundred years in use, then at least "close to it."

Neither is old home-workshop machinery nonexistent. There is nothing startlingly new about the do-it-yourself or hobby concept, and a great deal of light machinery was especially built for this purpose. From time to time the collector is afforded the opportunity of acquiring a treadle- or pedal-powered scroll saw, lathe, or other unit that originally was made for hobbyists of the last half of the nineteenth century.

When considering old machine tools, the matter of power sources also engrosses the collector. Here, too, is a promising field of small steam engines and boilers, early gas and oil engines, and hot-air engines, particularly the Ericsson Hot Air Engine—invented by John Ericsson, the builder of the *Monitor*. These engines, produced in many sizes, were one of the most popular forms of convenient light power and were manufactured and sold for many years after Ericsson's death in 1889. Not all of these old power engines were employed for driving machinery; many of them were used for pumping, home lighting plants, and like purposes, but all are worth collecting, although they require space that many collectors do not have available. A number of men have, however, filled barns or other quarters with such machinery, all important and interesting, and all too often almost of necessity doomed eventually to be scrapped if their collector has not taken steps to assure their preservation.

Here, too, might be mentioned many related devices, household and farm machines and tools, ranging from such comparatively small-sized household gadgets as mechanical apple peelers and corers and coffee mills, to pumps, windmills, and other large and hefty implements. Anything that in any sense is mechanical, mobile, or operational, regardless of bulk, is a sure bet for the attentions of some masculine collector. Indisputably there are men who collect such things as old windmills, but unfortunately, whenever such things are seen or spoken of, there is also the ever-present specter of what eventually is to become of them. In all too many cases, collecting is in actuality more a stay of execution than an assurance of permanence, and it all adds up to the fact that this, rather than the initial gathering in of such specimens, is the real if often unpleasant nub of the matter. This volume can offer no solution; it can merely point up the problem. Still, assuredly it is better to have collected and enjoyed something for a time than never to have collected at all.

THE TRANSPORTATION COMPLEX

Anything that has to do with transportation in any form, whether a clipper-ship trade card or a button from the uniform of a trolley-car conductor, to an actual automobile, boat, or locomotive is a matter of prime and extremely widespread masculine collecting interest. There are collectors who are interested in everything to do with transportation, but most generally the fever manifests itself as a particularized interest in one or at best two aspects, automobiles most frequently combining with some one other. There are men who are loco about locomotives and everything else to do with railroading, men who look with favor on ships and shipping and everything related to the nautical, men who are aeronautic buffs, a comparatively limited group of men whose bent lies in the field of horse-drawn vehicles, and, of course, those whose field is automobiliana.

Usually when a man becomes interested in automobiliana, aeronautica, railroadiana, or the like, his interests encompass everything to do with the field, including, if possible, the collecting and housing of the actual full-size articles in question. This obviously requires a certain amount of storage space; there is little point in collecting, preserving, and restoring—such full-size vehicles being, as already noted, one of the few areas in antique collecting where restoration is usually regarded as acceptable and even at times necessary and desirable—an old automobile, airplane, or locomotive unless you have room to house it and protect it from the elements when not in use. Furthermore, you will probably want some place to operate it. Public roads are available for the automobile collector, and the air for the man who collects and flies old airplanes. (A number of antique airplanes are admittedly more restoration and reconstruction than original, but this often is absolutely necessary when, as usually is the case, the owner intends to become airborne from time to time in his relic.) Even the waters around us are available for collectors of old boats, a group concerning which not too much is heard but which actually exists and appears to be on the increase. But if you own an old locomotive or trolley car that you want to restore and run, you really need not only a place to house it, but space enough for at least a few hundred feet of track, preferably even more. Furthermore, with a trolley car you also need not only a source of power but an overhead wire system that must be maintained, which makes things even much more difficult and complex, and though at first thought the reverse may seem true, all things considered, it is probably much simpler to own and operate your own steam locomotive than your own trolley car. One solution in either case, if you are fortunate enough to live near enough to one of the few established operating railroad or trolley-car

This locomotive, shown with 1879 coach, recent station re-creation, and antique windmill, was originally used on the Nevada Central Railroad. This locomotive, as well as the one shown in the color illustration, were built by Baldwin in the early 1880s.

Ward Kimball

museums, is to arrange to house your prize on its premises and, presuming it is the same gauge as the track, be able to run it on occasion over its right of way. There are, nevertheless, men who have succeeded in bringing to realization that perhaps greatest and seemingly most impossible of all dreams, to own their own private full-size railroad with locomotive, rolling stock, and enough track to make it worthwhile to run from A to B and then back up to A again and start over.

As a matter of fact, the available supply of real steam locomotives is now stretched pretty thin, so quickly and totally did the diesel take over, although few if any men would dare to think in terms of really big steam locomotives, something in the line of a narrow-gauge industrial or plantation engine being about what the practical man has in mind even when he allows his imagination to churn up about such possibilities. One man actually had to import a narrow-gauge train from Ireland. Another, who was both wealthy and foresighted, actually gathered up something like a hundred locomotives—mostly small industrial and plantation locomotives from the Southern states and Central America in the 1950s. Bear in mind, these were one hundred real steam locomotives, albeit small ones. All unfortunately were unceremoniously scrapped when he died suddenly, although all of them probably could have been sold to collectors, given a little time. Of the steam-locomotive situation as it existed in 1969, which is by coincidence exactly a hundred years after the North American continent was linked by the first transcontinental railroad, Ward Kimball, who owns two three-foot-gauge locomotives and houses a third for a friend on his Grissly Flats Railroad, observes, "Any ambitious reader who gets a hankering for a steam locomotive is due for a disappointment! Most have been found and purchased—even in faraway Hawaii and Central America." Still, it will be seen that he says "most," and everyone may be entitled to hope that somewhere, forgotten in an industrial plant or sitting on an overgrown jungle siding, there may still remain a little puffer with his name on it.

AUTOMOBILE COLLECTING

However, if for any of a number of reasons entirely apart from locating one, there is to be no locomotive in your life, then at least there is readily available the old automobile. Owning and enjoying an old automobile today presents few problems at all, so long as you do not allow yourself to become engulfed in the ridiculous automobile snobbery that most unfortunately infects a portion of the hobby, but which in truth is more vocal than widely accepted. Admittedly it would be nice to own an old Duesenberg, or a Cord 810 or 812, or some other vehicle to which has imperishably been affixed the cachet of accepted "classic." This, in a nutshell, is what almost everybody who approaches the subject with an open mind is prepared to admit is wrong with automobile collecting, the ridiculous overweening desire of some enthusiasts, one way or another, to divide old cars into recognized sheep and goats, classics, antique cars, special-interest cars, and the like. For the most part, it adds up to the fact that whatever the external and mechanical merits of the cars placed on the preferred list, they originally were made and survive in quantities too minute for the average man ever to hope to own one.

The average man often is much wiser and more practical than the self-appointed arbiters of so-called taste, and the average man subscribes to the theory—and rightly so, it would seem—that any old car is well worth seeing and saving, that any old car that he would enjoy owning and driving is worth his acquiring and maintaining, and that there is more than enough historic worth and inherent fascination in many an old car other than in those on some supposedly universally recognized "cream list" for there to exist no question as to their collectability. There may be some who will retort that all this amounts to the proverbial sour grapes, and perhaps there is some element of truth, no matter how slight, to this accusation.

Nevertheless, the vast majority of collectors of old automobiles seem fully to agree with this reasoning. Take the Ford Model A, of which 4,000,000 were manufactured from 1928 to 1931, keeping in mind as a comparison that less than five hundred Duesenbergs were produced in all from 1921 to 1937. Probably every man would like to own a Duesenberg, although a great many would perforce feel more than a little chary about taking one out on the road. But obviously, even if every Duesenberg ever made survived, less than half a thousand men could own one. On the other hand, according

A 1903 Ford Model A, the first automobile built by the Ford Motor Company, an eight-horsepower, two-cylinder, chain-driven vehicle.

Norman F. Schaut

to William A. Hall, long a Ford Model A enthusiast and founder and for eight years National President of the Model "A" Restorers' Club, there were in 1969 still between 80,000 and 100,000 Model As in existence. Although, admittedly, the Duesenberg as an overall make and the Ford Model A are extreme opposites and perhaps in using them as examples the comparison is being carried a little too far for the sake of emphasis, the basic point certainly is clear enough: The collecting of old automobiles may be fenced in with a complexity of recognition signals as a rigidly circumscribed field for a very few, or it may be a hobby open to any man who cares to participate. Furthermore, it might be asked whether the purpose of old automobile collecting is merely to render homage to a limited number of makes and models or whether first of all it is a fun hobby, and secondly whether its purpose is not also to a considerable extent to preserve and record the overall history of the automobile and of the automobile industry. From the latter standpoint, it might well even be argued that a Ford Model A is a more important artifact in many ways than a Duesenberg, a concept that no doubt will seem to many downright shocking and even impious!

As a matter of fact, there exists no general agreement as to what constitutes an antique automobile, and thereby certainly a collectable old car. The three leading American collector's clubs have widely varying interpretations, one recognizing it as applicable only to automobiles made prior to 1916, another to cars built before 1930, and the third that to merit the designation of an antique an automobile must be at least thirty-five years old. As pointed out earlier in this book, collectors are unlikely to pay much heed to legislated definitions of what comprises an antique. For what it is worth, most states that issue special license plates for antique automobiles calculate that an antique car is one twenty or more years old, which certainly is at least more in accord with the general outlook of the public and most collectors of old cars, although the fact is that there are certain cars less than twenty years old that are more or less universally recognized as, if not antiques, then at least as having a special collector's desirability for one reason or another.

In short, secure your favored old car, do what is necessary to it to put it into good and safe shape, enjoy it, drive it, and show it at auto-

One of the most glamorous and desirable of all old automobiles, and possibly the single best-known antique automobile specimen in America, Tony Koveleski's 1914 Stutz Bearcat Speedster. This car represents a good example of proper and meticulous restoration.

A. J. Koveleski

The automotive interests of the Rev. Richard E. Matera centers in Hupmobiles. Pictured here are his 1925 sedan with an unusual three-door body style, there being only one door on the left side, and his 1927 coupe.

Rev. Richard E. Matera

Owning a real fire engine of that bygone era before almost everything was covered over or concealed by streamlining is, not surprisingly, the ambition of many men and one realized by some collectors. This is a 1914 American La France four-cylinder, seventy-five–horse power, 350-gallon–capacity automotive pumper originally used in Venice, California.

Ward Kimball

mobile collector's meets if you wish, and, preferably, leave the arcane debating about definitions, classification, and recognition to others. In the case of antique automobiles, rest assured that the average hobbyist finds the intuition and definitions of the proverbial man in the street concerning such matters the most accurate and acceptable. As an added thought, it might be said that, while old commercial trucks seldom seem to excite too much interest, although they assuredly are collectable, a very special status and aura automatically appears to attach itself to the man who actually owns an old fire engine! Such a man is, of course, immediately recognized as one of those rare and unusual individuals who actually has realized an almost universal ambition. Owning an old fire engine is almost as good as owning an old steam locomotive and, if it is an automotive fire engine, probably for most a great deal more practical!

SIDELINE COLLECTING

Garage space is always the problem with collecting old automobiles. Some enthusiasts find a solution in owning but one old vehicle

A World War I French Spad biplane in flying condition and, as the photograph indicates, frequently flown today. It is painted in the colors of a member of the famous Lafayette Escadrille.

Cole Palen's Old Rhinebeck Aerodrome, Rhinebeck, New York, Frank K. Reuss Photograph

Greetings from the Sky

Rodgers in the Vin-Fiz Flyer
from New York *to* Los Angeles — *for* the Hearst $50,000 ocean to ocean flight

A souvenir of the first transcontinental flight. This is one of the slips dropped by Calbraith P. Rodgers, whose biplane was sponsored by Vin-Fiz, a soft drink, during his famous 1911 flight. The flight, with thirty stops enroute, covered forty-nine days, with an actual air time of three days, ten hours, and four minutes.

George S. Indig Photograph

at a time, lavishing work on it until it has been brought to a high state of perfection, showing it and enjoying it, and then disposing of it to another collector, and starting in all over again on the restoration of another vehicle. Many, for one reason or another, cannot collect real vehicles and, along with those who do, participate in collecting everything that they can accommodate that relates to their particular transportation interest, be it airplanes, automobiles, boats, railroads, or what have you. These are all more or less open-end interests with no limits really in sight as to what can be collected or how much can be accumulated: catalogs, nameplates, parts, models, and so on. Some things are common to all these interests, such as catalogs and other literature, while other fields usually can relate to only one. The collecting of automobile maker's insignia, for example, is confined to automobiles, although railroad enthusiasts somewhat similarly collect the much bulkier and heavier builder's plates from locomotives. Trolley-car transfers and tokens comprise a category for collectors of railroadiana, although some enthusiasts have extended their interest to those used on buses. The same thing has happened to a certain extent among collectors of railroad and trolley-car employee's uniform buttons, and presumably, if it has not been done yet, eventually there will be collectors of airline uniform buttons, both on the part of those who collect uniform buttons in general and those who specialize in aeronautica.

Sailing-ship and whaling relics are prime favorites among nautical enthusiasts, and such collections may embrace nautical instruments, already discussed, and sailor craft work, which is referred to in Chapter XII. These are both important aspects of nautical collecting, but the category extends to many other things, including ship's papers, prints, books, and any portions of old ships and ship equipment that a collector may be fortunate enough to obtain, the figureheads from old sailing ships being an especially prized grouping among not only nautical collectors but collectors of old wood carvings as well. Ship's tools and the tools of shipbuilders comprise a favored specialty of tool collectors. The indisputable fact is, of course, that a good deal of this material is becoming difficult to locate and obtain, particularly for the collector who arbitrarily insists only on the oldest, but it seems safe to say that it still is possible for anyone who wishes to specialize in this field to gather together an interesting and worthwhile collection. While nautical antiques are all too often taken to relate only to sailing ships, steamboat material is equally collectable save in the viewpoints of those who, for one reason or another, wish to restrict themselves to sail, nor are relics of old powerboats by any means neglected. There are, as already mentioned, a few collectors who actually own and maintain complete old vessels, steam and naphtha launches and even small sailing craft.

An interest in fire engines and fire fighting naturally leads to the collecting of anything relating to the subject, whether the hobbyist is or is not numbered among the fortunate few who can own an old engine. A certain amount of old firemen's equipment such as parade helmets and parade torches impinges also upon the political-collecting category. The collecting of insurance antiques is another fairly widely favored specialty which for obvious reasons is closely related to both fire and police antiques. Many collectors of material relating to fire fighting do not extend themselves into the collecting of insurance relics, but it is reasonably safe to say that almost all insurance collectors also collect fire-fighting material. One of the best-known groups of fire and insurance antiques is comprised of the so-called fire marks of the eighteenth and early nineteenth century, metal plaques placed upon buildings to show that they were covered by a particular insurance company which would make the exertions of the volunteer fire companies of the day worth their while. A number of old fire marks have been reproduced in recent times, some in telltale aluminum.

The collecting of police relics is another specialized category that properly should be mentioned here, although less widely followed than that of fire-fighting antiques. It is not generally realized that police relics include a most important group of fine ivory carvings, in the form of the parade batons widely used as presentation pieces from about 1885 to 1910. These were usually given to captains and higher ranks and were modeled on the regulation day stick of the patrolman, made of rosewood or mahogany but with their knobs, grips, and bottoms made of carved ivory and sometimes embellished with gold shields. It was also the custom to present sergeants and those of higher ranks with a billet (which usually in popular parlance is corrupted to "billy") carved entirely of ivory. Before ivory collectors fully realized the existence of these parade batons and billets, most of them were in the hands of police collectors.

Any early police badge made of copper is a rather desirable collector's item. Copper was the original material employed and, according to Jay Irving, probably the leading collector of police antiques, regardless of what anyone may tell you about "Constable of Police" or "Constable on Patrol," it was the copper badges that gave rise to "copper" and "cop." At the time the copper badges were first introduced in the mid-1840s, they were worn by members of what were still known as the day watch and the night watch and were worn on civilian clothes as a mark of identification.

CHAPTER VIII

Miniatures
and Samples,
Models
and Toys

The chapter title itself should suggest that here the collector is in an area where word meanings and categories can overlap; where one collector may classify a specimen under one subject and his fellow may retain the same article under another. In a sense, all are related and the problems involved are chiefly those of definition and interpretation. The operative word is "miniature," almost all of the articles that will come a collector's way in this area are miniatures of something, and the definitions become matters of either original intention or use. The most diffuse word is "samples," which easily can mean different things to different people.

SAMPLES

A sample may be a full-blown example of something—whether a card as carried in the sample book illustrated or an anvil—being offered for sale. It can also be a segment of a product—such as the window sash holder pictured, or a swath of cloth to illustrate the material from which a suit will be made. Or a sample can be a miniature, real or dummy, to illustrate a product or a package, or actually to provide a taste. American folklore is filled with tales of the traveling salesman, usually in relation to the farmer's daughter, but anyone who seriously sits down to study the actual history of the traveling salesman and his art finds there is amazingly little solid material. Salesmen speak of carrying their "samples," opening their "samples," showing their "sam-

Two pages with colored sample cards pasted on from an agent's sample book of calling, comical, and other cards put out in the late nineteenth century by the Columbus Card Company of Columbus, Ohio. This book was intended for direct retail selling.

George S. Indig Photograph

ples," but apart from a relatively few surviving sample cases and their contents—usually of the segment or miniature type unless the product was a small one—there is very little that tells us exactly what kind of samples and how many most salesmen carried or had shipped ahead of them from town to town. It is unfortunate, for a whole important facet of Americana threatens thereby to sink almost without trace.

The best information that can be garnered is that, in more cases than not, the samples were of the example type, full-sized and complete articles, although the salesman may well not have carried or shipped samples of his full line. Thereby vanishes one part of a popular tradition, that which repeatedly delights in assigning to every small or miniature item that cannot otherwise be satisfactorily identified the explanation that it must have been a drummer's sample. Most of these so-called samples therefore actually were miniatures of other types or models or toys, although on occasion a salesman may well have carried a working model of something that was too large to transport in actuality and such attributions are almost always questionable, to say the least. In the past thirty years, the writer believes he has seen offered or been offered himself almost a dozen model railroad car trucks each allegedly the sample of the Fox truck supposedly carried about by Diamond Jim Brady. Only one was even a model of the Fox truck, and every one could, although in one or two instances with a certain difficulty, be identified as a truck fabricated for model-railroad hobby use, mostly in the 1920s and later.

Salesmen's sample cases are interesting and collectable as business antiques, but such cases, when empty, unless elaborately especially fitted, usually have about as much impact and interest as an old pair of shoes. However, any sample case with samples, any set of samples, or any sample book with contents is an extremely interesting and highly desirable business antique. They are by no means anywhere near so common as might be implied from I. Warshaw's statement quoted in Chapter VI. The fact is, although it does not materially diminish from their interest and value, that the greater portion of surviving sample books are, like the one illustrated, not the tools of professional full-time drummers, but, rather, the sort of thing distributed to those who sought to make a little extra money in their spare time by taking orders for cards, stationery, and similar merchandise.

If a product or package miniature contains or contained the material indicated on the label, it was either a sample or an item smaller than the normal size, such as the cakes of hotel soap. Such samples were usually given away free at promotional exhibits or distributed by mail in response to requests elicited by advertising. Collecting samples in this manner was a widespread hobby not only among youngsters but among adults as well at one time; in the 1920s many people actively competed to see how many offerings of samples they could locate and how many different samples they could collect. Such a collection would be of considerable interest today, from the standpoints of business antiques, packaging types, and as samples themselves.

If a miniature package obviously—as in the case of the Libby cans pictured—or apparently was a dummy, simply a package and not a sample, it may have been employed for some direct commercial promotion. Most likely, however, it was something furnished or at least paid for by the manufacturers of the real thing for use as part of the equipment of a toy store or toy kitchen cabinet. In some cases, actual samples were furnished with such playthings, but more frequently dummy miniature packages only. These, too, are of substantial collector's interest today from more than one point of view.

Miniature dummy containers and samples, all evidently from the 1920s. The salmon can and the salt box are each two inches high. The Libby cans are dummies, as may also have been the Corn Flakes and H-O Oats boxes. The Kitchen Bouquet, Gold Medal Flour, and Worcester Salt are actual product samples.

George S. Indig Photograph

Inasmuch as a miniature of anything invariably has a built-in appeal, any of these miniatures is rated as desirable, often more so even than the full-sized article it emulates, somewhat on the principle that a full-grown St. Bernard the size of a spaniel will attract far more attention than a full-grown spaniel of normal size. There also exists a very large body of collectors of miniatures as such, who accept anything so long as it is a miniature, regardless of whether it is old or historic, or was made last week especially for sale to collectors of miniatures.

Then, too, there are samples in the form of preproduction handmade samples of various mass-produced articles. Any collector who can secure such a handmade sample in the category of antiques in which he specializes feels assured that he has obtained an outstanding prize indeed.

MODELS

As in the case of samples, models may take many forms and the word may mean different things to different people; it may even, in some instances, more or less correctly be taken to refer to an original

A beautifully crafted one-inch scale working model of a harp-frame Amoskeag steam fire engine of the 1860s. This model was constructed by F. A. Wardlaw in 1912–13. Burning cannel coal and operating on fifty-five pounds steam pressure, it was capable of throwing a stream of water for forty-six feet.

The Smithsonian Institution

full-sized specimen in the sense of a handmade sample shown to the trade, the "original model," or even a "demonstration model." For the most part, however, "model" is recognized as referring to a *ex post facto* miniature rendering of something that already exists in larger size. The pertinent questions, depending on the individual collector's particular viewpoint, is whether it is a good model or a bad one, an old model or a fairly recent one, a working model—in the case of something whose prototype is functional—or merely a dummy or a display model, and also, in connection with each of these queries, whether it is a scale model or not, and just how detailed a model it may be. There then arises the point as to whether the collector is seeking models that are themselves historic or whether his prime interest is in the quality of his models, regardless of their background or age. A deep gulf divides these two viewpoints.

A good model, good in the sense that it is an accurate miniature rendering of its prototype is generally one in which every part is built to scale and in proper relationship to every other part. Scale is measured in terms of the dimension used in building the model that corresponds to a dimension on the prototype. Thus a model on which one inch equals one foot on the prototype is described as a one-inch scale model; a model on which one-eighth inch equals one foot on the prototype is a one-eighth-inch scale model. This relationship of model to prototype sometimes optionally is expressed in terms of size or proportion, although this latter is not the form favored by those familiar with models and model making. Novices employing the size or proportion usages occasionally incorrectly refer to them as scale. A one-inch scale model properly is a one-twelfth size model; a one-eighth-inch scale model is a one ninety-sixth size model. Obviously there is a great deal of difference between a one-eighth-inch scale model and a one-eighth size model; a one-eighth size model would be one built to one-and-a-half-inch scale.

"It was built by an old sailor," saith the dealer of a model ship, or "by an old railroad engineer" of a model locomotive. Mildly interesting, perhaps, if true, but to the knowledgeable collector never the imposing recommendation it supposedly constitutes, but usually the exact opposite! The fact is that such men usually build extremely poor models of the very things with which they seemingly should be best acquainted. This seeming paradox has long been known to those familiar with models and model making as either a trade or an avocation. It was initially pointed out to the present writer in the 1930s by the late Harold V. Loose, then managing editor of *The Model Craftsman*. It is at first a somewhat disconcerting thought, entirely opposed to that which most of us have been brought up almost automatically to accept, and it is an interesting psychological point.

A sailor in building a model ship will almost invariably not only distort the proportions of the model so as to make the sections where his duties customarily place him much larger than they should be, but will lavish considerably more time and detail on those sections. A ship model built by an officer will almost always reveal a materially enlarged and detailed quarterdeck; a gunner will exaggerate and overdetail the gundeck, guns, and ports, and an old ship model built by a topman will fairly scream this fact by the nature of its rigging, crow's nest, and so forth. This is never done intentionally; the builder always feels certain he has constructed an exact model, but subconsciously the portion of a ship where he serves seems to him by far the largest and

An approximately ½-inch scale model locomotive, tender, and car built almost entirely of wood by a locomotive engineer in the early 1900s. It displays the typical characteristics of such engineer-built models in its oversize cab, in addition to which the lack of proportion of and attention paid to the car is obvious.
George S. Indig Photograph

most vital. Similarly, a locomotive engineer or fireman will almost invariably make the cab of his models much too large, while a brakeman building a model of the same locomotive will concentrate his attention and exaggerations on the end sections, where his duties compel him to spend most of his time. There are exceptions to this on occasion, of course, but it will be found to hold true in most cases. Such exaggerated models could form the basis of an interesting collection in themselves as comprising an unique area of pseudo folk art, but the collector seeking old models that are excellent as examples of the model-making art will be wary of anything built by the proverbial "old sailor," "old railroad engineer," and their fellows.

Apropos of this, during the 1920s and early 1930s a great number of crude and rather heavy-handed wooden ship models, usually with "antiqued" parchment sails, were imported from Europe, mostly allegedly *Santa Marias* and *Mayflowers*. They are known as "radio models" because a chief outlet was radio stores and the general idea was that such a model was the ideal topping for a console radio. Many of these turn up today, usually to be offered as models built by one of those proverbial model-building "old sailors." They undoubtedly form a chapter, if a brief and not very heady one, in the history of commercial model making, but it would seem that they might be equally or even more suitably gathered and preserved by radio collectors.

As far as the relationship of the age of a model and its quality as an example of model-making skill is concerned, there always were model makers whose workmanship would rate high at any time and in any context. At times, however, the requirements of their customers were not so high as they might be today. As a general thing, acceptable standards of model making have continually increased. A great many models that were considered extraordinarily fine examples a hundred, or even forty or fifty years ago, would appear run-of-the-mill or even crude today. The collector who seeks either old or contemporary models because of what they represent historically must accept much of this basis that he probably would not consider worthy if his sole criterion was to be the quality of the workmanship and the amount of detail in a model. The man who seeks not so much old models as he does models of old prototypes—two distinctly different things—may accept or reject specimens on the basis of a different set of standards. In any case, a model does not have to be very old to be properly rated as an antique model; models built thirty or forty years ago usually are regarded as "old" models from a collecting standpoint.

Whether a model is capable of working is still another matter, but it should be observed that many working models are necessarily not scale models or that frequently portions at least of the working parts cannot be accurately built to a small scale and at the same time made to function properly. A good number of old models were built as working models for mechanical-demonstration purposes in schools or for the teaching of shop apprentices. They comprise an interesting and rather distinct category in themselves. Again reverting to the matter of miniaturization as such, any working model that is extremely small is automatically a collector's item of considerable interest and a potentially distinct collecting category. A number of model makers have always been endeavoring to construct the smallest working model of this or that, often with surprising results, although such models frequently of necessity are not scale models as such, for example, the working steam engine using a five-cent piece in the base and the boiler made out of two thimbles, and the little coal-fired model locomotive evidently roughly based on George Stephenson's *Rocket* pictured here. The stationary steam engine is 3⅜ inches high and was made using a homemade bow lathe by a hospitalized World War I veteran, Edwin Husson. The specified amounts of fuel and water for its proper operation are eight drops of alcohol and ten drops of water.

A model of the Conowingo Hydroelectric Generating Station located on the Susquehanna River at Conowingo, Maryland. The model represents a cross-section through the dam and powerhouse and is typical of industrial models frequently constructed for display and demonstration purposes.

The Smithsonian Institution

A cut-away demonstration model of a horizontal stationary steam engine of the late nineteenth century. This is a model of a Thompson & Hunt "Buckeye" engine and is typical of miniatures developed for sales promotion and classroom demonstration purposes.

The Smithsonian Institution

Two working models notable for their small size. The vertical steam engine with its boiler made of two thimbles stands 3⅛ inches high, while the locomotive is reputedly the smallest coal-fired model ever built. The steam engine was constructed by a World War I veteran; the history of the locomotive has not yet been traced.

Mr. and Mrs. Charles A. Penn, Bumble Bee
Trading Post, Bumble Bee, Arizona, Carstens
Publications Photographs

An even smaller model steam engine was known to the late W. J. Bassett-Lowke, the boiler with the engine next to it both fitting entirely under a thimble! However, this model was incapable of generating steam itself and could be operated only by means of compressed air supplied from an outside source, while the Husson engine is a true working model steam engine. All of this raises interesting questions as to what truly does constitute a working model and whether the fuel must duplicate that of the prototype. The steam locomotive is thus interesting not so much for its small size but because it actually makes use of coal for fuel, not alcohol, as is customary in small steam models. Its date and builder have not yet successfully been traced, but in the mid-1930s at least it was regarded as the smallest coal-burning model locomotive known.

The public dispersal of a great number of the original old United States patent models which once were required to be submitted with every application for a patent has made still another particularized and once seemingly inaccessible class of models available to collectors, although what were regarded as the most important and significant

Since the release of the majority of the early United States patent models by the government, a number have reached the hands of private collectors. This is a group of such patent models built by inventors applying for patents on railroad equipment in the 1860s.

Ward Kimball

models were retained by the government. However, surprisingly to many, the fact must be noted that the various attempts to merchandise these patent models never appeared to attract anything approaching the enthusiasm on the part of collectors that had been anticipated. As a result of a series of sales and auctions starting in the late 1930s, fair quantities reached the hands of collectors, and specimens and groups of specimens appear from time to time. It can only be said that it is obvious that, merely because something is an original patent model, it is not looked upon by most collectors as thereby monumentally rare and desirable. On the other hand, when a specialized collector is fortunate enough to have acquired or to be able now to acquire patent models pertinent to his particular category, they can become very important and worthwhile additions indeed—patent models of tools for the tool collector, of toys for the toy collector, of railroad devices for the collector of railroadiana, and so forth.

This may suggest—and correctly—that the overall collector's outlook on models is often uncertain and surprising to noncollectors. The fact that a model originally took a certain number of man-hours for an expert craftsman to build often bears no relationship to its present-day value at all. In short, comparatively few old models have an intrinsic value in terms of the original cost or the cost of duplication at today's prices, and a good many models will go begging for purchasers at a price that is considerably below their original cost. This is particularly true of a great many models of stationary steam engines. On the other hand, an old model that somehow particularly strikes the fancy of collectors may command a surprisingly substantial price. All this makes for old model collectings being a rather uncertain business all around, at least from the standpoint of prices and values. What also astounds many is the relative desirability of many out-and-out toys as compared to many fine models. It may be difficult to find a purchaser for a finely wrought handcrafted steam engine, for example, while what appears a relatively poor toy rendering of a similar steam engine may readily be sold to a toy collector at a figure that seems out of all relation either to its intrinsic worth or in comparison to a fine model steam engine. But this is precisely the point, not only are there infinitely more toy collectors than model collectors, but the established background of mass-production and a knowledge of what was manufactured makes toy collecting infinitely less of a hit-or-miss proposition than model collecting, plus the fact that very seldom in any area of antique collecting are values set and purchases made on the basis of a more certainly established scale among knowledgeable collectors than in the field of toy collecting.

Before turning to toy collecting, however, one other and comparatively new facet of model collecting should be mentioned, combining as it does the art of fine model making as such, the collecting of models, and the collecting of antiques. This is the collecting of scale models of antiques. In short, if you like models and like antiques, you can make or purchase and collect models of antiques, either as a part of a broader antique collecting pattern or as a hobby in itself.

Toys

Possibly no other segment of antique collecting has been organized, categorized, and stratified as has the widely popular one of toy collecting. It is perhaps necessary to look to stamp collecting to find a parallel where so much interest has been evinced and so much research expended in learning the minute details of what has been manufactured, and in all possible major and minor variations; what is and is not popular, and all the potential mutations of relative rarity and desirability. This obviously is one of the great attractions of toy collecting among men; the collecting endeavor is so completely logically based that even its many complexities and as yet not fully explored areas become, in the eyes of most men, positive advantages rather than deficiencies. In any case, what has been said here should not be taken to imply in any way that toy collecting leans toward the unduly sobersided; on the contrary, it is distinctly a fun hobby. The point is that the novice who is anxious to learn can—barring falling into the hands of some charlatan—orient himself quickly and with a good measure of certainty such as is found in few other widely popular collecting categories.

Of the differences and distinctions between toys and models, one could write at excessive length without producing definitions that would totally satisfy to the last man each and every purist point of view. Yet the distinction is more or less implicit and, for the most part, readily recognized and accepted by collectors.

Many toys are in themselves models, of varying accuracy and detail. This is especially true in the case of many of the most popular collector's categories of toys, such as trains, steam engines, horse-drawn vehicles, and similar toys that are based on or at least inspired by actual prototypes. Some toys are, in fact, very good models as models, either or both from a standpoint of appearance and function. Yet a more or less essential difference is that a toy originally was made and marketed as a plaything for children, whereas a model usually was fabricated, primarily at least, as an adult artifact. Often the degree of fidelity of a toy to a prototype is more one of spirit than scale accuracy; a toy often gives more creative range to the artistic ability of its designer and, more often than not, is the better a toy for this than a model. A simile is often stressed that compares a toy to a painting and a model to a photograph, and all things considered, this is a good comparison, although admittedly it can be carried to extremes that defeat its essential validity. In most cases, from the standpoint of a collector, a model is something that is more or less individually handmade while a toy is

A French brass model cannon of the eighteenth century, formerly the property of General Joseph C. Swift, who was a member of the first class graduated from the United States Military Academy at West Point, that of 1802, having previously served with the Regular Army as a cadet.

West Point Museum

a mass-production item. There were, of course, a number of specimens usually classified as models that were produced in fairly large identical quantities and which usually are still of interest to a collector of models. In contrast, while there were on occasion handmade, individually crafted toys, few toy collectors would give such specimens house room. To be collectable, other than in the case of such desirable specimens of experimental or sample models of toys intended for production, an old toy must have been mass-produced, in exactly the same manner as a collectable postage stamp must have been issued by a recognized government for a legitimate postal purpose.

There is also a recognized distinction in intent and use. A model may have been designed and produced for hobby use and still remain properly classifiable as a model. A model may even actually have been used at times by a youngster as a toy, yet this does not alter its collector's identification as a model. The French eighteenth-century model cannon illustrated was a model and was owned by General Joseph G. Swift, who was graduated from the United States Military Academy at West Point, New York, in 1802. The fact that it is known that General Swift later gave it to his grandson as a toy and that it was played with as a toy does not in the least alter its identity as a model or its collector's interest solely as a model. It would be of interest only to a collector of old models as such or a collector of military equipment, although the latter might conceivably collect both toys and models relating to his speciality. However, this miniature cannon, whatever its other virtues and relative desirability, would definitely not be of interest to a toy collector. On the other hand, there are numerous instances of articles originally made as toys that were purchased and used for other purposes than that of children's playthings; nevertheless, from the collector's standpoint, they remain toys.

The situation is graphically summed up in the photographs of the two open trolley cars, both based on similar or perhaps even identical prototypes. One, however, is obviously a toy, manufactured in 1910–13, and desirable and collectable as a toy, although it might also often and without any great breach of propriety be referred to as a "miniature trolley car" or a "model trolley car." The other specimen is equally obviously a model, constructed in the 1930s, and desirable and collectable as a model. As cited in the case of the French model cannon, both of these trolley cars might well be collected as part of a collection of trolley-car material in general or a broad railroadiana collection, but only one would be of interest to a toy collector and only the other one, of interest to a model collector.

Categories of Toy Collecting

Yet it should not be assumed that toys are collected only for their nostalgic or romantic values, or even in the broader and probably more popular context as relics illustrating the history of the toy industry. True, these things enter not inconsiderably into the picture and to the interest in and attractions of toy collecting, but many men are drawn to old toys because of the mechanical complexity and ingenuity and the mass-production know-how that are importantly represented in many of the most popular categories. Furthermore, many of these categories carry important historical connotations of the times and manners and an overall picture of life at the periods during which they were manufactured. A toy of, say, 1870 or 1910 is in many ways more char-

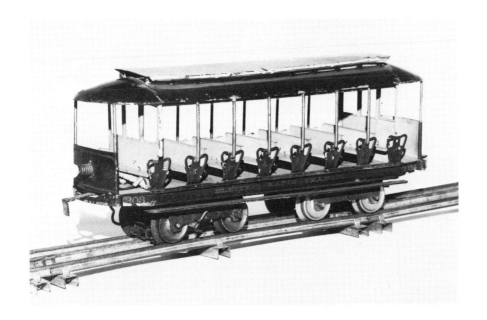

Both of these 2⅛-inch-gauge replicas of an open trolley car may properly be referred to as models, but they illustrate the generally popularly accepted differentiations between toy (top), a Lionel mass-production article of 1910–13, and scale model (bottom), a hand-built car constructed in the 1930s.

George S. Indig Photographs

acteristic and accurately reflective of 1870 or 1910 than almost any other artifact that could be named.

The accepted collector's classification of toys can be somewhat complex and often given to overlapping for among the most popular collector's categories will be found those classified according to prototype —such as trains, automobiles, or boats; according to the primary material from which they are manufactured—such as tin or cast iron; and according to the method by which they are powered—such as clockwork, electricity, or steam. There can be all sorts of broad or narrow subcategories or cross-categories imaginable, depending on what a collector chooses to concentrate, such as cast-iron trains or clockwork-powered tin toys. There are also methods of classifying and specializing, or at least of giving primary attention to, toys by periods, by manufacturers, or by countries of origin. Most of the desirable collectable toys, as of the time of writing, were manufactured roughly from 1840 to World War II, although already many collectors are starting to push the terminal date of their active interests forward in time somewhat and collecting many of the specimens of the later 1940s and even the 1950s. What customarily is recognized as the true Golden Age of toys, however, dates from the Civil War to the early 1930s.

The universally recognized greatest of all toy manufacturers was Ives, whose dates coincide almost exactly with those mentioned immediately above as marking the limits of the Golden Age, a circumstance by no means surprising considering how importantly the Ives products contributed to the fact that this era was the Golden Age. Ives was importantly active in almost every major collector's category but most particularly in clockwork toys, cast-iron toys, and toy trains. Any Ives toy is *ipso facto* highly desirable and collectable. However, so much was produced by them in more than sixty years of production that this does not also—at least not yet—mean that every Ives product is now necessarily either rare or valuable. In short, there still exists room in this area for the novice collector to acquire a fair sampling at least of Ives products, although naturally the opportunities diminish somewhat with each passing year. Many of the older Ives toys, in common with most nineteenth- and early twentieth-century toys are not marked with the name of the manufacturer, and toy collecting usually requires a considerable amount of study and research in order correctly to establish the identity of a particular specimen.

A classic American clockwork tin toy of the 1870–90s, manufactured by Ives. The legs of the horse move independently in a perfect trotting motion as the toy runs along the floor. Collectors deem Ives toys the best and most desirable of all makes.
G. William Holland Collection

Two late nineteenth-century American cast-iron horse-drawn pull toys, a walking horse and sleigh, and a dray. The sleigh was manufactured by Ives and a comparison of the detail of the design and the caliber of the castings and finish with those of the other unit will provide a good idea of why Ives products are so highly regarded in comparison with ordinary makes.

A. J. Koveleski

From the standpoint of geographic specialization and limitation, it can be fairly said that the vast majority of the most desirable old toys are those manufactured in the United States, Canada, and Great Britain, toy collectors above all others being aware of how grossly exaggerated and embellished is the hoary legend of Continental European toy-manufacturing superiority. In many cases, there is relatively little collector's interest or value in Continental toys, although they are not infrequently dumped on unwary beginners. In certain categories, such as trains, automobiles, and steam toys, the Continental toys occupy a fairly well-accepted status of recognition of a certain level of collector's interest among those who base their collections broadly, but almost always at a more or less overall secondary level of desirability. In toys, as in other collectables, size, gaudiness, original selling price, and other superficialities do not in themselves automatically confer high value and desirability. There are a number of highly prized and valued European toys, but, in short, the beginner in toy collecting should proceed very cautiously in acquiring such specimens and not allow himself to yield too readily to either visual or verbal siren songs concerning such specimens.

In the writer's *The Handbook of Old American Toys,*[1] the subject was broken down into sixteen definite categories, plus a miscellaneous seventeenth category, which were based on more or less accepted collector usage at the time and still generally valid for the classification of toys according to a system that embraces all major types. However, for the purposes of this summary, the following groupings may be suggested as best covering the most popular, interesting, and widely collected categories, bearing in mind the ever-present factors of overlapping and potential cross-collecting:

Categories based on material: tin, cast-iron.

Categories based on prototype or specific nature: trains, automobiles, mechanical banks, mechanical cap pistols.

Categories based on form of power: clockwork, steam, electricity, friction.

---

[1] $4.95, Mark Haber & Co., Box 121, Wethersfield, Connecticut 06109. *The Toy Collector* also is suggested and the various titles in *The Complete Book of Model . . .* series, all presently in print, each contains historical material on the toys and models relating to the specialty enunciated in the title.

Most of these are self-explanatory, but three—mechanical banks, animated cap pistols, and friction power—seemingly call for further explanation. A mechanical toy bank is a bank, usually but not necessarily fabricated of cast iron, wherein the deposit of a coin is accomplished by, accompanied by, or followed by some action, usually of one or more moving figures. Mechanical banks should not be confused with registering banks, which usually contain a certain measure of mechanism but wherein the function of the mechanism is simply to record the total amount of coins deposited. An animated cap pistol is one in which the firing of the cap is caused by the movement of a figure of a person, animal, or object mounted on the pistol. In short, an animated cap pistol was intended not as a good replica of an actual firearm, but as a sort of comic action piece. Friction toys are those powered by means of a heavy flywheel that is set spinning and then transmits its momentum to one or more wheels of the toy so as to propel it along the ground. Reference should also be made here to pull toys, or toys without any means of self-propulsion, intended to be pulled by a child. Pull toys are seldom if ever regarded as a definite collector's

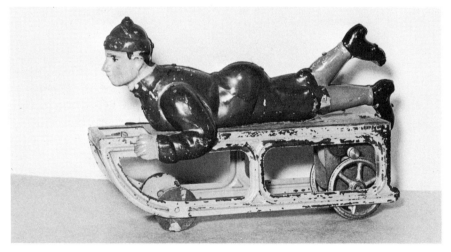

Most friction toys were locomotives, trolley cars, and automobiles, but a few novelty items were produced, such as this boy on a sled introduced in the World War I era but continued well into the 1920s. It was manufactured by the Dayton Friction Toy Works of Dayton, Ohio.

Leon Perelman

category in themselves, but the term is well understood as identifying a specific type of toy which may be constructed of tin, cast iron, wood, or other material and which takes the form of a miniature automobile, locomotive, horse-drawn vehicle, or other wheeled unit.

Popularity and Trends

For the most part, men prefer toys manufactured of substantial materials and either or both displaying in themselves or reflecting from the prototypes from which they are derived mechanical ingenuity and industrial progress. Thus, not unexpectedly, probably the most widely collected category of toys is that of toy trains. This includes, in the case of the later track trains, not only locomotives and cars themselves, but everything that was manufactured to help make up a complete miniature railroad system: stations, tunnels, bridges, signals, track, and so on. Toy-train collecting, when followed to the broadest extent, involves segments of most of the other popular toy collector's categories. There are toy trains made in whole or in part of tin or cast iron, and

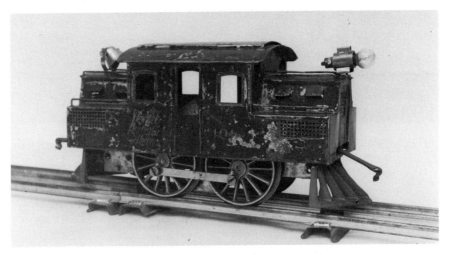

Early electric trains are probably the most widely collected category of old toys. Pictured here is a Lionel New York Central–type locomotive (although lettered by the manufacturer for the New York, New Haven & Hartford Railroad) made 1910–12.

George S. Indig Collection

One of the first toy automobiles manufactured in the United States, a Hafner clockwork-powered model manufactured in the opening years of the twentieth century. It features a working steering tiller, plush-covered seats, sheet-metal body, cast-lead wheels and running gear, and rubber tires.

A. J. Koveleski

there are toy trains powered by clockwork, steam, electricity, and friction, as well, of course, as pull toy trains. By far the greater number of train collectors, however, are most interested in clockwork and electric track trains, the specimens representative of the equipment that for decades made the toy train truly the king of boys' toys, and thereby, not surprisingly, today the most popular category of all toys among men collectors.

A good second in overall popularity is displayed by toy automobiles as a collecting category, although this has so many recent and even current collecting overtones that a considerable part of the hobby is pursued on a basis that, regardless of how broadly definitions are attempted, removes some of the interest at least from anything that with any justification can be termed antiques collecting. There are, however, many specialists who do limit the period from which they will accept specimens sufficiently to make a substantial part of these collections properly classifiable as antique toy collections. This problem does not exist with most other popular types of toy collections, tin and cast iron as a basis are materials seldom met with in production in recent years, and in any event enthusiasts collecting on the basis of specializing in such materials or specializing in such forms of power as clockwork or steam seem to find little difficulty in limiting that which is acceptable to their collections in terms of a reasonable time span. It is only the old toy-automobile collecting enthusiasm that seems to bubble over to any considerable extent and at times takes in really recent and even contemporary specimens.

Mechanical-bank collecting is a much publicized category, and not alone for the seemingly high prices that many banks command, but if only partially at least for this very reason, it is not so widely pursued as is toy-train collecting and toy-automobile collecting and other popular specialties. This is not to say that each particular category does not usually have its prime collector's items whose values—particularly inasmuch as they often apply to articles of what to many collectors seems comparatively recent date—often amaze those not yet conversant with the ins and outs of toy collecting. This in its turn automatically creates a situation wherein, in order for enthusiasts to continue to collect in the most popular categories, not only the date spans of what constitutes an "antique toy" must ever be brought forward but also there is an increasing tendency to find not only acceptability but even surprising value in toys of lesser calibers than those to which knowledgeable toy collectors, even in the very recent past, for the most part restricted themselves and which, regardless of recently developing trends, must inevitably always carry the greatest interest and desirability.

There can be little doubt that toy collecting is the most actively bubbling pot in all of masculine antique collecting and evidently will continue to occupy that role well into the unforeseeable future. So widespread and ever-increasing is interest in toy collecting that what is happening is that almost any obsolete toy that fits within one of the more popular categories is almost automatically collectable and is collected, to a large extent regardless of caliber, desirability, or age. Perhaps such toys are not collected with any great measure of verve or enthusiasm, at least on the part of more aware individuals, but they are nevertheless collected. Such specimens often change hands at prices that, to most toy collectors of not very long ago, would have seemed absolutely unbelievable for articles that many of them literally would not even have deigned to accept as gifts. The result, as the 1960s drew to a close, was that not only were many toys that had been manufactured hardly more than a decade earlier being collected as, if not "antique," at least as sufficiently "old" to warrant such attentions, but that a surprising number of such toys were starting to show up at antiques shops and shows. Once an article or group of articles is somewhat widely merchandised in this manner, there are few who will take it upon themselves to cavil at the applicability of referring to them as "antiques." It cannot be said with any accuracy to what extent those offering such recent toys for sale are conscious of their actual age—in all fairness it must be admitted that almost any toy that has been too strenuously played with by a child can very rapidly take on a superficial appearance of considerable antiquity.

There are many who inveigh against the collecting of such toys, either on the grounds that many of them simply are not yet old enough to warrant such interest or because, in the case of those that are of a parallel age with long-accepted toy collectables, they are not of sufficient stature to warrant such attention and enthusiasm. Anyone who would attempt to comment judiciously upon the situation is on the horns of a dilemma. On the one hand, it would seem only proper that in any field of antiques collecting some standards of acceptability be maintained, based either or both on age or merit, even though admittedly it is desirable that the restrictions founded upon age ever be advanced with the passing of time. On the other hand, the history of antiques collecting is littered with the limbs which various commentators climbed out upon and cut off behind them by asserting that this or that was not and never could be worthy of collecting.

CHAPTER IX

Theatrical, Musical, and Political Antiques

Somewhere on the fringes of almost every man's memory there exists a passing circus parade. This may seem a rather curious circumstance in a great number of cases, for many who firmly possess this recollection are too young ever actually to have witnessed such an event, but it is indicative of the powerful fascination with which the circus and everything about it seems to grip all males. The collecting of circus material—"circusiana," in token of the collector's penchant for tacking such endings onto things of particular interest—is therefore natural enough. It forms a popular category in itself apart from the collecting of most theatrical and even showmen's antiques, although to some extent it stands closely linked with another specialty, the collecting of material relating to the history of zoos and menageries. The latter is one of the so-called quiet or little heard-of categories of collecting, devoting itself to the history of the exhibition and importation of animals; most of its collectables are of paper, as also to a large extent are those of the circus collector.

Often the two specialties overlap and complement each other neatly. Take the case of Mr. Quick's hippopotamus:

First the poster of G. F. Bailey & Company's "Circus & Menagerie," which portrayed in glowing colors some twenty-four-plus hippopotami. In fact, there was a diminishing line of them seemingly running off into infinity in the background. It was probably not necessary to inform most showgoers of the third quarter of the nineteenth century that

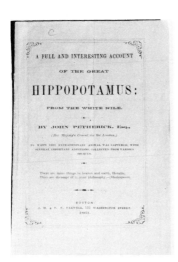

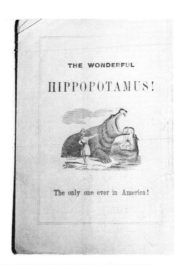

Mr. Quick's hippopotamus, the first in America. Top, the front and back covers of a booklet issued in 1861, when it was exhibited in Boston. Below, a poster of G. F. Bailey & Co's Circus & Menagerie after G. C. Quick and his hippo had joined the show. Note that the circus poster is an elaboration of the art work on the back of the 1861 booklet.

George S. Indig Photographs *(top)*
Ringling Museum of the Circus,
Sarasota, Florida *(bottom)*

Messrs. Bailey & Company did not own or exhibit two dozen of these behemoths, although from the poster even the most cautious person might be excused for expecting at least a pair. There was one hippopotamus and it was Mr. Quick's, seemingly the first in America. The show title was, in fact, quite honest about this, presuming always, of course, that one was literate enough to know that "hippopotamus" was a singular noun, but most viewers of the day probably took the *s* ending as indicative of the plural. The show title—for the 1857 season, according to some accepted circus chronology—was the mouth-filling "Grand Metropolitan Quadruple Combination Consisting of George F. Bailey & Co.'s Circus, Herr Driesbach's Menagerie, G. C. Quick's Colossal Hippopotamus, and Sands, Nathans & Co.'s Performing Elephants."

However, *A Full and Interesting Account of the Great Hippopotamus From the White Nile* by John Petherick, Esq. ("Her Majesty's Consul for the Loudan"), also illustrated and from the files of a menagerie collector, refutes this dating and tells in detail the story of Quick's hippopotamus, assertedly purchased by him from Petherick for $20,000. The booklet is dated Boston 1861, at which time "Bucheet" was being exhibited in a store in that city. According to Petherick's account, the hippopotamus, then only a day or two old, was captured in April 1858, and hence could not have been with Bailey's show in the season of 1857, nor could the title of Bailey's show have been the cited one in 1857. By 1861 "Bucheet," which the booklet explains is Arabic for "fortunate" or, colloquially, "lucky dog," would only have attained approximately a third of his total eventual weight and size. In any event, the poster is most probably from the mid-1860s to the mid-1870s, and the two pieces undeniably make an unusual pair. It will also be seen that the two central hippopotami on the poster derive from the woodblock on the back of the 1861 booklet with the figure of the keeper omitted.

The George Fox Bailey of the poster, incidentally, was not the famed Bailey of Barnum and Bailey. The latter, James A. Bailey was in fact born James Anthony McGinnis, who went to work when he was less than thirteen for Frederick H. Bailey, the advance agent for the Robinson & Lake Circus, in 1859 or 1860, and subsequently adopted his employer's name. The Lake of the Robinson & Lake Circus, incidentally, was the gentleman whose widow, a little more than a quarter of a century later, was to become the wife of Wild Bill Hickok just a few months before Wild Bill went off to be dealt his aces and eights in Deadwood.

G. F. Bailey was the son of Hachaliah Bailey, the Somers, New York, farmer who gained fame exhibiting "Old Bet," often incorrectly referred to as the first elephant in America. This Bailey worked for Aaron Turner, one of the "Flatfoot" circus operators, married Turner's daughter, and eventually took over the Turner show. He did become connected with Barnum as the manager of Barnum's show in 1876–80 during the period that it was a "Flatfoot" operation. According to that fount of circus knowledge, Joe W. Mc Kennon, acting curator of the Ringling Museum of the Circus,

The "Flatfoots" was an organization of animal show and later circus operators from around the Somers, New York area. They organized in 1835 and had operations into the eighties. Their opposition was the most ruthless of all the combines. Fact is, if a show wasn't a member of their group, it just did not play in their territory for a period of over twenty years. The term "Flatfoot" originated in this way: When a show not in the trust

The "Lion's Bride" bandwagon of the Hagenbeck-Wallace Circus. It was originally built in the winter of 1904–05 for the Carl Hagenbeck Trained Animal Show by the Bode Wagon Works of Cincinnati, Ohio. In 1906 the animal show became a part of the Hagenbeck-Wallace Circus.

Ringling Museum of the Circus,
Sarasota, Florida

started to come into the monopolized territory they were warned, "We put our foot down flat, and shall play New York State, so watch out." "Flatfoots" was applied as a derisive title at first, but not for long. After a few wreckings it became a title of respect.

Thus, briefly, some of the many interlocked fringes of circus history connected with but a single poster, and an example not only of the complex lore of the circus that engages the attention of innumerable collectors of circusiana, but also, in a broader way, a suggestion of what can lie behind almost any collectable item in almost any category. This is why collecting, to be fully savored, must be regarded as consisting of a great deal more than merely gathering in and preserving specimens or even merely of savoring their superficialities!

CIRCUS COLLECTABLES

To own an old circus wagon undoubtedly ranks as the epitome of circus collecting, and there may still be a few old wagons hidden around the country awaiting a zealous hobbyist. The pedigree of most circus wagons is something to be traced much like that of a dog. Most of them were used over a considerable length of time and often passed from one show to another in the course of various maneuverings and combinations. This is the main reason that there still exists a possibility, however faint, of a collector's turning up an unknown wagon stashed away in the barn of some descendant of a former circus man. However, candor necessitates stating that the chances are somewhat slim today, and, outside of a museum, an old circus wagon is a rather inconvenient thing to own, and it certainly will not tell you as much about circus history as will the run of posters, programs, and other paper material that a collector is much more likely to come across and will find far easier to house. However, when a great many old circus wagons finally were broken up, their elaborately carved figures and decorations sometimes were removed and saved, and these sometimes appear on the market, although often there may be some question as to whether these offerings truly are what they are purported to be.

The circus poster is undeniably an art form in itself, equally an important category of historical advertising material with a special flamboyance all its own. Most circus posters—and theatrical posters in general—were based on a standard twenty-eight-by-forty-two-inch sheet of paper, hence the terms "half sheet," "four sheet," and so on to refer to the size of a poster, the larger posters being pasted up of a number of separate sheets. A "half sheet" poster could be either twenty-one by twenty-eight inches or fourteen by forty-two inches. There were exceptions at times, of course. The 1897 Barnum and Bailey poster pictured is an odd twenty-nine by thirty-seven inches. For the most part, though, circus and theatrical posters go by the standard sheet sizes, and the collector should bear these sizes and terminology in mind. Most of the posters that the average collector will have the opportunity to acquire will be half-sheets and full-sheets, with occa-

 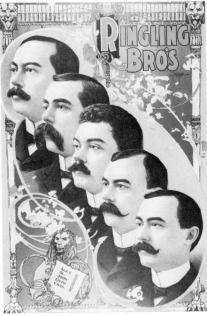

The ever-entrancing glory of the circus poster. Two rival 1897 posters that provided a portrait gallery of then competitive circus greats, Barnum and Bailey, and the Ringlings. The basic design of this Barnum and Bailey poster was used for many years with slight changes, there being probably between fifteen and twenty variations in all.

Ringling Museum of the Circus,
Sarasota, Florida

Two throwaways of the early 1880s distributed by the W. C. Coup Show, a puzzle card and a dummy note on the "First National Amusement Bank." Coup was as well known and as ingenious in his day as Barnum; he achieved a "Four Ring Circus" by placing a smaller ring inside the center of his three rings.

G. William Holland Photographs

sional odd sizes such as those just mentioned. Few posters that were pasted up in more than one sheet were likely to be salvaged by boys after a show had passed, but a good number of half-sheets and full-sheets were secured in one way or another, and, of course, a number of examples of all sizes that never were pasted up have managed to survive. There were samples and printer's waste and there was almost invariably some boy to latch on to any odd poster that anyone had around. Which is not to imply that old circus posters, not even those of thirty or so years ago, are by any means common, but they are obtainable from time to time.

Programs are naturally much more readily obtainable, as are handbills and advertising throwaways of various kinds, but a circus collection need actually be limited only by the ingenuity of its owner. It should be realized, however, that it is not exactly the kind of material that, if an enthusiast decides to make it a specialty, he can go out and readily buy in quantity in the open market the next day. The wise collector will, in fact, probably devote a considerable amount of his energy to gathering fairly recent material to be put aside against the day when it, too, is old enough to be of importance.

In retrospect, the history of the American circus undoubtedly is dominated by the figure and legend of P. T. Barnum. This is unfortunate in a way, for he was, in fact, a relative latecomer to the form of entertainment with which his name is forever coupled. Others pioneered the circus, and even in his day there were other names equally as well known in different parts of the country, such as W. C. Coup, for instance, two of whose novelty throwaways are illustrated. It was, in fact, Coup who was Barnum's manager and partner in 1871–75 when Barnum first began his big splash in the circus world (he had had an earlier show in the late 1840s and early 1850s) and who invented the system of loading flatcars from the ends that made the transportation of circuses by rail practical. It was of Coup, not Barnum, that the famous story was told in the 1880s—various towns being specified, according to the teller—of the owner of the new theater who entered his premises after the painters had finished and beheld an unfamiliar visage looking down on him from above the stage. Upon being informed that this was William Shakespeare, and the reasons for his presence, his comments were abrupt: "Shakespeare? Never heard of him! Paint him out and paint in a picture of W. C. Coup!"

THEATRICAL ANTIQUES

Much that has been said concerning circus antiques holds true for the similar and related category of theatrical relics, although there are perhaps somewhat broader possibilities in the way of articles relating to specific actors and actresses, playwrights and producers, and an overall far greater availability of material if the collector is concerned with the theater in general. Theatrical collecting as such embraces not only the legitimate theater but extends to include musical and vocal performances, vaudeville and burlesque, and the performing arts in general. It also extends to the collecting of sheet music, although the type of sheet music a great many men collectors specialize in is that related to a specific subject of particular interest, such as music relating to the railroads, political sheet music, or war songs. Apropos of the last, this may be the most suitable place to observe that in recent years anything pertaining to World War I has become of considerable interest to collectors, and sheet music holds a perhaps more important role in this category than with any of America's previous or subsequent conflicts. There are not only the war songs as such—endless attempts being made by songwriters to achieve something that might prove another "Over There"—but, often scarce and certainly little known, the immediate postwar songs, sometimes through the sale of which it was intended to raise funds for the assistance of veterans, such as the now almost forgotten 1919 "They Acted like the G.A.R.'s," published by the Legion of Allied Veterans of the Great War, Inc., and "Yankee Girl, I'm Coming Back to You" of the same year, dedicated to Major General Clarence Edwards, commander, and the 26th (Yankee) Division, illustrated here.

It is possible and often popular to channel a theatrical collection toward material relating to a single favored star or team, from Junius Brutus Booth to Southern and Marlowe, from Weber and Fields to Helen Hayes. It is still surprisingly easy to provoke a heated quarrel among stage buffs as to the relative attractions of such bygone ladies as Lily Langtry, Adah Isaacs Menken, and Lillian Russell. A very good case, based on the extent and ever-greenness of her memory, can, however, be made out for the proposition that America's true all-time sweetheart is Jenny Lind, who, it generally is agreed, was by no means an outstanding beauty even by the standards of the mid-nineteenth century, although there is a general belief, perhaps a legend in itself, that when she opened her mouth and sang, seemed to be transformed. Also, Jenny Lind was in the western hemisphere only for some twenty-one months, from September 1, 1850 to June 1852 and, despite frequent

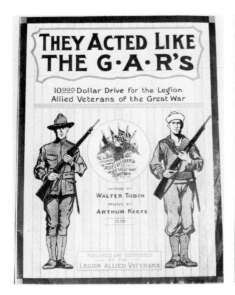 

Immediate post-World War I sheet music, "They Acted like the G.A.R's" and "Yankee Girl, I'm Coming Back to You," both put out in 1919 and sold to raise funds to assist veterans of the Great War.

George S. Indig Photographs

invitations, never returned. But in addition to her own attributes, Jenny Lind has had two things going for her. One was her initial sponsorship in the United States by Barnum, and the Barnum legend in itself is sufficient in the United States to add luster to anything it touches; if Jenny Lind appeared the greatest possible theatrical attraction to P. T. Barnum, that alone is enough. The second was that, in the motion picture, *The Mighty Barnum,* released in 1934 and now frequently shown on television, Jenny had the good fortune to be enacted by one of the most beautiful of actresses, Virginia Bruce (Barnum was played by Wallace Beery). When Jenny Lind is mentioned to most American males today, the image they conjure up is not that of the lady of her photographs or even the somewhat enhanced features of the contemporary statuary, but that of the blonde beauty of Miss Bruce. Anything connected with Jenny Lind is highly collectable and, as the illustrations indicate, there is a considerable variety of material to be found, often suitable for collecting as a part of a number of different popular categories. The letter to the man who sent her money for a daguerreotype would be a valued addition

Two busts of "The Swedish Nightingale," Jenny Lind, each about nine inches high. The bust at the left is of bronze and is labeled "Jenni Lind" (sic). It was made by Sautschek and dated 1863. The bust at the right is of French Haviland china and is correctly marked "Jenny Lind."

W. Porter Ware

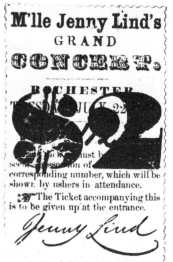

A ticket to one of Jenny Lind's concerts on her famous and only American tour, 1850–52. This ticket was for Rochester, New York, July 22, 1851. Each ticket bore a facsimile of her autograph.

W. Porter Ware

for any photography collection,[1] the police collection of Jay Irving prizes a letter from the then Chief of Police of New York regarding tickets to her first American concert, any empty Genin hatbox is regarded as a prime Lind-Barnum item. The hat store of John N. Genin was on one side of the entrance to Barnum's Museum and, when the tickets for Jenny Lind's first American concert were auctioned off, Barnum counseled Genin to purchase the first one for any price necessary for the sake of the publicity that would thereby befall him; hence the collector's value that attaches to any Genin hat or hatbox. Jenny's own image, however, is to be collected in a variety of forms, daguerreotypes (despite her chariness as expressed in the pictured letter as to allowing strangers to have them), pipes, eyeglass cases, commemorative bottles and flasks, music, bronze and china statuary, prints, and other forms. Reputedly, she is the lady in the sleigh in front of Barnum's Museum in the well-known print "Sleighing in New York," but it seems certain that this popular identification is a completely erroneous one and simply another manifestation of the Jenny Lind legend.

There is a surprising variety of theatrical statuary, particularly busts of famous figures, awaiting the collector who can locate them. One particularly interesting group, both to theatrical and to book collectors, is that comprised of what variously is known as Shakespearean porcelain, Shakespearean china, or Shakespearean figurines. The last is not quite fully descriptive, for although the most interesting pieces undoubtedly are the miniature full-length figures, the group also includes busts, toby jugs, and other forms. The earliest and best ones appeared in England in the second half of the eighteenth century. Their making continued well into the nineteenth century, and from time to time ever since additional pieces have appeared, most having been made in Great Britain, where their fabrication goes back to the early days of Bow and Chelsea-Derby. These latter, as are some of the later figures, are porcelain, of course, but many of the later pieces were produced in less expensive materials. Most are painted, some of the better

---

[1] This and numerous other previously unpublished Lind letters is included in *The Lost Letters of Jenny Lind* by W. Porter Ware and Thaddeus C. Lockard, Jr., London, 1966. It is obtainable in the United States for $4.50 from The University of the South Supply Store (Book Department), Sewanee, Tennessee 37375.

ones with considerable artistry and often making use of extraordinarily beautiful colors, the Derby blues in particular being famous among these wares in general. Some of the nineteenth-century Staffordshire-ware figurines are rather sketchily decorated, however, and the Parian items, with the exception noted below, are always left undecorated in imitation of marble. The Parian figures date from the late 1840s onward.

There are numerous full-length statuettes of Shakespeare, usually leaning on a pedestal and pointing to a sheet of manuscript on which appears—even in some of the Parian ware—a somewhat garbled quotation from *The Tempest*. Certain of the earlier figures are definitely identifiable as portraying specific actors in favored roles, most particularly James Quin as Falstaff and David Garrick as Richard III. The Quin figures seem to have been the most popular with contemporary purchasers and certainly are today among collectors. They range in height from about nine to fifteen inches, portraying Falstaff at the moment of the "What's honor?" speech, and the detail sometimes extends to legible writing on a bill for a capon, sauce, and sack sticking out of the doublet pocket. Quin (1693–1766) was considered the first actor in England until the appearance of Garrick, whom he later supported at times, and was particularly noted for his portrayal of Falstaff. Other early figures include King Lear and Shylock (as a pair of figurines), and a design long popular that is customarily identified as "Andromache Mourning Over the Ashes of Hector," which, collectors of this specialty seeking as many possibilities as they can, customarily is accepted as a Shakespearean figure from Troilus and Cressida.

Other figures include Antony and Cleopatra (as a pair of reclining figures), Henry VIII, Macbeth and Lady Macbeth, and Hamlet. Some of these designs appear to be of fairly recent origin. Richard III always was a popular subject, although the early vigorous figure of David Garrick of the eighteenth-century design subsequently gave way to a cottage ornament portraying Richard in his tent, in which the tent becomes the most apparent portion of the molding. The range of known subjects is not too extensive, but there is almost endless variety by way of manufacturer, size, material, and pose for most of the pieces. Probably the best collection of this material on display in the United States is that in the Folger Memorial Library in Washington, D.C.

Shakespearean figurines. Left, late eighteenth-century Chelsea-Derby figure of James Quin as Falstaff. Center, Chelsea-Derby figure of Shakespeare pointing to lines from The Tempest. *Right, nineteenth-century Staffordshireware figure of Richard III awakening in his tent.*

George S. Indig Photographs

From Shakespeare to the medicine show may seem an enormous leap, but another particularized and highly interesting phase of what must, if only for want of any better classification, be included among theatrical antiques are those relating to medicine shows. They are important not only in themselves as a form of once popular but now vanished entertainment, but equally because of their connection with the popular avocation of bottle collecting, as well as with industrial history and advertising antiques. In many cases, the medicine show of the late nineteenth and very early twentieth century was a highly organized theatrical enterprise, charting its travels with as much care as the circus, actually sponsored by big bottlers, and a far cry from the traditional hit-or-miss faker immortalized by O. Henry in "The Gentle Grafter" or portrayed in dozens of motion pictures in what Hollywood classified as "a standard Raymond Walburn or Berton Churchill part." Medicine shows were once big business, usually carefully scheduling their appearance in towns when big crowds would be drawn in by the concomitant stand of a carnival, circus, or fair, and heralding their arrival and performances with a storm of curious and interesting literature.

An example of what may be collected in the way of medicine-show materials is found in the four-page *Guide to Health* of which the front and back pages are illustrative of the promoters of Kickapoo Indian Sagwa, a product familiar to most bottle collectors, and associated nostrums. The Kickapoos were the traditional and most popular tribe among the makers and vendors of assorted Indian remedies. Just why the Kickapoos has always been rather puzzling, and there have been various suggested explanations, but Frederick J. Dockstader, Director of the Museum of the American Indian, believes the main reason was simply that the name "Kickapoo" had a certain ring to it. Circulars of this type were rubber-stamped in each town, giving the location of the medicine show. The specimen illustrated bears the words "FREE EXHIBITION/Union St. Near Bridge" stamped above the heading employing, for the second line at least, a set of movable rubber type. Investigation reveals that the performance in question took place in Springfield, Massachusetts, in 1896. The circular submits much curious material, including highly debatable medical lore, an injunction to purchase only genuine bottles bearing the signature of Healy & Bige-

 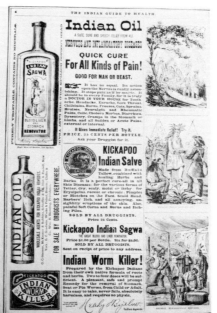

Front and back pages of a four-page circular distributed in the 1890s as advance publicity for an Indian medicine show, the place being rubber-stamped adjacent to the pointing finger at the top of the first page.

George S. Indig Photographs

low, who are described as "Indian Agents," woodcuts of friendly Kickapoos giving their beneficent Sagwa to the agents, and, in contrast, the Kickapoo scalp dance, and another entitled "The Death of Custer," the fatality in this case being portrayed as taking place in a deep woods. The implication intended evidently is that Custer came to this end solely because he was in a weakened condition through failure to take his Sagwa regularly.

A rather lengthy essay could, in fact, be written or an entire collection based on the commercialization of Custer over the years.

ANTIQUES OF THE SCREEN

Many do not realize how important a part was played in public entertainment by the professional lantern-slide showman in the last decades of the nineteenth century, but, in effect, these shows were the motion pictures, television, and even newsreels of their day. The collecting of professional magic lanterns and slides therefore is an important aspect of the overall collecting of theatrical material as well as a specialty in itself, most particularly insofar as the collecting of slides is concerned. In addition, some of the mechanical or animated slides are important historical forerunners of the motion picture itself. This professional lantern and slide material should by no means be confused with toy magic lanterns and slides, a subject in which there is comparatively little interest among toy collectors, which is not to say that they are not secured and retained by some general toy collectors, but it is a warning flag against the prevalent tendency to push these toy lanterns and slides to novice collectors as something very desirable.

Just the opposite obtains in the case of the professional lanterns and slides—they are widely regarded as extremely desirable. This may be due in part to the fact that, while most toy lantern slides were rather trashy and grotesque objects of continental European origin, the professional slides, many of which were made in the United States and Great Britain, were prepossessing, quality items of an entirely different nature. Furthermore, many of the professional slides are of extraordinary historical interest, especially to Americans, and most notably in the case of the innumerable Civil War slides.

The professional magic lantern slide of the nineteenth century—originally known as a "slider"—was mounted in a wooden frame about 7 inches long, 3¾ inches to 4 inches high, and about ⁵⁄₁₆ to ½ inch thick. The glass slide itself usually was circular in form, about 3 inches in diameter, and almost always beautifully colored. Most slides from the mid-1850s on were manufactured using a photographic process capable of reproducing drawings and paintings. The principal manufacturers appear to have been William Y. McAllister and James W. Queen & Company of Philadelphia, and T. H. McAllister of New York, although it seems probable that many of their slides were from a common production source. The subjects of the regulation slides were almost endless, and their catalogs included thousands of slides of American and foreign views, Biblical scenes, illustrations of novels, portraits, scientific specimens including microscopic objects, history, and also horrifying pictures used by temperance lecturers.

The all-time big lantern-slide subject was the Civil War, the slide-making process having been brought to its full level of perfection just in time fully to chronicle the conflict. There were no less than nine

A twenty-seven-inch-high late nineteenth-century professional magic lantern manufactured by Benjamin Pike & Son of New York. The three slides are, counter-clockwise, a standard circular slide (under the dropped lens cover); an animated slip slide; and an animated lever slide of a deer drinking, its neck and head raising and lowering as the lever is moved.

George S. Indig Photograph

hundred sixty slides in the Civil War series cataloged by Queen in the years immediately following, and although the line gradually was thinned down as time went on, many of them were long standard. The list included persons and events that today are hardly remembered even by specialist historians but which obviously were the subject of widespread common interest and knowledge in their day. These slides were, in fact, the newsreels and television newscasts of their day, and countless professional exhibitors made their way around the country putting on shows, leaving their itineraries with their supplier so that the slides with the latest hot news could be shipped to them each week. For example:

No. 90. Infernal machine discovered in the Potomac near Aquia Creek.

No. 91. Wilson's Zouaves in the covered way on the land front of Fort Pickens.

No. 92. Lieut. Hall's compliments to the Secessionists.

No. 93. Battle of Hoke's Run—Col. Starkweather with his Wisconsin Regiment.

Inasmuch as the manufacture of these slides was carried on in the North, there were many allegorical and comic slides directed at the South, such as:

No. 766. The Furlough South (Comic). Rebel returns to the bosom of his family. Being clad in the stolen uniform of our gallant defenders, he is mistaken by his wife for a "Yank," and received accordingly.

The movable or mechanical slides are of especial interest as precursors of the motion picture. They are mounted in wooden frames similar to the regular slides and may include a movable slip or lever or a complex crank and gear mechanism. There were also chromatrope slides, such as the Washington Chromatrope with Stuart's painting in the center surrounded by revolving stars and stripes, and, perhaps most interesting and complex of all, sets of movable astronomical diagrams demonstrating the solar system, the phases of the moon, the eccentric revolution of a comet around the sun, eclipses, and so forth —every projectionist his own planetarium. The movable astronomical slides seem always to have been sold only as complete boxed sets of ten or so slides. (There also were ordinary, nonanimated astronomical slides which should not be confused with the ones with actual motion produced by means of a crank and rack-work.) Another special class of slides was made up of dissolving view slides and dissolving chromatropes which could be satisfactorily projected only by means of special dissolving view or stereopticon lanterns. Dissolving view slides were sold in matched sets of two to six slides. The collector who finds an isolated dissolving-view slide likely will find it puzzlingly incomplete until he properly identifies it for what it is. There were a few animated slides, some even with cranks and gearing, made for toy magic lanterns. As toy slides, they are considered relatively desirable, but the collector will have no difficulty distinguishing them by their smaller size and flimsy construction from professional slides.

MECHANICAL MUSICAL INSTRUMENTS

Old musical instruments of regulation patterns are collected, but seemingly not widely or very often in more than a halfhearted manner. There seems to be something almost inherently depressing in somebody's old clarinet or tuba. On the other hand, anything that makes music mechanically is extremely widely and enthusiastically collected by men. There was once a great deal of contemporary ridicule directed at mechanical music by those who found the whole concept of having a machine imitate that which a live musician was capable of performing, but the shoe is on the other foot today collectorwise and possibly there is even some little feeling of guilt concerning this favoring of devices that in many cases may have put real musicians out of work that operates to make the idea of collecting the instruments of these men seem, as suggested, disheartening.

Other than those obviously intended for home use, mechanical or automatic musical instruments may or may not be coin-operated. Also, some of them, such as a number of the band organs, originally were furnished as more or less integral components of amusement-park devices, such as merry-go-rounds. The word "nickelodeon," incidentally, may have a varyingly broad or restricted meaning according to individual interpretation. Some apply the word to any coin-operated amusement or entertainment device, such as peep-show motion-picture

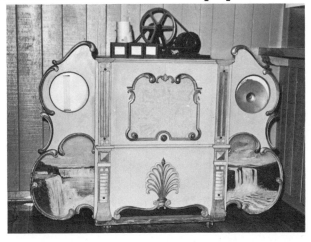

A forty-four-key band or fair organ measuring seven feet three inches in width and weighing six hundred pounds, circa 1920–25. Manufactured by the Rudolph Wurlitzer Manufacturing Company, North Tonawanda, New York (Model No. 106). One of the paper rolls used in this organ may be seen standing upright on the top.

Ward Kimball

machines as well as musical instruments; others take it as meaning only a coin-operated mechanical music maker, while still others believe its use properly should be restricted solely to coin-operated player pianos. The list of mechanical musical instruments is a varied one, and besides the best-known types, a considerable number may be found, such as automatic violin players, banjo players, and harp players, and there are a number of complex specialized and combination devices that successfully reproduced the original playing of an artist with amazing fidelity.

Player pianos usually employ paper rolls for their programming and actuation, motion being secured by foot-pedaling in the case of the majority of instruments intended for home use, while those built for public places were electrically operated. Sometimes additional effects were included in such player pianos intended for public use, such as a mandolin attachment. If there are sufficient attachments, the player piano is considered an orchestrion, or, in effect, a mechanical orchestra, the orchestrions usually departing from any resemblance to a piano as such and often becoming extremely large and complex, with all sorts of mechanical musical effects possible. However, it should be kept in mind that there are instruments properly classifiable as orchestrions that still retain a basically piano form with exposed keyboard, and there are instruments properly designated as forms of player pianos that are built in straight-fronted cabinets and that have no exposed keyboard.

There also are various forms of automatic organs, some being large pipe organs for use in public places and known variously as dance organs (usually for indoor use) and the louder band organs or fair organs. There were also, of course, the large—sometimes enormous—theater organs, although these were only sometimes equipped for automatic playing. All types of organs and, in fact, any keyboard-played musical instrument are popular collectables among those who can house them. Due to their complexity and construction, any piano organ is in a sense a mechanical musical instrument, although that term usually is reserved for use as a synonym for automatic musical instrument, albeit there are also those who maintain that, correctly, a mechanical musical instrument is only one that is operated by a clockwork mechanism, such as are most music boxes, and from an overall standpoint of both

An eleven-and-three-quarter-inch-long late nineteenth-century Swiss cylinder-type music box that plays four tunes, manufactured by E. Touffoirs of Acier.

George S. Indig Photograph

A Regina disc-type music box of the early 1890s, with several extra records at the left, manufactured by the Regina Music Box Company of Rahway, New Jersey.

Ward Kimball

antiques collecting and ordinary technical terminology, there is much that can be said in favor of this viewpoint.

As to the music boxes, this group of automatic instruments is relatively familiar to most people, particularly the cylinder music box, one of the earliest and most popular forms. (Aside from music boxes, the great period of automatic musical instruments was the early twentieth century, many among the types most popular with collectors today being manufactured in the 1920s and even the 1930s.) In the 1890s and early 1900s another type of music box attained fairly widespread use, the disc music box, as typified by the Regina. Machines of this type made use of interchangeable metal discs to actuate selectively the teeth in a musical comb. Roller organs or paper-roll organs are also closely allied to music boxes as being automatic instruments intended largely for home use, although their music is furnished by organ reeds rather than by a musical comb. Various methods including paper rolls and metal discs were employed to select and sound the programmed notes, the great period of roller-organ popularity being the 1880s and 1890s.

In the collecting of automatic musical instruments, the gathering of additional paper rolls, discs, or whatever originally was employed in any given instrument usually also assumes an important role. The owner of such an instrument or instruments usually wants them to be in playable condition and to be able to play them from time to time, and extra rolls usually are gathered for actual use rather than merely as historical relics. The field of automatic musical instruments is one of the few areas in antiques where restoration is generally regarded as acceptable and even in some cases desirable, at least to the extent of making an old unit serviceable. It is again possible today, also, to purchase newly manufactured rolls suitable for use in certain types of old automatic musical instruments.

PHONOGRAPHS AND RECORDS

Many enthusiasts tend to regard old automatic musical instruments and old phonographs as part and parcel of the same hobby. However, beginners frequently express surprise when they find that this is far from invariably being the case. A moment's reflection will reveal the reason for this: a phonograph is not truly a musical instrument itself but rather a machine for reproducing music and other sound, although to many this appears a rather thin distinction. Unquestionably, in terms of specialized hobbies in themselves, there are a great many more collectors of old phonographs and phonograph records than of old automatic musical instruments and associated materials. There has long existed a most active and widespread hobby of collecting old phonograph records, although mainly in terms of old opera and band recordings for replaying, a hobby accompanied by much debate as to which pressing and label may truly give the best rendering of a specific artist and piece, opera being a point of especial interest among these collectors.

However, this is far from all there is to the lure of old phonographs and records. Most of those who collect them as antiques are intensely interested in the machines themselves and in old records, cylinder or disc, either essentially as examples of types and labels or for their content, which may include the same interests as those held by the type of collectors mentioned in the preceding paragraph, but, among men at least, are just as likely, if not even more so, to run more to comic dialogues and sketches, popular songs, and, perhaps even most of all, to historical recordings. This last group of collectors not only busy themselves in what historical personages were recorded and seek specimens of the original records, as well as in some instances of re-recordings, but also frequently indulge in the perhaps pointless pastime of making up lists of persons whose life spans were such that their voices might easily have been recorded and preserved forever and sharing with each other their lamentations that no one possessed the necessary combination of foresight and verve to see to it that such recordings were made for historical reasons. Their prime example and regret probably is the Empress Eugenie, who survived until 1920; every man who collects phonograph material would seemingly make much of a record of the voice of the legendarily beautiful consort of Napoleon III.

There are in fact two legends that continually pass among succeeding groups of collectors, evidently possessing a curious attractiveness for the minds of such enthusiasts. One concerns the premature invention of photography in the eighteenth century, but the failure to discover suitable means permanently to fix the images. This story evidently stems from the experiments of Thomas Wedgewood and others around 1801 to make photographs from paintings on glass and from projected silhouettes. The second, and seemingly far more fascinating to many, tale relates to the supposed premature invention of the phonograph by a Frenchman who visited the White House with his machine during the Civil War and actually made recordings of the voice of Abraham Lincoln. His recording material, however, supposedly was so impermanent that a record could be played back but once and was then useless. Furthermore, supposedly his last record remained unplayed for some years until at last Edison ruined it in a bungled attempt to play it into one of his early machines so that it could permanently be preserved. The origin of this story apparently comes from garbled accounts of the Phonautograph, a device invented in 1857 by Leon Scott, that would make a graph of the human voice but not a playable recording.

Of Presidents of the United States, recordings have been made of all since William McKinley. There also exists a record designated as a speech by McKinley, but the predominant opinion among phonograph collectors is that the voice itself actually is that of Len Spencer, a well-known professional phonograph performer (*Uncle Josh at the County Fair, Uncle Josh in a Hotel,* and so on). In any event, the number is rather slim and disappointing in view of what we might have had, for it would have been possible to have had recordings of the voice of every President since Andrew Johnson, or more than half. There are, however, other historical recordings of even greater collector interest. Probably the most interesting and desirable of all American historical records is that made by Columbia in 1918 under the label *Nation's Forum.* On one side of the disc, accompanied by his facsimile autograph molded into the material, is a brief address by General John J. Pershing, *From the Battlefields of France* ("Three thousand miles away, an American Army is fighting for you . . ."). The other side contains the address *Loyalty* by former United States Ambassador to Germany James W. Gerard. This is of extreme historical importance, containing in Gerard's own voice the account of his famous conversation with the German foreign minister, Zimmermann, that noted telegram fancier, in which Zimmermann threatened the rising of 500,000 German reservists residing in the United States and Gerard replied that there were in the United States 500,001 lamp posts on

The label of From the Battlefields of France, *the phonograph record made in France during World War I by General John J. Pershing. Perhaps the most interesting of all historical phonograph records, the other side carries the address* Loyalty *by James W. Gerard.*

George S. Indig Photograph

which they would be hanging the day after the attempted rising. In his verbal account of the event on the record, however, there is an interesting slip that evidently passed unnoticed; Gerard gives his figure as "501,000," or perhaps that actually is the figure he gave Zimmermann.

Of the talking machines themselves—phonograph, now so widely used as a generic name, originally was, of course, merely one specific brand, along with Graphophone, Gramophone, Victrola, and so on— little in particular needs to be said save that there is a multiplicity of types and models sufficient to keep the collector busy for many years, and that many are still easily come by. That and this one other important point: Most of the later machines, and this probably includes virtually all of the disc machines, were sold substantially as complete, finished units of a particular type. Much confusion can be created in attempts to study and categorize the earlier cylinder machines, however, particularly in the case of the Edison Phonographs. In the early 1900s a number of machines that originally played only the two-minute cylinder records were converted to play either two- or four-minute records by means of conversion kits provided by the factory. In some instances, this conversion was done by the dealers before machines in stock were sold; in other cases, it was done on models already in the hands of individual owners. Similarly, there was considerable alteration in this period of the horns of the Edison machines, many machines originally furnished with small horns being converted to large horns by attaching a bracket that would hold the crane for a large overhead-

A British-made "Peter Pan" portable Gramophone, ca. 1912. Although it plays a standard-size record, the machine completely folds up into its leather-covered box measuring six inches high, four and a half inches wide, and seven inches long.

Ward Kimball

An Edison cylinder phonograph, originally manufactured in late 1906 to play two-minute records only. It was updated by the dealer within the next four years using factory-supplied components in the form of a stylus that also played four-minute records, and a large horn.

W. van Roosbroeck

supported horn to the back of the machine. There are thus many possible variations and the collector must determine his own standards of what may constitute a proper variation within the scope of his individual collection. The Edison Home Phonograph illustrated, for example, manufactured late in 1906 according to the serial number, has been fitted with a conversion turnover stylus assembly for playing either two- or four-minute cylinders dating from 1908 or 1909, and a new horn, crane, and bracket dating around 1909–12.

It will be seen that not all cylinder records, even when of the same diameter, are interchangeable or can be played on any machine on which they seem to fit physically; the four-minute cylinders have finer grooves and twice as many per inch as the two-minute cylinders. (There also were larger-diameter cylinder records.) This also is true of disc records; Edison discs—as well as cylinders—have vertical or "hill and dale" modulation, while Victor and a number of other records have laterally modulated or "needle-cut" records. Manufacturers of disc machines frequently made optional reproducers for other types of records than their own make; Edison also, from 1926 on, had alternate reproducer arms for playing their regular discs or their long-playing and thicker Diamond Discs. The latter type of discs may be seen in place on the turntable of the Edison disc machine pictured.

POLITICAL ANTIQUES

The retention of old political-campaign items, particularly buttons relating to Presidential campaigns, is almost a reflex action with countless Americans, as distinct from the actual purposeful collecting of political material in general or campaign material in particular. A surprising number have kept the buttons they wore in every campaign in which they were old enough to vote; if your man won, your button obviously played its part in history; if he lost, the button is a nostalgic memento of vanished hopes and efforts. An enormous number of men must, however, be seriously collecting old campaign buttons as a purposeful hobby as evidenced by the seemingly amazingly short time in which campaign buttons—despite their apparent plentitude—become acknowledged collector's items. Naturally, interest centers chiefly in Presidential campaign materials, or in the earlier campaigns of men

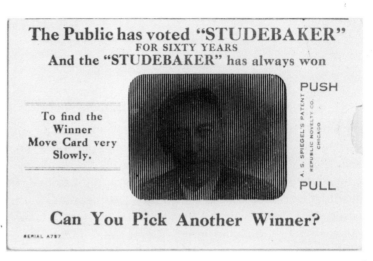

A photographic transformation card of the 1912 Presidential Campaign, distributed by Studebaker. By pushing or pulling the slide, the pictures of the three candidates appear—Woodrow Wilson (shown here), William Howard Taft, and Theodore Roosevelt.

G. William Holland Photograph

who eventually were nominated for the Presidency, with a certain definite interest also in important senatorial, gubernatorial, and mayoralty campaigns. Understandably, however, there is relatively little interest in the "Joe Smith for Alderman" type of thing, most people neither knowing nor particularly caring about the who, when, and where of Mr. Smith's effort.

A careful distinction must be made between actual campaign buttons and other campaign material, and political material as such. Both are highly collectable, but a great many specimens that seem at first offer likely to be campaign material, while assuredly political material, are seen upon investigation by no means actually to have figured in a campaign, and rather to be of a commemorative or even a memorial nature. The most widely collected campaign material are buttons, badges, and ribbons. The use of buttons in political campaigns, relating either to a particular candidate or a party, is usually credited with taking hold in the United States in the 1830s, although there are those who find evidence of considerably earlier use of political or semipolitical campaign buttons, and there certainly are at least some such buttons of a political if not of a campaign nature. In any event, it does not appear that campaign buttons, as a widely distributed and recognized political adjunct, came into use until after the Civil War, the more common form for some time continuing to be the cloth campaign ribbon or badge.

There were also many other widely employed forms of campaign material in the late nineteenth and early twentieth century. Some, such as collar boxes—and even imprinted paper collars, watch fobs, and cane heads were, given the customs of masculine attire of the times— evidently especially favored. However, almost anything that could be cheaply made was adapted for campaign purposes or especially fabricated, and there are a great number of specific novelties that the political-campaign material collector can endeavor to locate and obtain, such as the noisemakers in the form of a miniature wooden faucet for the 1891 New York State gubernatorial candidacy of Jacob Sloat Fassett (faucet-Fassett), none of which evidently were found workable upon delivery and presumably for the most part scrapped, and the 1896 McKinley soap dolls. Political parade material almost forms a category in itself, the now legendary torchlight parade not only having long been an actuality in itself but also the support of an industry that produced parade torches (also employed in firemen's parades), special hats, capes, uniforms, transparencies, and paper lanterns, the general use of some of this material continuing into the early twentieth century. Political caricature also provides a collecting category in itself.

Akin to political collecting in general there also is the collecting of recruiting and patriotic posters and similar material put out in wartime, World Wars I and II in particular having resulted in a great deal of this type of material; a few farsighted individuals starting to build comprehensive and now important collections of posters immediately after if not actually during World War I. World War II seems to have contributed a totally unique phenomenon in the form of a considerable number of patriotic buttons of varying sizes. The first of this material appeared shortly after December 7, 1941, with "Remember Pearl Harbor" buttons and buttons bearing a picture of General Douglas MacArthur, then continuing through most of the war with a startling number of buttons, some quite large, which were hawked at parades and patriotic rallies and sold in novelty shops, and ranged from the simple injunction "Win the War" to commemorative items such as "One Down and Two To Go," marking the surrender of Italy. Well over one hundred different buttons of this period are known and, as noted, their appearance on so prolific a scale seems unique to World War II.

CHAPTER X

Sports, Games, and Amusement-Park Devices

Taken all in all, it is somewhat surprising that more publicity has not been given to sports antiques and that the numerous men who make a hobby of collecting them have not far more widely heralded the obvious enjoyments of their avocation than generally has been the case. W. Porter Ware, that man of widespread collecting interests, and the redoubtable Nat Fleischer of *Ring* magazine are two well-known exceptions to this, but they and a few others are the proverbial exceptions that prove the rule. For reasons that are somewhat difficult to evaluate, sports collecting has to date been a category that for the most part must be numbered among the "silent" antiques hobbies. Perhaps one reason for this situation is that on the occasions when sports antiques have been publicized, attention to a large extent has been directed to the equipment known to have been used by one particular champion or another. In baseball, for example, much attention has been directed to balls autographed by or bats used by such mighty men as Ty Cobb or Napoleon Lajoie, rather than to assemblages of material illustrating the history and development of the baseball or the baseball bat as such. Perhaps many collectors who do not and probably never will own one of Babe Ruth's bats or a pair of Jim Jeffries' boxing gloves feel that the real merit in sports collecting can lie only in the possession of such personally identifiable relics.

Obviously this cannot be true nor should the concept be permitted to take any wider hold than it may now possess. While certainly every man would take keen pleasure in owning such personally associated specimens, this is far from what the collecting of sports antiques is all about. It is, in the main, the purposeful collecting and study of contemporary equipment—for, as most men are aware, sporting goods have continually changed over the decades as does everything else, and of associated items in the form of posters, tickets, catalogs, prints, books, toys, trophies, statuary, and so on. In fact, in sports antiques, as in so many other categories, the range of potential collectables proves upon investigation to be infinitely broader than most enthusiasts would at first imagine.

In any event, there already unquestionably exists a host of active collectors of sports antiques, little publicized as they may have been. For evidence of this it is necessary only to consider the fact that there are book dealers who specialize in the subject and who regularly issue not merely sales catalogs of what they have available in books, manuals, and other paper material, but even more tellingly, lengthy lists of their specific wants, covering virtually every sport imaginable. A recent want list from such a specialist bookman enumerated over five

There are those who believe that golf derived from a Dutch game known as kolf. *The point is debatable, but clubs and balls used in* kolf *such as these fifteenth-century specimens W. Porter Ware is examining in the United States Golf Association Museum and Library are most desirable sports antiques.*

W. Porter Ware
Howard Coulson Photograph

A four-man bicycle, built in 1898, of the type usually designated a "Quad." It could be ridden for pleasure but was also favored for use in pacing a bicycle rider seeking a speed record.

The Franklin Institute

hundred sought-after specific titles, plus general material, before reaching the tenth letter of the alphabet in the headings under which they were classified and which included Archery, Athletes, Badminton, Baseball, Basketball, Boxing, Canoes, Clubs, Coaching, Cricket, Cycling, Exercise, Falconry, Fencing, Football, and Golf. It is safe to say, name your sport and there exist numerous collectors and collectables, from baseball and boxing (two favorites) to bicycling and skating.

It is true that many collectors of old bicycles and motorcycles may look upon themselves and be looked upon by others chiefly as vehicle collectors, but bicycles and motorcycles also are properly sports antiques and are collected from that standpoint as well. Investigation of the possibilities of collecting sports antiques often surprises many in its revelation of how much material there is available that overlaps into other and much more widely publicized fields of collecting, such as bronzes and prints, and, as exemplified by these, how much sports material in fact results from endeavors and sources that most people think of as primarily artistic. Yet this should not really be in any sense astounding, for the athlete in all ages attracted the skills of artists working in various mediums and continues to do so. Furthermore, there was always a vast market for such prints and other work for display in clubs, barbershops, saloons, and other places where men tradition-ally gathered. It is therefore only to be expected that there should exist so much graphic and sculptured sports material.

A good example, or perhaps more properly an exceptional one, for it is regarded as one of the most outstanding of sports antiques, is found in the remarkably well executed bronze of John L. Sullivan knocking down Billy Mitchell which appears as the frontispiece of this book. The statue, which is 16½ inches long, 14½ inches high, and 5 inches wide, catches Sullivan at the moment of dropping Mitchell in

Old punching bags in the collection of Nat Fleischer. The bag in the center, used by John L. Sullivan from 1882 through 1892, represents one of the earliest types of heavy punching bags. It was fabricated for Sullivan by the famous William Muldoon and contains an inner bag filled with ashes and sawdust.

W. Porter Ware

Howard Coulson Photograph

a bare-knuckle bout held on March 10, 1888, on the estate of Baron Rothschild at Chantilly, France. Sullivan had been the World's Heavy-weight Champion under the Revised London Prize Ring Rules since 1882 and—a little realized point—was to remain the bare-knuckle World's Heavyweight Champion until his death in 1918, the 1892 fight with Corbett which Sullivan lost being fought with gloves under the Marquis of Queensberry Rules. The 1888 fight with Mitchell went thirty-nine rounds and ended in a draw. A little more than a year later,

Sullivan beat Jake Kilrain—himself, as is the case with most noted pugilists, the subject of statuary—in seventy-five rounds at Richbourg, Mississippi, in the last bare-knuckle championship bout.

The 1888 bout also was for the World's Heavyweight Championship, being held on private property before an invited audience because prizefighting was then against the law in France. Among those invited to the event was the noted sculptor Emile Hébert (1828–1893) in order that the contest might be immortalized in bronze, Hébert being reported to have made a great number of quickly executed sketches during the contest for reference in his subsequent work. The resulting bronze statues were presented by Baron Rothschild to a number of his friends who had attended as a souvenir of the occasion. Just how many were cast is unknown. One, now in the Fleischer collection, was long a prized possession of Richard K. Fox, the publisher of the *National Police Gazette,* although it has never satisfactorily been clarified whether Fox attended and was presented with the statue by Rothschild or whether he subsequently managed to purchase one and displayed it to suggest that he had been present. The specimen illustrated herein is in the collection of Mark Haber, who managed to locate and secure it in the 1940s. However, the point is—and this is an important point—that a fair number are known to have been made, although no one can tell how many may still survive, and the possibility always exists, as it does with all desirable specimens that originally were produced in multiple, for additional specimens being found by other fortunate collectors. This would hardly militate against the desirability and value of the presently known examples, but it is one of the factors that tend to make such things as this so much more alluring and interesting in the view of most men collectors. While there is admittedly ever a certain and often not inconsiderable attraction in owning something of which only one exists and no one else can possess, most men feel there is an equal if not even greater appeal in items such as the Sullivan-Mitchell statue where every interested collector has at least a chance.

Sports Statuary and Prints

A fair, perhaps even in the eyes of many a considerable amount of sports statuary was made and exists, mainly bronzes of specific notable

A nineteenth-century French bronze of a hunting dog by P. J. Mene. This is a fine example both of these old miniature bronze statues in general, and of one type of such statuary that a specialist in sports antiques can find. It measures eleven inches in length.

Mark Haber, Andrew B. Haber Photograph

individuals or of generalized scenes or of hunting dogs. In addition, there must be considered the statuary and relief figures that appear on many trophies, a great many of them of stock designs and of varying materials, including silver.

As has been suggested, the field of prints relating to sports is of great magnitude; to the collector who attempts to essay it as a specialty it usually appears almost endless. N. Currier and Currier & Ives alone put out well over a hundred prints of distinctly designated sporting subjects and, by an easy extension into related areas such as Western scenes, the total issued by them alone can be raised well over two hundred, still not taking into account the stock posters they supplied in great numbers for races, trotting meets, and similar events. The Currier sports prints range from the very well-known and highly desirable "The American National Game of Base Ball," depicting a game at the Elysian Fields, Hoboken, New Jersey, where the first formal championship game was played between the Knickerbockers and the New Yorks in 1846, to the rather obscure "Ball-Play Dance by the Choctaw Indians." Some of the Currier sports prints were issued in series of two or four each, such as "American Feathered Game"

("Mallard and Canvas Back Ducks," "Partridges, Woodcock and Snipe," and "Wood Duck and Golden Eye"), "American Field Sports" ("A Chance for Both Barrels," "Flushed," "On a Point," and "Retrieving"), and "The Life of a Hunter" ("A Tight Fix" and "Catching a Tarter"). "A Tight Fix," depicting a hunter desperately defending himself with a knife against a gigantic enraged bear while his companion seeks the opportunity to get in a shot from a distance, is one of the best-known of the Currier & Ives prints, and at one time an example sold for the highest price ever paid for one of their prints. While the Currier product ran heavily toward hunting scenes, it also included a good number of racing, prizefighting, and other sports prints.

The firm, incidentally, was active over a much longer period than most imagine, dating its founding as 1834, although prints were not immediately published, and not terminating its activities until 1907. By the latter date most of its prints were hopelessly out of style, but from about 1840 into the 1890s, the firm was one to reckon with. From the proportionate makeup of its range of sports prints, it is obvious that

A bust of Christy Mathewson, the famed New York Giants pitcher. It was executed by Gertrude Boyle Kanno, who is reported to have watched Mathewson in action at the Polo Grounds over a number of years before undertaking this outstanding example of sports statuary.

National Baseball Hall of Fame and Museum,
Cooperstown, New York

the main outlet for such prints was to persons who intended to use them to decorate bars and barbershops. The latter establishments had, of course, a ready source of pictorial embellishment in the aforementioned Richard K. Fox's *National Police Gazette,* but there was a recognized distinction between the use of such clippings and the purchase of formal prints, although Curriers originally sold for as little as fifteen cents and the top retail price for the largest colored prints was three dollars. There were hundreds of other printmakers active in the United States in the latter two-thirds of the nineteenth century and most of them contributed abundantly to the flow of sports prints, not to mention numerous ones produced abroad.

Prizefighting prints make up a category in themselves and one that was popular even before the middle of the eighteenth century, when evidently most if not all of them came from Great Britain. There are prints going back at least to John Broughton, who in 1743 created the Original London Prize Ring Rules. The print of these rules tagged "As agreed by Several Gentlemen at Broughton's Amphitheatre, Tottenham Court Road, August 16, 1743" obviously does not necessarily have to date from 1743 as it usually is so identified, nor to be the very first of the boxing prints, but it is old enough, as is the mezzotint of Broughton and George Stevenson, usually dated as 1750. The great era of prizefight prints seems to run from the last decades of the eighteenth century and well through the nineteenth, when at last the craft of photography to a large measure took over their purpose.

A great deal of serious attention was at times paid to these prints on the part of sportsmen, many of them being reviewed and criticized in contemporary sports publications. In an article on prizefight prints appearing in the May 1951 issue of *The Antiques Journal,* Paul Magriel quotes in full a review of the aquatint by Charles Turner after a painting by Thomas Blake that appeared in *Annals of Sporting* shortly after the print was placed on sale in 1821. Admitting that Blake's purpose had evidently been to create a "grouping together of all the most celebrated pugilists, second raters, and millers of the Fancy," the review then took him to task in several hundred words for numerous specific errors, anachronisms, and artistic failings, and noted "there is such a thing as posterity, as youth growing up, who will look at this picture, as a refresher of their memories, and that they will be led astray,"

A PRIZE FIGHT.

THE AMERICAN NATIONAL GAME OF BASE BALL.

Sports prints are legion and can comprise a special category all their own if desired. Top, an 1820 British print, "A Prize Fight," by H. Alken, published by T. McLean, and, bottom, the famous Currier & Ives print, "The American National Game of Base Ball."

The Old Print Shop

finally granting that, if Mr. Turner would print a broadside "explanatory of the liberties he has taken with historical truth, probability and facts," the picture might then be "admissible among the Fancy at half-a-crown"—the selling price being three pounds.

It is interesting to observe that once Currier & Ives had gotten fully under way with their prizefight prints, many of the bouts and boxers they depicted were British, these prints evidently commanding a wide market in Great Britain as well as in the United States. Most of their pugilistic prints incorporated considerable explanatory and statistical material, including the information on *The Great Fight for the Championship* in 1860 between Heenan and Sayers that "the battle lasted 2 hours 20 minutes 42 rounds, when the mob rushed in & ended the fight."

Uniforms and Equipment

When Bob Fitzsimmons arrived in San Francisco from Australia in 1890, he was wearing a high silk hat. The hat has been preserved and, along with a photograph of Fitzsimmons wearing it, is presently in the collection of Nat Fleischer, to whom Fitzsimmons presented it. There are other examples of articles of clothing preserved in other collections of sports antiques, shoes, caps, shirts, and even complete uniforms. They are undeniably historic, but seldom too easily come by, present problems in proper preservation, and in any event, a great many men very evidently feel there is something not a little tawdry and depressing in attempting to collect and preserve old clothes. Whatever the reasons, relatively few sports collections appear to go in very extensively for old wearing apparel, although there are some notable exceptions. To a considerable extent, however, this evident reluctance to dabble in old clothing seems to run through most forms of masculine collecting where it might well enter into the picture as closely as it could in the collecting of sports antiques.

Aside from commemorative material such as prints and statuary and the highly popular and almost endless array of paper material, the thing evidently most widely collected by sports antiques enthusiasts is the equipment actually used in the sport itself, whether that sport be baseball, archery, golf, tennis, football, cricket, lacrosse,

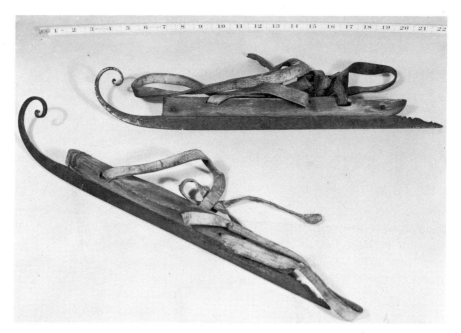

Old ice skates are another very popular sports specialty among collectors. This is a pair of early racing skates, about 1800–20. The overall length of a skate is nineteen inches.

W. Porter Ware

Beadle's famous dime publications were not confined only to the famous dime novels but extended to sports manuals, as evidenced by this 1867 manual on curling and skating. Early manuals relating to all sports are eagerly sought by collectors.

W. Porter Ware

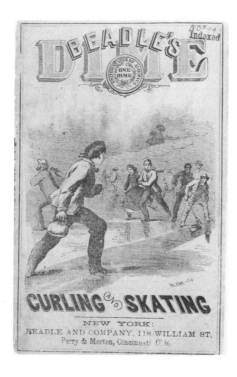

The last baseball autographed by Babe Ruth. This particular ball is, of course, a permanent museum exhibit. Other balls autographed by Babe Ruth occasionally become available to collectors and are naturally considered highly desirable specimens for a baseball or general sports antiques collection.

National Baseball Hall of Fame and Museum,
Cooperstown, New York

curling, ice skating, fishing, croquet or what you will. An interest in hunting antiques naturally manifests itself usually in the collecting of old firearms. Once a collector gets involved in collecting sports artifacts, whether relating to one sport, several, or even a general assemblage, the range of possibilities is endless. Furthermore, much of this material is relatively small, at least small enough for a still prodigious supply of old balls, bats, racquets, clubs, and similar things to remain as yet uncovered and awaiting the questing enthusiast. There are museums devoted to various sports, the most notable, of course, being the National Baseball Hall of Fame and Museum at Cooperstown, New York, as well as notable private collections, but as already indicated, a vast amount of collecting and study remains to be done to illustrate and record the development of sports equipment of all kinds.

Take the baseball, for example. There are numerous collectors of baseballs, from the standpoint both of autographed balls and of the evolution of the ball itself, but as with dozens of other types of sports artifacts, there still remains an enormous opportunity for collecting and researching the development of the baseball. Just how many different baseballs, taking into consideration both models and manufacturers,

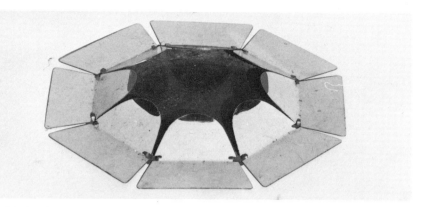

The "Golfers' Putting Disc," an eight-lip indoor practice cup, ca. 1920, manufactured by The Golf Shop Company, Chicago, Illinois. Old golf clubs, bags, balls, and everything else pertaining to the game are becoming increasingly popular sports antiques.

George S. Indig Photograph

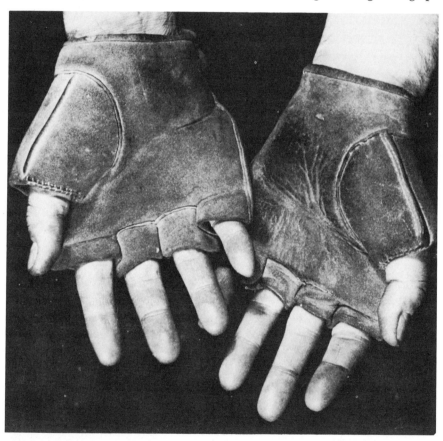

Early fingerless catcher's gloves, worn on both hands in the 1870s. When found in reasonably good condition, as in the case of these specimens, old baseball gloves are prime sports collectables.

National Baseball Hall of Fame and Museum,
Cooperstown, New York

actually have been manufactured over the decades evidently has not been estimated. A study of balls in existing collections as well as old catalogs of sporting goods suggests that the number must have been astoundingly large and that the collector who set out to collect baseballs on this basis and—hopefully—to study their history would have an enjoyable and rewarding lifetime pursuit ahead of him. Typical catalogs of the 1880s, for example, offer from a dozen to two dozen distinct models, and some expand the range still further by offering an alternate selection of many of the same balls but with red leather covers, one of the now almost forgotten, short-lived enthusiasms of the game. They were evidently once manufactured in fairly large quantities, yet there is an automatic temptation to pose the question, just how many present-day baseball collectors possess even one red baseball?

In any case, this is but one particular article, and the point is really not so much the relative scarcity—or perhaps even lack—of red baseballs, but precisely what part did the red baseball play in the development of the game. The matter need not be too heavily underlined, and the point being made here should be clear: at present there exists a vast potential for the purposeful collecting and accompanying study of the antiques relating to virtually every sport, although admittedly a few fields, such as bicycling and hunting, have been rather well explored, albeit more from their connections with other categories of antiques than as sports antiques as such. The accompanying photographs should provide at least an idea of what can be done in the direction of sports antiques, as well as suggesting why sports antiques may well become one of the most widely and enthusiastically pursued categories in the years to come.

GAMES AND GAME EQUIPMENT

Games may not be sports in the strictest sense, but the relationship of games and gaming to sports antiques should be fairly obvious, and it is rather difficult dogmatically to attempt to separate the two for there is much overlapping. For instance, are billiards classifiable only as a game, or as a sport as well? Games frequently and confusingly overlap with toys, and often it is only a matter of use rather than of equipment that determines whether a game is properly classified and collected as a toy or as a separate category closely related to sports.

An interesting Civil War period game, published by Charles Magnus of New York. "The object in view," according to the rules, "is to run between the lines of the blockading squadron and to reach Wilmington, N.C.," which is located in the center of the maze.

George S. Indig Photograph

Some games and game equipment are obviously not toys, either by virtue of the mode of play or because of the type of equipment involved. Once again, the interested collector must make his own guidelines and patterns of collectability within the framework of his own outlook and inclinations. Then, too, the matter of puzzles can provide the collector with problems of classification if he permits them to do so. Nevertheless, analysis of minor details and distinctions apart, the average collector or potential collector of the subject has a pretty good idea of what games and game equipment—adult games, if you will— should and should not include. This is certainly not to say that, if desired, a collection cannot be built up that embraces all types of games, although it may seem a little incongruous to some to find things like boxed sets of such juvenile standbys as "Peter Coddle's Trip to New York" and "Old Maid" cheek by jowl in a collection with poker chips and roulette wheels. On the other hand, there really is no evidence that adults did not play "Peter Coddle" at one time or another, although it may perhaps reasonably be assumed that they were not the same adults who habitually did business with Richard Canfield at his Saratoga Casino.

The collecting of poker chips is a rather widespread if relatively little noted hobby among men. Like old fountain pens, they are things that men seldom discarded, and innumerable men who do not think of themselves as collectors at all take some little pride in assemblages of sample chips they have gathered from various places they have visited. The collecting of game counters as a whole was once a rather

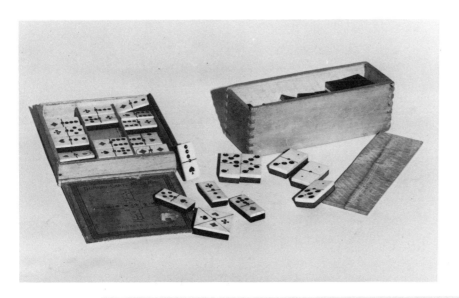

*Two boxed sets of late nineteenth-century dominoes: a French set (left) intro-
ducing playing-card-suit symbols into the game, and a standard set. Also pictured
are three games of the late nineteenth and early twentieth century, including the
board for an 1893 Chicago World's Fair game.*

George S. Indig Photographs

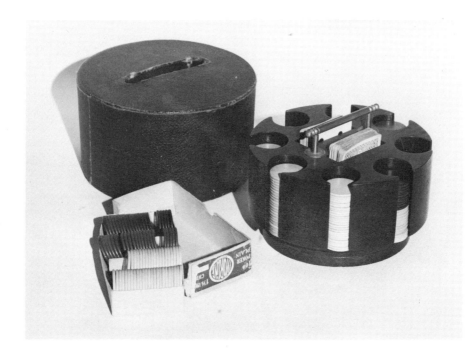

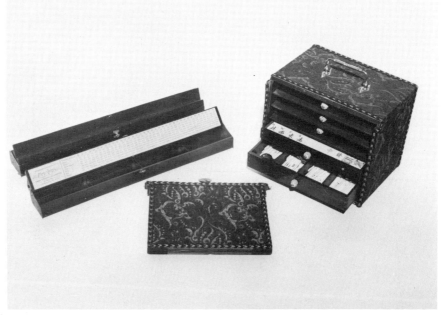

Top, a revolving poker or pinochle set of the early 1900s, together with poker chips of the same period. Bottom, an elaborate Mah-Jongg set, together with two racks, a relic of the great Mah-Jongg enthusiasm of the 1920s.

George S. Indig Photographs

widespread enthusiasm, although the emphasis was for the most part on European pieces, and some of this enthusiasm may also have been of the aforementioned travel-souvenir type of collecting. However, there was considerable outright antiquarian interest in game counters and counter boxes if they were sufficiently old or elaborate. Americans in particular—although they certainly did not avoid specimens of other eras—seem to have taken a curious especial interest in counters of the reign of King George III. In any event, European counters and boxes, of both the George III period and later, were and on occasion are to be found in a variety of materials including real and imitation gold, silver, ivory, porcelain, tortoiseshell and other materials, as were other artifacts associated with the gaming tables of London, Bath, and elsewhere.

That some of these articles displayed a high degree of artistry and craftsmanship is undeniable, although, to a certain extent at least, there were the exceptions. To anyone who has studied the subject even superficially, it is apparent that materials of more than nominal value, and workmanship of considerable caliber, whether reflected in actual handcraft or in mass-production manufacture, were at times lavished upon game equipment. It is possible to get together a fairly extensive and interesting collection of old chessmen, dominoes, dice, checkers, and similar material, and there are many related areas that merit exploration. In recent years, for example, there has been noticed a measure of increasing collector's interest in Mah-Jongg sets and equipment, although the Mah-Jongg craze manifested itself in the United States only in the 1920s. However, the 1920s already are more than far enough removed from us in time for much that was then produced to be recognized now as collectable antiques.

However the matter may be cut, there is no doubt that the most widely and enthusiastically collected group of material associated with games and gaming—which in their everyday use are not by any means synonymous but both of which may in many instances relate to the same thing—are playing cards.

THE DEVIL'S PICTURE BOOKS

Despite their ubiquity and their great popularity as a collector's item, no one really is certain when or where playing cards originated.

The ever-popular story which is still frequently cited is that they were invented in the last decade of the fourteenth century specifically for the amusement of a "mad king," Charles VI of France. This identification means nothing to most people, but if it is put into the context that Charles VI is the French King of Shakespeare's *The Life of King Henry the Fifth*, it becomes somewhat more interesting albeit none the more accurate. There are those who insist that cards did not appear in Europe until the fourteenth century; others who believe they arrived there some hundreds of years earlier. All serious students of the subject now agree they originated long before in Africa or Asia and that their use did not become widespread in Europe until early in the fifteenth century. There are those who can make out a good and serious case for cards having originated in Egypt in Biblical times or at least being known and used there then. From time to time also there crops up the story, which evidently carries considerable appeal to the mystically attuned, that playing cards are based on and contain a secret record of the Great Pyramid, or, optionally, that the Great Pyramid and playing cards both contain the same secret record of man's knowledge of the ages. This theory attracted a good deal of attention around the turn of the century, was much heard of again in the 1920s, when there was great excitement over the discovery and opening of King Tut's tomb, and seems destined to be revived every twenty years or so well into the future. It is one of those tales in which, if read with an open uncritical mind, the average person is willing to find much superficial logic and fascination. Everything else aside, however, its tellers cannot decide—and find no inconsistency in the fact—whether a deck of cards properly consists of fifty-two or fifty-three (including the joker) cards. Both numbers are critical to the theory which has it that the slope of the Great Pyramid is at an angle of fifty-two degrees, and that the slope is two hundred twelve feet high, that figure being fifty-three multiplied by four. In any event, the fifty-two-card pack is the Anglo-Saxon pack, which originated only a few hundred years ago in England, earlier packs having either a lesser or a greater number of cards.

The study both of playing-card history and of playing-card collecting is naturally complicated by this variation in pack size, as both and especially the former are complicated by the fact that the actual use of many of the early packs is highly uncertain. It is probably as incorrect to state that all of the early decks of cards were used for divination and other mystical purposes rather than in the playing of card games as it is to designate them all unquestioningly as playing cards, unless the latter term is to be accepted as having a much broader meaning than presently is accorded it. The matter of the number of cards that comprise a given deck is naturally of much interest to those who collect old cards in this manner, there being a great deal of difference in the desirability and value of a complete deck and one that lacks one or more of its cards. Most decks of playing cards range from thirty to fifty-two cards (again the question arises as to whether the joker is counted and, further, whether the additional advertising or scoring-information cards included in many fairly recent decks must be retrieved in order to qualify the deck as truly complete).

With the exception of the tarot decks, the Anglo-Saxon decks are probably the longest, with our standard forty-eight-card pinochle deck and fifty-two-card poker decks. The tarot cards were among the first widely used in Europe, appearing in Italy late in the fourteenth or early in the fifteenth century, presumably from the East. "Tarot cards" is really redundant; "tarots" alone is the correct form, the name supposedly—and in speaking of the history of playing cards the prudent commentator will make much use of such qualifying terminology— deriving from the Italian *tarocco*, indicating that the backs were decorated with diagonal crossings.[1] It is frequently stated that a pack of tarots consists of a total of seventy-eight cards, four suits of ten numbered and four court cards, twenty-one superior or trump cards (*atouts*), and a fool, the last coming down to us as the joker. Supposedly the modern Anglo-Saxon deck of fifty-two or fifty-three cards derives from such decks, the *atouts* and four court cards being eliminated, twenty-five from seventy-eight leaving fifty-three. Some writers include the fool as an *atout*, making twenty-two such cards, but come out with the same total of fifty-three by noting that of the *atouts* only the fool is retained.

The fact is that there were four distinctly different types of tarots,

[1] However, Mrs. Mary W. Baskett, Curator of Prints of the Cincinnati Art Museum, where the John Ommke Playing Card Collection is housed on permanent loan from the United States Playing Card Company, writes: "The Museum has indexed its fifteenth-century Italian Tarot cards as 'Tarocchi Cards' since they are thought to be the trump cards in the game of Tarok ('Tarocco')."

Le Monde (The World) and Le Fou (The Fool) from a French tarot deck, ca. 1800, this being one of the tarot decks in which The Fool is not included among the numbered atouts *or trumps. Bottom, early double-head court cards from an American deck of the 1870s, the cards still square-cornered and without indexes.*

The John Ommke Playing Card Collection on permanent loan to the Cincinnati Art Museum from the United States Playing Card Company the decks consisting of fifty-four, sixty-two, seventy-eight, or ninety-seven cards. The seventy-eight-card deck is the earliest, and the fifty-four-card deck is a subsequent "short" version of it, retaining the twenty-one *atouts* and the fool, as well as the sixteen court cards, but eliminating twenty-four of the numbered cards. The ninety-seven-card deck appeared late in the fourteenth or early in the fifteenth

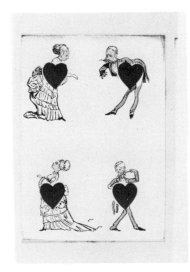

Examples of special decks of playing cards. Left, the four of hearts from an American comical deck of 1877. Right, the back and two cards from the special deck of cards commemorating the Pan-American Exposition at Buffalo, New York, in 1901. Each card shows a different Exposition building.

The John Ommke Playing Card Collection on permanent loan to the Cincinnati Art Museum from the United States Playing Card Company *(left)*
George S. Indig Photograph *(right)*

century, and the sixty-two-card deck followed late in the seventeenth or early in the eighteenth century. The confusion in regard to the status of the fool card is due to the fact that in the original seventy-eight-card deck and the fifty-four-card version thereof the fool was not an *atout*, whereas in the ninety-seven- and sixty-two-card decks the fool is counted as an *atout*.

While early tarot (tarots are still manufactured in Europe) decks and other worldwide card types are of interest to many collectors, playing-card collectors in the United States and Great Britain naturally to a great extent center their interest upon the so-called Anglo-Saxon decks. It is not possible to assign exact chronological progressions to the development of these cards; there not surprisingly was considerable overlapping of styles. However, the following general progression in basic styles in our decks may be noted: decks with full-figure court cards (although double-headed court cards are found in early eighteenth-century tarots); decks with double-headed court cards; and decks with an identifying letter or number and symbol of the suit in two corners. The last type of cards are known as "squeezers," as they enabled the player to squeeze the fan of cards together into a much smaller and more convenient compass while still plainly showing him exactly what cards he held. Squeezers seem to have appeared in the United States in the 1850s, but the style was still far from universally adopted for a number of years thereafter.

Much attention customarily is paid, especially in brief introductory discussions of the subject, to decks in which the usual court cards are replaced by symbolic figures, such as Virtue, or actually identifiable personages, their purpose being to eliminate references to royalty during revolutionary times, to provide political caricature, or simply to commemorate individuals. Such cards are always interesting and usually relatively scarce and desirable but by no means invariably the tremendous rarities many beginners regard them. There are also many commemorative decks for events such as world's fairs, and it should also be noted that there are a number of decks that are not in a sense playing cards as they lack the standard suit markings and cannot be used for regular card games, although in most cases they can be and are intended to be employed for special games.

Invariably the kings, queens, and jacks have returned to the realm of playing cards. The point is often made, and it is not only over-exaggerated but has never been entirely valid, that card players are among the most ingrained of traditionalists and fiercely resent any attempt to change or modernize the cards simply for the sake of traditionalism. This is not true, as witnessed by the immediate and widespread acceptance of decks slightly narrower than the regulation size for convenience in playing games where a great many cards may be held in the hand at once (a matter of gender is involved here, too, for while bridge decks may be made narrower and accepted, no one would think of attempting to put out pinochle decks in the narrower form). The reason for refusing to accept changes usually has a very practical basis. Instant recognition is of great importance or at least convenience in play, hence no one cares to change the style of the court cards or to have to pause and think properly to identify a substitute figure. Using four separate colors, one for each suit, would have little practical value for a number of reasons, the most obvious being that the additional colors either would be too light to serve any purpose in poor light or would have to be so dark as to have no value in distinguishing them readily from the standard black and red. Repeatedly efforts have been made over more than a hundred years successfully to merchandise round playing cards, the presumed advantage being that no matter how a hand was picked up the cards would automatically be in playing position without requiring any additional alignment, an advantage more than overcome by the fact that it is more difficult to mix and deal round cards than conventionally shaped ones. Substantially smaller- or larger-size cards, including miniature decks, have never been looked upon as anything but novelties because of the greater difficulty of mixing, dealing, and holding them. Playing cards thus continue substantially unchanged not because of unthinking resistance to change but for purely practical reasons.

There are several ways in which playing cards are collected, the two basic systems being as entire decks, preferably with the case, or by retaining one sample card from each deck. In the latter instances, if the faces of the cards enter into the collecting scheme at all, the preferred card naturally is the ace of spades, which carries the identification of the maker as well as, often, other information. (Make a bet with someone sometime as to the number of colors in which the ace of spades in a given deck may be printed; at times there appears a small identifying number in blue, not black, whose variation in color almost always passes unnoticed, in itself a perfect demonstration of why printing decks with each suit in a different color is pointless.) Some collectors, however, prefer to collect the jokers. Whether the ace of spades or the joker is collected, the enthusiast also, of course, has an example of the back of the given deck. There are, however, numerous collectors who collect only from the standpoint of the design on the back of a card and to whom, for this purpose, any card from a deck is equally good.

While collecting entire decks would seem the most logical and interesting form of playing-card collecting and in any event that most calculated to preserve historical material in a proper manner, it cannot be gainsaid that there are not certain practical advantages to collecting backs. For one thing, it matters little whether a deck that is obtained is complete or not. For another, any deck provides the hobbyist with dozens of duplicates for ready trading with other collectors of backs. As a result, a collection of considerable size usually can be built up very rapidly. There also enters into the picture the matter of housing the collection. The collector of complete decks has far greater bulk and must keep his decks together, preferably in the original tuck cases or boxes. The collector of backs only can and usually does mount such specimens in albums, where they can readily be handled and examined. Withal, however, it is impossible to commend the collecting of playing-card backs alone. Perhaps it would be incorrect to call it a frivolous form of collecting, but most men would almost certainly feel it is lacking in much of the serious historical approach that is found in other modes of playing-card collecting and particularly in the collecting of complete decks.

AMUSEMENT-PARK DEVICES

There are men, as already mentioned, who collect such things as real locomotives and windmills. There also are men who collect amusement-park and carnival rides; men who own, if often they must be stored in knocked-down condition, actual old merry-go-rounds and Ferris wheels and similar equipment. It is scarcely necessary by this

One of the "Liberty Bell" slot machines, generally greatly predated. This cast-metal machine with wooden base carries no maker's name and is identified by the bell bearing the date "1776" below the coin slot. It probably dates in the 1920s.
Mr. and Mrs. Charles A. Penn, Bumble Bee Trading
Post, Bumble Bee Arizona, Hogan Smith Photograph

point to have to underline that, however undeniably fascinating and worthwhile such collecting activity may be, it inevitably presents storage problems of a nature with which the great majority of collectors, no matter how enthusiastic they may be, are unable to cope. The average hobbyist who is interested in preserving and studying amusement devices must of necessity concentrate on the smaller forms, mainly coin-operated machines of the type that not only appeared in amusement parks as such, but in city penny arcades, hotel lobbies, and other points. These machines are closely akin to two other groups already discussed, vending machines and coin-operated automatic musical instruments, as they are also related to coin-operated games of chance, or what are sometimes referred to simply as "slot machines," although there are a great many coin-operated machines that might also qualify as properly describable as slot machines. In any event, a number of people, not excluding many collectors, apply the term "slot machine" without any effort at precision.

Most collectors who to any extent collect one type of coin-operated machine tend to collect all types, although there are some specialists.

There also are some closely related machines that were produced so as to work without requiring the insertion of a coin, which are part and parcel of this overall collecting category. In some cases, they are identical to the coin-operated machines but without the coin-operating mechanism. Their status is not quite certain in all cases. Some may have been made in this form for home use. Others may simply represent machines from which the coin-actuating mechanism was removed and retained when the machines were disposed of by the original owners. Others may have been employed for "come-on" use outside penny arcades or for other purposes.

Coin-operated machines seldom are as old as they often are supposed; usually they merely seem so from use and abuse. There is much uncertainty, confusion, and both accidental and deliberate misattribution concerning the history, dating, glamorizing, and purveying to collectors of conventional game-of-chance slot machines. It would seem, for example, that few if any were actually used in the gambling hells of the old West, contrary to what some fondly imagine, although, of course, the precise validity of this statement will depend upon what exact period any particular individual cares to regard as "the Old West." It has been asserted, and perhaps not wrongly, that some of the confusion attendant upon their history can be traced to rival slot-machine manufacturers' promotional claims and their endeavors to cover the trails of infringements. Certainly many if not most of the machines a collector is likely to encounter are by no means as old as they are generally believed to be. Apropos of the matter of age in regard to all coin-operated devices, much is often made of the coin slot as evidence that a machine must be at least a hundred years old because the United States penny assumed its present size in 1856 and no large cents were minted after 1857. A large slot on a coin-operated machine of the type that normally would be a penny-actuated machine simply indicates that the machine was manufactured originally to fill an order from a country where the coinage differed from that in the United States. Canada, for example, minted large cents as recently as 1920. Also, in recent years, a considerable number of old coin-operated machines evidently have been brought back for sale to collectors from Mexico and Central and South American countries.

These coin-operated machines (and this is particularly true of the penny-arcade types such as fortune-telling machines with wax figures), however glamorous they may continue to appear when left in their original settings, usually massed in brilliantly illuminated penny arcades or boardwalk and amusement-park stalls, almost invariably take on a rather tawdry and even depressing appearance when removed and displayed by a collector. This is perhaps inevitable, for many of them were maintained in use over several decades. Interesting and worthwhile as they are, to avoid undue disappointment, the collector must be cautioned that almost invariably, when removed from the bright lights, music, and crowds of their original setting, they may well seem to fade, much as does a flower taken out of water.

CHAPTER XI

Books and Other Printed Collectables

Book collecting is a long-established and long-honored avocation, but a great deal of what is presented on the subject to novices tends to suggest that it was hardly prepared with the writer's feet on the ground. There are probably few literate people today who are not aware, whatever their other interest—or total lack of interest—in old books that a Gutenberg Bible or a First Folio Shakespeare is, to say the very least, a rather desirable and valuable thing. Somewhat fewer, perhaps, but still a very substantial number of people are knowledgeable of old book matters at least to the extent that even such a relatively slight and flimsy thing as a first edition of Edgar Allan Poe's *Tamerlane and Other Poems*—for it is essentially a pamphlet of about forty pages measuring but 6⅜ by 4⅛ inches—can, in the context of the financial terms of reference of the average man, be a quite heady thing indeed. But talk of such things, and other rare and astronomically expensive books, unless accompanied by a properly administered antidote, is sufficient to scare most would-be collectors away from bibliographical pursuits even before they start.

At the start, therefore, let it be emphasized that every old book is not rare; every first edition is not by the fact that it accords with this overglamorized description automatically valuable, and that there are trends and places in book collecting that can provide enjoyment for every form of interest and purse. There will always be some, of course,

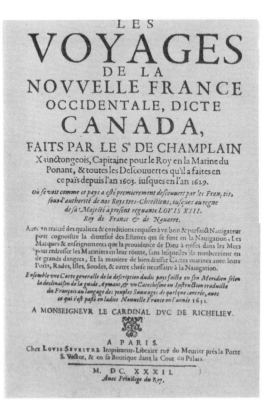

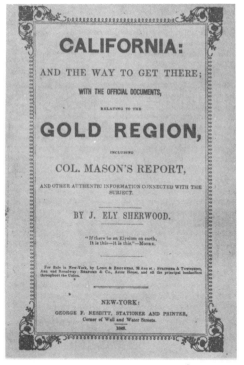

Two very interesting examples of early Americana—albeit one was published in France—both relating to travel. Left, the title page of an account of voyages to "New France," Paris, 1632. Right, a report on the discovery of gold in California, New York, 1848.

The American Book Collector

who will shake their heads in surprise and despair to learn that there are substantial numbers of men collecting in areas where the valued authors are not William Shakespeare or Edgar Allan Poe, but Victor Appleton, Allan Chapman, H. Irving Hancock, and their peers. Of the latter group, the first two names in fact were house pseudonyms controlled by the Stratemeyer Syndicate. If Victor Appleton rings a bell, it is probably because this was the name used on the longest, most popular, and—in the view of many—best of the pre-World War II boys' book series, the Tom Swift series. If you think Appleton is out of place in company with Shakespeare and Poe, even in the area of book collecting, bear in mind that Tom Swift, in company with Long John Silver and a few others, was a primary influence in getting many of the members of the generations now reading this volume to realize that there could be something very exciting and worthwhile to be found between the covers of books and to become readers and, subsequently, in many cases, book collectors. This is not a very stylish pronouncement today in some scholastic and literary quarters, but it is difficult to deny its essential truth.

WHAT TO COLLECT AND HOW

There are probably three basic approaches to book collecting: to collect by authors, to collect by subjects, and to collect books as outstanding and interesting examples of the bookmaker's art. The reasons that books are collected are varied and obviously do not exclude decorative usages, but apart from collections primarily based on the book as a progressively developing artifact in itself and in terms of the history of printing, of the reproduction of illustrations, and of bookbinding, it can be said that the chief reasons for collecting books are to preserve them, read them, and to gain information from them. In short, most book collectors are men who like to read and possess a zest for gaining enjoyment through reading and a desire to expand their range of knowledge. At times, preservation and reading may appear to conflict; all books are relatively fragile things, and many old books and pamphlets are very insubstantial, obviously requiring great and continual care in handling and housing. In the case of books that have attained sustained popularity and continued reprinting, there is little problem, for a collector can carefully house his valued specimens and make use of other and less valued editions for ordinary reading enjoyment.

This is eminently practical in the case of a book such as the first edition of Robert Louis Stevenson's *Kidnapped*, pictured here, or any book of which a reading copy is obtainable easily and inexpensively.

A copy of the first published edition of Robert Louis Stevenson's Kidnapped, *London, 1886, in the original binding, right, together with the solander case made to receive it, foreground. The case is made to appear as a book itself when shelved. At the left is the protective wrap that is placed around the book before it is inserted in its case.*

George S. Indig Photograph

However, it is not possible in the case of many old books and pamphlets, a few obvious examples of which are illustrated. Our basic assumption must be—and it would seem unquestionably the correct one—that to a major extent books and particularly items of historical interest and importance are collected not only merely for their physical possession, for filling an empty and awaiting niche in a series as it were, somewhat akin to an empty space in a stamp album, but at least to some extent to be read, enjoyed, and studied. Handling then becomes a problem. Regardless of how careful a person is, and over how long a period no material diminution in condition becomes apparent, it is extremely difficult if not impossible for an item that continually is handled not eventually to show some signs of cumulative deterioration.

One solution, in the case of specimens that it seems likely will be referred to frequently, is to make a copy for reading use by means of one of the inexpensive copying processes now available. In some cases, it is now possible to secure offset reproductions of certain old and scarce books and pamphlets. When they are available they are desirable things to have for day-to-day use, whether a collector possesses an original or not. While there is now a continuing stream of emissions of such reproduction copies, usually by means of photo offset, the number of titles that are thus reproduced is and probably always will remain relatively small in comparison to the overall number of books and pamphlets that have been published and a matter of limited chance of just how many items in a given collector's field, if any, will thus become available. It should be noted that such publishing of facsimile copies of old and desirable books, although only somewhat lately attaining really extensive proportions, is by no means entirely an innovation of recent years. Pictured here is a facsimile edition of *Paradisi in Sole Paradisus Terrestris* by John Parkinson, a gardening book of over 600 pages reproduced from the edition of 1629 by Methuen & Co. of London in 1904. Such reprints naturally at times take on an eventual collector's value and status of their own.

Admittedly, every desirable old book has a certain intrinsic value of its own simply as a physical specimen, and there are many who will very sincerely propound that this really is the basis and whole of book collecting, the gathering and preservation of such specimens merely to this end. There also have been and are collectors who gather so many

The title page of a facsimile edition of Paradisi in Sole Paradisus Terrestris *by John Parkinson, a gardening book originally published in 1629. This reproduction copy, itself now an item of interest to collectors, was published in London in 1904.*
George S. Indig Photograph

books that they cannot hope to use them as a reading library. This may not be a manifestation of mere hoarding; many men have in some such manner gathered collections relating to a number of subjects that eventually were made available to all through presentation to libraries or which, in some cases, formed the basis of a library in themselves. Yet in this discussion it seems best to suggest that the book collector direct his attention either to books of interest to himself in terms of reading enjoyment or to books from studies of which he may justly expect to derive information relating to a subject of interest. Naturally, book collecting may be pursued as an independent hobby in itself or in conjunction with one or a number of other interests.

TERMINOLOGY AND TECHNIQUES

It is possible for the would-be book collector to get involved in a great mass of specialized designations and terminology, often expressed in catalogs of dealers in books by abbreviations. It would be impossible to give anything approaching a comprehensive glossary here, but there are two basic matters, size and binding styles, that experience has shown are most particularly confusing to beginners and which should certainly be explained here. The sizes of books usually are expressed in traditional terms and abbreviations relating to the number of times the original large sheets of paper on which a book was printed were folded to create the individual pages. As a ready guide, it may be kept in mind that the higher the number in the abbreviation, the smaller actually is a given book. Thus, a folio (Fø) size book is over 13 inches high, a quarto (4to) is over 12 inches, an octavo (8vo) is over 9 inches, a duodecimo (12mo) is 7 to 8 inches, a sextodecimo (16mo) is 6 to 7 inches, a vigesimoquarto (24mo) is 5 to 6 inches, and a trigesimose-cundo (32mo) is a book 4 to 5 inches high. There also are some other larger and smaller sizes referred to on occasion. The Audubon bird

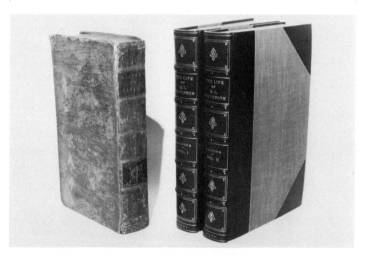

Types of bindings: left, full leather; right, half leather. A three-quarter leather binding has a greater proportion of leather along the top of the binding; a quarter leather binding has substantially less leather along the top and usually has no leather corners.

George S. Indig Photograph

prints, for example, were published as an elephant folio, 23 inches high. The most frequently met sizes are the duodecimo—the *Kidnapped* pictured is this size—and octavo, of which the present book is an example.

Bindings are referred to as full, three-quarter, half, and quarter, these terms usually in particular referring to the relative amount of leather in a binding as contrasted to the remaining portions covered with cloth or paper. A book with a full binding is one completely bound in leather. Three-quarter bound indicates that the leather on the spine and corners fill approximately three-quarters of the total space along the top of the binding; half-bound indicates the leather fills about half of the top, and quarter-bound indicates that the leather extending sidewise from the back of the book fills only about a quarter width of the top. Usually there are no leather corners on quarter-bound books. The same terminology can also be applied to clothbound books, half-bound indicating that the cloth fills about half of the top, with the remainder covered with paper, and so on.

Condition and originality are naturally of great importance in book collecting, as in most categories of antiques, and completeness is also of enormous import, a missing page or even a missing flyleaf greatly reducing the value of a book. By the same token, if a book originally was published with a dust jacket, the presence of the dust jacket substantially enhances the value of a specimen. There was a period in book collecting not too long ago when little attention was paid to the presence or absence of dust jackets and there are probably still some collectors and dealers who would still argue as to the importance of the dust jacket, and whether or not it should affect the value. Naturally, a great many old books that originally had dust jackets are found with the jackets missing. There now seems little room for argument that the presence of a jacket enhances the desirability and value of a specimen, although few if any collectors would refuse a book they otherwise desired because the dust jacket was missing.

Today the desirable form of binding among collectors is invariably the original one in which a book was issued. Again, this was not always so, and many early collectors as a matter of course rebound their acquisitions in fine leather bindings. Of course, at the time books were issued, many ordinary purchasers who possessed the means automatically had the publisher's binding removed and the book rebound. In the view of most book collectors today, such contemporary bindings are acceptable, but a specimen in the original publisher's binding is always regarded as more desirable by far. These facts need not inhibit the collector who likes to see good leather bindings on his shelves so long as he is willing to attain this goal by having a protective solander case made for an individual book and suitably bound. Such a case at once serves to provide a desired appearance of fine binding on the shelf, for the back of the case resembles a bound book; to protect the book from dust and other damage; and at the same time to retain and preserve the original binding for its historical importance and collector's value. Such a solander case, which includes an internal folding cloth and board protective wrap for the book itself—as distinguished from an ordinary slipcase in which the book slides directly into the case—will be found shown in the photograph of the first edition of *Kidnapped.*

A number of nineteenth-century books of interest to collectors were originally published in parts, that is, in a number of separate and periodically issued paper-covered pamphlets. They range from such things as Dickens' *The Pickwick Papers* to the pictured *Circle of the*

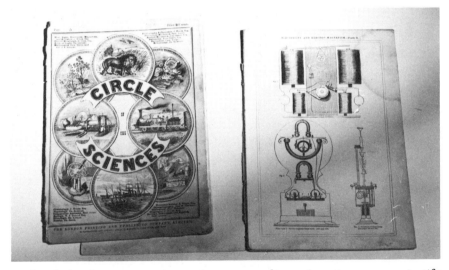

Circle of the Sciences, *an interesting compendium of contemporary scientific knowledge published in parts in London in the mid-1860s. The cover of one part is shown here, together with a plate from another, illustrating an electric clock mechanism and, lower right, an electric lamp.*

George S. Indig Photograph

Sciences. The reader subscribed to the work and when he had received all the parts in installments, he had the complete book in the form of twenty or so pamphlets. At this point, some of the more affluent subscribers would have the parts bound into a complete book, the covers (wrappers) of the parts being removed and discarded in the process. Any book that originally was thus published in parts is of considerably greater collector's interest and value when in the form of the original separate parts than when they have been bound together into a volume or volumes.

PATHWAYS OF COLLECTING

An enormous amount of study has been undertaken in connection with books, work which continually is being carried forward. Where the work covers the authors or fields of particular interest to a collector and have been published, either as books or in magazines, they are of tremendous value to every interested hobbyist. A good bibliography, describing in detail the various editions and impressions of a

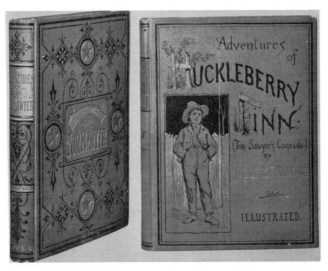

Two interesting and highly desirable American first editions of Mark Twain classics. Left, the first issue of the first edition of The Adventures of Tom Sawyer, *Hartford, Connecticut, 1876. Right, the first edition of* Adventures of Huckleberry Finn, *New York, 1885.*

The American Book Collector

given book, together with the points that distinguish them is of inestimable use. To refer once more to the pictured first edition of *Kidnapped,* for example, the accepted source for which to turn for information would be *A Bibliography of the Works of Robert Louis Stevenson* by Colonel W. F. Prideaux, as edited and supplemented by Mrs. Luther S. Livingston. Here three primary editions of *Kidnapped,* or, to give it its complete title, *Kidnapped: Being Memories of the Adventures of David Balfour in the Year 1751,* in book form are listed and described in detail. These are the proof edition, a few copies of which were issued in wrappers in 1886 in order to secure copyright; the first published edition, also 1886, and the first illustrated edition, 1887. The book pictured is the first published edition. To be more precise, it would be the first published British edition, for there also exists its first publication in the United States, which would be the first American edition. It should not be taken from its use here as an example of a number of points raised that the first published British edition of *Kidnapped* is an extremely rare and valuable book; it is a good book, to be sure, but its appearance is due to its applicability as an illustration of the matters under discussion.

The first edition has, nevertheless, become more or less the symbol of book collecting. There are many books in which the first edition is not rare; there are also many books that exist only in a first edition— often undesignated as such (and even on occasion erroneously designated as such), which in any case is where the application of bibliographical lore, if it already exists, or its uncovering on your own if it does not, comes into play. But it should be said that there are many collectors of recent or modern first editions, and that this is just as much a worthwhile facet of book collecting as is the collecting of old first editions.

Writing in the November 1962 issue of *The American Book Collector,*[1] its editor and publisher, W. B. Thorsen, advised in an article directed to beginners and would-be collectors:

Let the millionaires fight over the Gutenberg Bibles, the *Don Quixotes,* and the *Tamerlanes,* there are many fields open. . . . American history from

---

[1] *The American Book Collector* is the only American magazine published for private book collectors. The address is 1822-C School Street, Chicago, Illinois 60657, and the subscription price of $7.50 per year for ten numbers, or $1.00 per copy.

the discovery by the Vikings to Dos Passos *ad infinitum* is the meat on the bookseller's block today. Early voyages, the Indians, overland journals, cowboys and badmen, cattle drives, the West, the South, all the fifty states, the hamlets, the towns and the cities, pioneers, railroadiana, everything Americana seems to be in demand—and the prices for rare items are soaring.

Apropos of the last, it should be observed that book collecting is one of the few fields where there is a price guide available that has some real relevancy and practicality. The *American Book Prices Current*, issued annually, lists prices of all books that realized more than $5 at public auctions.

As to what Mr. Thorsen says, all true enough, although he is in a broad way still speaking of what many would consider somewhat better books. There are many fields—some directly or indirectly mentioned by him, some not—of intense potential interest to men who collect or would like to collect books both for their own sake and in connection with other collecting interests. Local histories, mentioned by Mr. Thorsen, are of great pertinence in researching many fields; often the only adequate early accounts of industrial enterprises exist in such histories, even though it is no secret that some of these volumes at least involved certain elements of commercialism at the time of publication as to which notable local individuals and enterprises might or might not be included. Similarly, early city and state directories contain a tremendous amount of meat for the researcher on almost any topic who can and will dig it out.

There exists a fascinating and, to a large extent, unplumbed collecting field for men in the numerous nineteenth- and early twentieth-century books, technical, semitechnical, and popular, dealing with commerce, mechanics, manufacturing processes, business methods, and related subjects. Some examples are illustrated herein. The obsolete volumes on such matters can prove a treasure trove to the researcher, and a general collection built along these lines, a fascinating and potentially important assemblage of material pertaining to such matters. Some volumes of this type are still relatively easily come by; some are scarce and now command fairly good prices; others can frequently be picked up even today for modest sums. Many such books, once discarded as technically outdated and thereby supposedly worthless, are infinitely richer in information of value and interest to the collector-student in many areas than much more modern and supposedly all-

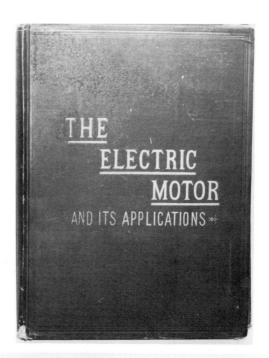

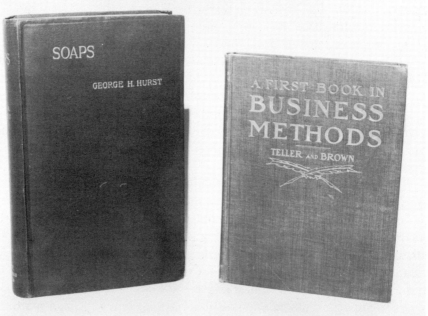

There is a vast, interesting, and worthwhile field awaiting the collector in the form of old business and technical books. Shown here are The Electric Motor and Its Applications *of 1888; a manual on soap making, 1907; and a 1911 textbook of business methods, including color plates of various commercial forms.*

George S. Indig Photographs

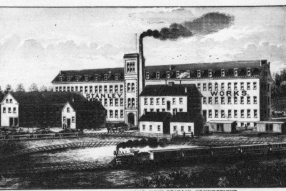

A *page from* Asher & Adams' New Columbian Rail Road Atlas and Pictorial Album of American Industry, *New York, 1875. The Asher & Adams' atlases with their twenty-five by seventeen-and-one-quarter-inch pages are a rich source of company and product history, factory views, and illustrations of products; in the instance pictured here, builder's hardware.*

Stanley Hardware, division of the Stanley Works

embracing accounts. Volumes on trades and manufacturing processes, frequently published in comparatively small editions, often are illustrated, if only for reasons of economy, with manufacturer's catalog cuts. The field is almost inexhaustible. It would appear one of the most interesting and promising areas for the man who is potentially interested in book collecting. Another interesting and favored field may be found in early illustrated and color-plate books dealing with subjects of appeal to men: exploration, history, sports, natural history, and the like. Nor should the fact that catalog collecting also is a form of book collecting be overlooked.

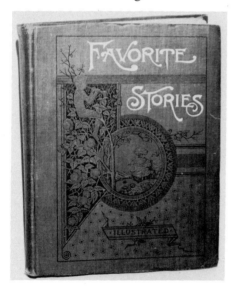

The cover and two pages from Favorite Stories, *subtitled* Happy Hours for Little People, *Boston, 1896, a late nineteenth-century collection of stories, poems, and illustrations adopted from various sources and intended for both boys and girls. It includes a color frontispiece.*

George S. Indig Photographs

The field of children's books in general—unitary volumes, sets, collections and annuals, toy books, and the like initially directed to youngsters of both sexes, and of boys' books in particular, has long been popular and is acquiring ever greater favor among collectors now that so many are aware of or finally accept the fact that to be valid collectables such books need not be very old, indeed, that perhaps the greatest interest of all to substantial numbers of collectors is held in the series books published early in the twentieth century. The so-called dime novels and related early boys' paperbacks have, of course, long been a subject for enthusiastic collecting by men. Many have been puzzled over the designation "dime novel," including Irvin S. Cobb in his essay "A Plea for Old Cap Collier," inasmuch as most remembered and today collected ones originally retailed for five cents. The answer is that the first ones did sell for a dime, the price subsequently being cut to a nickel or half-dime. The half-dime was an actual denomination of silver coin minted by the United States through 1873, the five-cent piece, or nickel, not appearing until 1866, and the designation "half-dime" long persisting in popular speech as the more common and readily recognized term for five cents. *Beadle's Half-Dime Library*, which Charles Bragin, a leading authority on the subject, considers probably the greatest of all dime-novel series, was not even instituted until 1877, four years after the coinage of half-dime pieces was discontinued.

Undoubtedly there have been some rather exaggerated stories passed into general circulation and acceptance tending to suggest that any old dime novel is of necessity worth a very substantial sum. There are examples that have commanded high prices indeed, but investigation indicates that most of the seemingly fabulous prices stated to have been paid have not been for single issues as common impression has it, but for extensive runs—sometimes in the hundreds of different issues— of a single continuing title. Even today most single copies of dime novels carry a relatively moderate price tag.

It is to some extent difficult to draw a definite line between the dime novel as such as its subsequent successors in the form of the pulp magazines. Some of the dime-novel series, such as *Brave and Bold Weekly, Old Sleuth Weekly,* and *Tip Top Weekley*, were published almost up to World War I. The dime novel, in fact, never truly died; it merely took on other forms, including the pulp magazines (also now

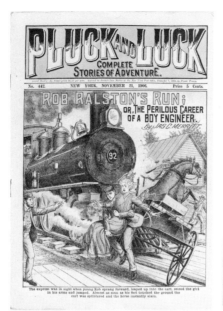

The dime novel—usually actually selling for five cents during much of the period of their greatest popularity—has long been an established men's collectable. Pictured are a typical 1906 issue of Pluck and Luck, and its counterpart of 1933, Detective Dan. *The latter contains one story in comic-strip form and a second in text.*

Ward Kimball *(left)*
George S. Indig Photograph

Two paperback delights of a type in many instances printed and reprinted for decades. Jesse James *was published in 1910, although at first glance many would assume it to be much older. The* Life of Bob and Cole Younger with Quantrell the Outlaw *is undated, but remained in print well into the 1930s.*

George S. Indig Photograph

eagerly collected), paperback books, and comic books. The comic book *Detective Dan* of 1933, which is pictured, is in essence a dime novel—with the price back to ten cents. Many of the early paperback Westerns remained in print much later than generally is realized, *Francisco Villa the Mexican Bandit* by "Capt. Kennedy U.S.A." not appearing until 1916 and even the *Jesse James* example illustrated bearing a 1910 copyright. Books of this type frequently are offered as extremely old, in some cases being pick-ups from earlier works and carrying no date. *The Life of Bob and Cole Younger with Quantrell the Outlaw*, illustrated, is one of a series of such books that remained in print and readily available well into the 1930s. An awareness of this fact does not make the books any less collectable, but it puts them into their proper context.

Magazines and newspapers are also highly collectable; it is in fact a question whether the dime novels, most of which appeared periodically, more properly are books or magazines. They can, depending on your outlook, be classified as either. Also deserving of mention here is the collecting of old comic strips and, among some, of the more recently introduced comic books, a somewhat surprising number of old comic sections having been preserved in one way or another.

BOYS' SERIES BOOKS

Boys' series books deserve special mention here as a popular men's collectable that has but recently come into its own or at least emerged into public view. The reasons for its popularity are obvious, these books having been extremely popular among boys who now make up the greatest proportion of adult men collectors. A number of men have indicated that they began the collecting of these books after reading denunciations of the type by school librarians and commentators on childrens' books, if only to reread them to see if time and memory had given them a gloss that they did not possess and if they were really as bad and potentially harmful as their detractors insisted. Unfortunately —or fortunately, perhaps—the detractors spoil whatever case they might have by invariably setting upon the Tom Swift books, because they were the most popular and best known of the genus, as their example. As a matter of fact, the Tom Swift books are generally well

Two volumes with dust jackets from two all-time most popular boys' book series.
Tom Swift in the Caves of Ice, or The Wreck of the Airship, *and* Ralph, the
Train Dispatcher, or The Mystery of the Pay Car, *both published in 1911.*

George S. Indig Photograph

plotted and well written; they stand up fairly well upon rereading
today and, at the time they were read by boys, could hardly have
helped but to be not only inspirational in themselves in directing many
boys to the possibilities of invention, manufacturing, and mechanics,
but also in inculcating a love of reading and of books in general. It is
now known that most of the Tom Swift books were written by Howard
R. Garis, a writer of some attainments, under the Stratemeyer Syndicate
house pen name of Victor Appleton. There may have been no Shake-
speares among them, but a number of other fairly good authors, including Clarence Buddington Kelland, plied the trade of authoring boys'
series books at times.

Admittedly, there were some books of this type that were pretty
awful, not surprising in view of the fact that there were over three
hundred different series, with no one knows how many actual authors
involved and about one hundred seventy-five known authors or pseudonyms recorded. Some of the series consisted of only a few titles. Tom
Swift, the longest, comprised thirty-eight titles in the original Grosset

and Dunlap series, with two additional ones, for a total of forty, appearing only in a later, short series of eleven issued by Whitman. The currently published Tom Swift series relate to the adventures of Tom Swift, Jr., purportedly the son of the original hero, and have no part in the original series.

With the publication of Harry K. Hudson's *A Bibliography of Hard-Cover Boys' Books*[2] in 1964, many things became much easier and clearer for the collectors of these books, and the Hudson bibliography, which actually is limited to the series books, is recommended to all who are interested in this field. Only a few further comments are required here, regarding a specialty gaining increasing favor among men, the collecting of series books relating to World War I. Many readers of the Donohue Boy Scouts Series (there were no fewer than thirteen Boy Scouts series issued by various publishers) have been puzzled by the blank space appearing in the listing of the books in the series where a slug of type obviously had been hastily pulled. The book that originally occupied this space was *Boy Scouts Under the Kaiser, or, Uhlans in Peril,* which was withdrawn when the United States entered World War I and most copies, both in stock and already in private hands, probably destroyed, although it might appear that in peril would be an ideal place for Uhlans to find themselves at the moment. A previous book in the same series, which the publisher seemingly could not determine was properly titled *Boy Scouts in Belgium, or, Under Fire in Flanders,* or *Under Fire in Flanders, or, Boy Scouts in Belgium,* contains a diverting episode wherein the naïve scouts are wandering around Belgium in the path of the invasion and invite a kindly German officer to share their campfire breakfast. They tell him of their plans to go to Berlin and see the Kaiser in order to get extradition papers for a criminal they are pursuing who has stolen the plans of United States fortifications! As the officer mounts his horse from the off side and rides away, they finally deduce that they have been frying bacon and eggs for none other than Kaiser Bill himself. Previously the boys had been chummy with General Joffre. There was nothing like being neutral in thought and in deed in 1915. As a token of the general

---

[2] $4.95, Harry K. Hudson, 3300 San Bernadino Street, Clearwater, Florida 33515.

caliber of the book, it should be remarked that the villain who has stolen the plans bears the astoundingly original name of "The Rat."

At the same time, H. Irving Hancock was writing his now-scarce four-volume *Conquest of the United States Series,* in an effort to awake the boys of America to its danger and to aid in the cause of preparedness. Hancock did not agree with the author of *Boy Scouts in Belgium* that the Kaiser was "friendly to the United States." The four Hancock volumes in this series portray a German invasion and conquest of the United States in 1920, the Central Powers having finished off the Allies in Europe, who had had to fight without American assistance. It has not been remarked that in his first two volumes Hancock simply paralleled the strategy of the American Revolution, the Germans first landing at and capturing Boston, and then moving on to New York. Hancock may be considered the military writer of the boys' series books, also writing, among other series, the *Annapolis Series,* the *West Point Series,* and the *Boys of the Army Series.*

Most men who collect the boys' series books relating to World War I also collect the girls' series books covering that conflict as well. Virtually every established heroine or group from Grace Harlowe to the Campfire Girls rushed overseas to serve as nurses or ambulance drivers. For reasons that are not quite clear, but possibly due to such titling as *Grace Harlowe with the Marines at Chateau Thierry* and *Grace Harlowe with the American Army in the Argonne,* the *Grace Harlowe Overseas Series* became popular with boy readers who usually would not touch a girl's book with the proverbial ten-foot pole. Grace Harlowe first appeared in the *High School Girls' Series,* which was a sort of counterpoint to Hancock's *High School Boys' Series.* In any event, following the war, in the subsequent Grace Harlowe books, *The Overland Riders Series,* the series was deliberately aimed at a joint readership of boys and girls. To further this end, a popular character, Stacey Brown, was borrowed from *The Pony Rider Boys Series* and moved into such books as *Grace Harlowe's Overland Riders Among the Border Guerrillas.* The acceptability of the Grace Harlowe books among boys was furthered by the fact that the author was Jessie Graham Flower. Most Americans are given to a reflex association of the name Jesse (even the Biblical one) or Jessie with Jesse James, and most boys, of course, do not realize that Jessie is the feminine form. This is not surprising; for years the sign marking the house in St. Joseph, Missouri where Jesse James was killed spelled the name as "Jessie James." To many boys the books appeared to be Westerns written by a man whose very name seemed certain proof that he knew a great deal about the Wild West and outlaws!

In connection with books, as well as printed matter of all kinds, it should be noted that old printing-trade relics are highly collectable and widely collected. These include old woodcuts and engravings, wood and metal type, type-specimen books, and, where possible, small presses and all sorts of related printing equipment. The greater number of men interested in this field simply collect and preserve the material; a few extend their hobby activities actually to undertaking some printing projects making use of the relics.

MAPS, PRINTS, AND LITHOGRAPHS

To be candid, the great difficulty with the extensive and purposeful collecting of old maps, prints, and similar graphic materials is the problem of display and housing. The collector of old books readily can gather hundreds or even thousands of specimens and safely and conventionally house them in bookcases, where they will be at once accessible and protected, as in any private library. There is no similar approach possible with maps and prints. A varying number—but always a comparatively small one—may be framed and hung. Some collectors have, in effect, covered the four walls of a room with framed maps and prints, even the walls of several rooms. Yet once any collector has gone as far in this direction as he can, what is left? Any extensive collection of maps or prints must be housed in cabinets or portfolios. They are relatively delicate things, always having to be handled with care and best handled as little as possible. There is nothing wrong in itself with a collecting hobby that requires that many specimens be kept packed away out of sight; many collectors in other categories find themselves in the same situation, but most of these collectables are not of the fragile nature of prints, nor of things that originally obviously were intended for display and which are at their best when they can

A British print of 1814, "Bonaparte in Trouble," a cartoon with suitable "Explanation" provided at the bottom so that no one can possibly miss the points of the Devil tempting Napoleon with the Russian Crown, the Russian bear, the British lion, and so on.

The Old Print Shop

"Coming to the Point," an 1854 print after a painting by William Sydney Mount. Prints of this type are sometimes referred to as "genre prints," indicating a picture of a scene from common life or one that tells a story, but that designation actually is little favored by many collectors.

The Old Print Shop

be properly placed and viewed from a distance. All this is not said to discourage the collecting of maps and prints, for they are not only decorative but interesting, worthwhile, and historically important in a number of ways; it is simply to underline that an enthusiast undertaking the broad-scale collecting of such material faces certain inherent problems not encountered in most other fields of antique collecting and for which in his earliest enthusiasm he may be completely unprepared.

Interest in maps and prints centers in many areas, and collectors may approach the subject in general from several viewpoints: method of production, artist, or, perhaps most frequently done, subject, such as marine, railroad, sports, and so on, and by printmaker or publisher. Nor should it be forgotten that some of the finest late nineteenth- and twentieth-century lithographs from the standpoint of both art and execution were put out as advertising posters and form a definite category in themselves, although one perhaps not appreciated by many collectors. The excellence of many of these pieces should not be surprising, for most of them were executed by the same artists and printmakers who produced purely decorative prints.

The collector who may seek to gather in material touching all bases will find himself faced with a considerable number of methods of reproduction, although in recent years, particularly with the publicity attending Currier & Ives prints, many have tended to regard prints as synonymous with lithographs. Among the processes employed besides lithography, which did not come into widespread use until fairly well into the nineteenth century, are woodcuts, metal engravings, etchings, drypoints, aquatints, and mezzotints, with perhaps further minor types or subtypes recognizable by the expert. Most of these methods continue in use even to this day, particularly for artistic conceptions that are—often by preference—to have very small printings, and there is no clear-cut line of progression from one method to another that largely replaced it to be traced out, save that lithography and steel engravings eventually largely took over the popular side of things and made great numbers of duplicate prints available at comparatively moderate prices.

For a long time, color prints were possible only by laying in the color by hand on each individual specimen. Gradually, in the later nineteenth century, the process of lithographing in color was perfected

THE LIFE OF A FIREMAN.

Two well-known and much-admired prints. Top, "Sleighing in New York," an 1855 print by D. Benecke, very frequently referred to as "The Barnum Museum Print" after the edifice in the background. Below, an 1861 print, one of a series of four Currier & Ives prints called "The Life of a Fireman."

The Old Print Shop

"And lo! as he looks, on belfry's height/ A glimmer and then a gleam of light!" *"The Landlord's Tale" (Paul Revere's Ride), the much-admired etching based on* Longfellow's Tales of a Wayside Inn.

George S. Indig Photograph

and replaced any need for hand coloring. The output of lithographs was prodigious. There were hundreds of printmakers active in the United States in the nineteenth century. The array that faces the collector today is almost endless, not only of works that were made as prints, but from the mass of smaller pieces that have barbarously been pulled from the old books and magazines that they originally illustrated. The latter, from a technical standpoint, properly have little interest to the collector of historical prints as such, but may well have interest to the individual who collects from the standpoint of illustrations relating to one or more specific subjects.

There are certain categories of prints that seem to be firmly established as staples, such as old American lithographs. On the other hand, there have always been certain elements of the faddish or transitory about many aspects of print collecting, with the relative popularity of various types rising and falling and rising again, perhaps not entirely without rhyme or reason, but at least with a certain measure of seeming uncertainty, particularly in the viewpoint of the collector whose collecting pattern was too much oriented toward the investment con-

An example of the colored railroad photograph of the late nineteenth and early twentieth century. Examples were once among the decorations of every major railroad station and travel agency. This 1898 example by the Photochrom Company depicts the crack Black Diamond Express of the Lehigh Valley Railroad.

George S. Indig Photograph

cept. In any event, it certainly makes good sense to say of the collecting of old maps and prints, best collect either from the standpoint of that which you like personally—which, after all, is good advice in any field of collecting—or else on a basis of things that impinge upon and assist and strengthen other collecting interests, the latter suggestion applying much more in the case of prints than of maps, which more or less naturally, apart from their purely decorative values, form a collecting category in themselves.

PICTURE POSTCARDS

Picture postcards comprise a vast collecting specialty in themselves. In fact, they have always been a popular collectable from one standpoint or another, enormous quantities being purchased either as souvenirs of visits or simply because, early in the twentieth century, at least, the collecting of postcards was an extremely popular hobby in itself. The picture postcard is by no means so old as some believe, its use not having been authorized by the United States Post Office until 1898, although it was in widespread use in Europe somewhat earlier, and there were also some previous issues in the United States. The history and claims for the invention of the picture postcard are respectively so complex and numerous that it is impractical to go into the matter here. Initially it was required that the entire face of the card be kept clear for the address, the pictorial matter and any message having to be placed on the reverse. In 1907 the use of the face of the card for both message and address was admitted to use in the United States, permitting the entire back of the card to be employed for the picture.

Initially the range of picture postcard types was rather extensive, including many greeting and comic card types, categories whose function in more recent times has largely been taken over by the special greeting card that is mailed enclosed in an envelope. At one period in postcard collecting, postally used cards were widely regarded as possessing an equal or even greater desirability than new cards, most especially when the place and date of the postmark tied in with the subject of the card. This outlook has many adherents today in certain phases of postcard collecting, although to a large extent the old interest

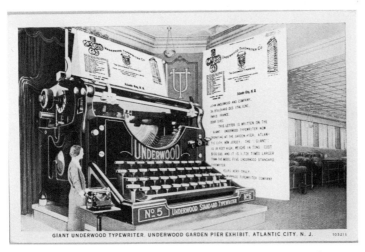

GIANT UNDERWOOD TYPEWRITER, UNDERWOOD GARDEN PIER EXHIBIT, ATLANTIC CITY, N. J.   103211

Postcard collecting has long been a popular hobby. This card of the 1920s depicts the giant eighteen-foot-high, fourteen-ton, fully working Underwood typewriter referred to in Chapter III, built in 1915, and for many years displayed on the Garden Pier at Atlantic City, New Jersey.

George S. Indig Photograph

in place and date has been taken over by the philatelic hobby of first-day-cover collecting. While certainly not rejecting any card simply because it has been postally used, most men collectors today would undoubtedly prefer unused postcards and, in the case where cards initially were sold in sets, the set in its original form complete with envelope or container and with the cards unseparated if originally vended in this form.

General picture postcard collecting is popular, but is as illimitable, if not more so, than the collecting of backs of playing cards. Most men who collect picture postcards specialize to at least some extent, among the most popular specialties being railroad scenes, and in fact, transportation of all kinds, fire engines and related views, factories and industrial scenes, world's fairs, military subjects, comic-strip-character cards, and sports. It is probably a rare man, however, who, having the collecting bent and collecting in one or more categories, does not also have at least a few old picture postcards of personal interest somewhere about the premises. He may not actively collect them as such, but he certainly has no thought of discarding them!

CHAPTER XII

Metalwork, Woodwork, and Other Crafts

It is to be hoped that nothing that has been said up to this point conveys the impression that men disdain or fail to appreciate individual artistry and craftsmanship. Nothing could be further from the truth. What has been affirmed is that most men are not bemused by the concept that there must be merit in something merely because it is handmade and, to reiterate, that most men are aware that there is as much if not more true artistry and craftsmanship in the processes that attend the bringing into being of a mass-produced article as in many artifacts of which only one of a kind can exist because it literally was handwrought. Furthermore, men frequently suspect—and often correctly—that many antiques traditionally accepted as handmade or even as folk art actually were factory-mass-produced. An awareness of this fact in regard to any given specimen does not, however, usually in itself detract from a male collector's appreciation of or interest in collecting the article. Often, indeed, such an awareness actually enhances this appreciation and interest. Although the idea may appear barbaric and shocking to some minds long accustomed to other tunes, there are today many articles collected by men only because they have ascertained that they were factory-made, in which formerly they took no interest because they were under the impression that they were handcrafted!

This chapter deals with a number of different things of current interest to men collectors. Some of them actually were individually crafted, some were mass-produced, and, to tell the truth, the exact origin of some of them has not been determined. Considerable research on this point still remains to be done and no doubt will be properly done in ensuing years. Suffice it to say that, with their direct know-how concerning how things are made, as well as their often highly developed intuition concerning such things, men collectors strongly suspect certain long-accepted handcraft categories and subcategories as having been mass-produced, and others in which they feel assured that for some articles factory production started a great deal earlier than previously had been thought, and that many so-called handmade, primitive, and folk-art specimens actually were factory-made. Often their designs deliberately were primitive or even downright crude not because they were individually made by untutored craftsmen but because such designs were most salable in certain parts of the country. There was often an element of planned provincial sales appeal in this, the merchants being able to assure customers that the goods were made locally and not in the big city, or even perhaps in another state. Nineteenth-century manufacturers were no less aware than those of today of the profits to be found in catering to the demands of specific markets.

Tin, Copper, and Brass

Tin has always been a favorite material among collectors, whether plain, hand-painted, or stencil-decorated. A particular cause for extensive masculine interest in tinware of all kinds and the history of its manufacture and commerce is the continually growing popularity of early tin toys. Most tinware, including so-called country tinware, was factory-made from an early date; in fact, there was never but a small amount of tinware—custom-made pieces—that was anything but in effect shop-made and mass-produced. (Incidentally, the appellation "country" applied to almost any group of antiques now tends to make men collectors grimace with suspicion that it is being grossly misapplied.) An early nineteeth-century tin factory, even if with only a dozen or so hands, was capable of turning out an enormous quantity of production tinware in a year's time. Much of it was painted and decorated, either freehand or with stencils. Sometimes, in the early days, this decorating may have been done by girls at home, but in

A twelve-inch-long painted tin box, probably manufactured in Connecticut in the early nineteenth century. While a certain amount of handwork obviously entered into the decoration of such pieces, they were actually for the most part production pieces and a far cry from the legendary individual "country" efforts.

Old Sturbridge Village Photo

most instances everything was done from start to finish in the factory. Such hand painting and decorating was relatively cheap and rapid, but a good example of the employment of production know-how of a high stage of refinement can be found in the twelve-inch-long box or chest illustrated. Many names have been applied to these chests, and of a certainty they could have been employed for many purposes, from kitchen use to holding papers. In any event, it is obvious that this particular chest was intended to be placed against a wall, for the back is undecorated.

The tin chandelier also pictured may have been a special item; it may also have been a stock number. In any case, it points toward two important matters. First, while the making of candles was to a large extent a home craft, the tin-candle molds into which they were poured, generally regarded as extremely old and scarce articles of Colonial days, were for the most part shop-fabricated and mass-produced throughout most of the nineteenth century. As seen in Chapter VII, the candle-mold stake was one of the six types of stakes still regarded as absolutely essential for the trade of tinner in the 1870s, and there

Two interesting candle-holding devices whose history, production background, and exact dating are speculative, but each of considerable interest in its own way. Either may date from the late eighteenth or early nineteenth century. Left, an adjustable wooden candle stand and, right, a tin chandelier.

Old Sturbridge Village Photos

were also then available stock machines for their far more rapid production than actually making them on the stake, the same tube-form-
ing machines serving to make either candle molds or ladle handles.
The second point brought up is that everything concerning lighting
is of considerable collector's interest, the only controversial point in
connection with this category being whether it should be limited to
candle holders and stands and early types of lamps, or whether it
should extend also to include electric lighting. Most men collectors
definitely feel that it should.

The material tin, and usually referred to by that name, employed
in tinware manufacture actually was not pure tin, but tinplate in the
form of sheets, these being ten-by-fourteen-inch sheets of iron covered
with a thin coating of tin to inhibit rust and to make soldering easy.

Other metals favored by early craftsmen and manufacturers were
copper, brass—both cast and in rolled form—zinc, and cast bell metal
and other alloys; pewter, britanniaware, and iron being separately discussed below. Bell metal usually was an alloy of brass and tin, sometimes with some copper or zinc or both added. There is a belief that

*Three middle or late nineteenth-century brass mortars and pestles, the smallest
mortar being only two inches in height. Brass mortars of this type and period
were employed not only in drugstores but were normal home furnishings used
for preparing both remedies and food.*

George S. Indig Photograph

bell metal always contained silver, stemming from the supposed tradition of vestrymen throwing silver coins into the mix at the casting of a new churchbell in the expectation of thereby giving it a more pleasing tone. Plain bell metal, *sans* silver, was, however, a standby of early manufacturers. The bell-metal skillet illustrated, marked with the name of the manufacturer, Gay and Hunneman, and dated 1794, is an interesting example of early and in fact pre-nineteenth-century commercial manufacture. In many instances, the appearance of such a date would indicate only the year the patterns for a given article were made, not the actual date at which a given specimen was produced.

PEWTER, BRITANNIAWARE, AND IRON

Pewter has always stood as a desirable collectable, complete with connotations of deft Colonial craftsmanship, while britanniaware frequently was regarded as a nineteenth-century mass-produced pretender with little or no collector's value or interest. The fact is there always were various grades of pewter containing differing proportions of tin,

An interesting example of late eighteenth-century American productivity, a skillet cast of bell metal, an alloy consisting largely or entirely of brass and tin, manufactured in the 1790s by Gay & Hunneman of Boston, Massachusetts.

Old Sturbridge Village Photo

A cast-iron potbellied coal stove, the "Railway King," measuring four feet in height and manufactured in the late nineteenth century, together with appropriate coal scuttle and shovel. As the name indicates, it was designed primarily for use in railroad stations.

Ward Kimball

antimony, copper, and lead. The supposed best grade of plate metal or plate pewter theoretically is mostly tin and should contain no lead, whereas the cheapest kind, Ley metal, on the other hand, contained a good deal of lead, although—again theoretically—the lead content should not be higher than twenty percent. By the end of the eighteenth century, the now much-sought early pewter was regarded as cheap and common. Britanniaware was developed both as an alloy of greater hardness, luster, and workability and also as a catchy sales name that would overcome the increasing resistance to pewter. To attempt to clarify a most frequently confusing point, there was never any one set formula for britannia metal any more than there was for pewter, but after the first third of the nineteenth century, britanniaware became a distinctly recognizable class of merchandise from pewter, the britannia metal often being fabricated in sheets which could be stamped or spun into desired shapes, and the ware often silver-plated. It was at the time regarded by about everyone as an improved and more desirable material than pewter, and it is difficult to disagree with this conception today. Nevertheless, on occasion, collectors still will find themselves

Late nineteenth- or early twentieth-century store and household equipment. The candy scales were manufactured by the Chicago Scale Company. The wooden-base coffee grinder is unidentified, but the larger grinder is a No. 2 manufactured by the Enterprise Manufacturing Company of Philadelphia, Pennsylvania.

Mark Haber, Andrew B. Haber Photographs

being told that pewter, even "late" pewter, is good, worthy, and collectable, while britanniaware is not! In time, the allure of the term "britanniaware" faded, and pewter regained popularity as a designation. In the channels of trade, even as late as the 1930s, many contemporary articles manufactured from various white-metal alloys customarily were designated "pewter" because of its traditional connotations.

Whatever the merits of any of the metals previously mentioned as collector's items, to an ever-increasing number of men the collectable metal *par excellence* is none of these but, rather, cast iron. Cast iron was the great material of the nineteenth and early twentieth century, at least in the United States, where there were good supplies of coal and ore readily available and labor was, comparatively speaking, expensive. These years were literally the Iron Age. The original costs of designs and patterns were relatively high, but once the master patterns for anything had been created, endless duplicates could readily be turned out in the foundry at low cost. The result was a flood of devices, ornamental and useful—or combining both attributes—fabricated in whole or in part of iron castings, which could be marvelously detailed when the particular product at hand and the spirit of the times called for it.

It would be pointless to list all the things made of iron, from small household appliances and decorations to panels intended to be interlocked to form complete building fronts. There are collectors of such large castings, constructional and architectural iron, ornamental lawn furniture and animals, mantelpieces, hat racks, stoves, and so on. Again, storage is a considerable problem, unless a few pieces are used functionally around the home. On the other hand, there are endless smaller articles that can be collected and studied purposefully and in depth, including tools, nutcrackers, cigar cutters, kitchen appliances and mechanical gadgets, and so on. The household gadgets make up an immense category in themselves, including as they do such illustrations of a nineteenth-century awareness of the desirability of labor-saving devices as cherry pitters, meat choppers, measuring faucets, coffee, spice, drug, and bone mills, ice cutters, ice-cream freezers (iron works in a wooden pail), lemon squeezers (invariably designated as such in an era before orange juice evidently was thoroughly appreciated), sausage stuffers, and fruit, wine, jelly, and lard presses. Some of these items, especially in their larger sizes, are not, strictly speaking, household artifacts, but were used on farms and in hotels and boarding-houses.

It is a safe rule that if any cast-iron device is animated, or if designs embrace miniature figures of people—comic or otherwise, or both—the articles are fairly widely collected and regarded as relatively desirable. An entire category can be built up of such specimens relating to tobacco: cigar cutters, plug-tobacco cutters, counter cigar lighters, for instance. Another specialty is animated nutcrackers. The period of the popularity of such cast-iron pieces did not end precisely with the close of the nineteenth century; many were manufactured in the early 1900s, but collectively they usually are referred to as Victorian iron-work, even though occasionally the actual material employed will be found not to be cast iron but some white-metal alloy. The fact is that the character and ornateness of the styling of most of these devices are very attractive to men, their often ornate design seeming a pleas-ant contrast to the starkness of modern design. This pleasing com-plexity of embellishment possible through the iron-casting process extends to articles in many other collected categories, such as tools, as exemplified by the plane pictured, sewing machines, and typewriters.

Another facet of ironwork collecting is represented by the gather-ing of old hinges, hasps, wagon hardware, and so on. This often in-cludes also the collecting of brass hardware as well. While some attempt to limit themselves to the earlier handwrought hardware, it is obvious that the mass-production pieces and most particularly the beautifully ornately cast Victorian and early twentieth-century hinges and other hardware are becoming of primary attraction and active interest to more and more collectors.

In connection with the foregoing reference to counter cigar lighters, it should also be mentioned that a number of men make a specialty of collecting early—and many not so early—pocket lighters. Somewhat similarly, many men specialize in old fountain pens and mechanical pencils, a rather colorful category. In the first four decades of the twentieth century, few men ever could resist the radiant claims of the boardwalk, country-fair, and street-corner sellers of inexpensive fountain-pen and pencil sets, and they evidently continue to exert a

Animated cast-iron appliances of the late nineteenth and early twentieth century. At the top is a Brighton No. 3 plug-tobacco cutter with figure thumbing its nose. The squirrel and dog are nutcrackers, the former unidentified, the latter manufactured by the Eschmeyer Company.

Mark Haber, Andrew B. Haber Photographs

Wooden kitchen appliances of the early nineteenth century of the type usually regarded as so-called primitive homemade gadgets but actually in most cases factory mass-produced. At the top is an evidently factory-made cherry pitter; at the bottom a press of uncertain derivation.

Madison Square Garden National Antiques Show

considerable residual attraction to this day. One man, a prominent sales manager, revealed, however, that he had originally taken up their collecting simply to have an icebreaker when he entered a prospect's office for the first time, having observed that it was a rare man who did not have one or more defunct in his desk drawer. He ended up with several thousand different specimens of old fountain pens and mechanical pencils, a sincere interest in them, and a comprehensive knowledge of the history of their manufacture and sale. Another man reported that he started collecting old pipes—another not uncommon masculine specialty—with much the same purpose, and in twenty years ended up in about the same position of knowledge and eminence as a collector as did the gatherer of old pens and pencils.

WOOD AND POTTERY

Wood and pottery products have not much attracted the attention of men up to now because it was widely accepted that so many of them were individually made, although it should have been obvious that in many instances at least this was hardly the case at all. It is becoming increasingly apparent that much of this material, as suggested in the opening paragraphs of this chapter, was not individually made but, often even in the late eighteenth century, was the product of fairly substantial manufactories.

This field is still so little explored in a scientific manner and still so clouded over by the traditional embellishments of the handcraft and pioneer-art legends that it is still not possible to say with any real authority whether many specific items were homemade, the one-of-a-kind products of custom craftsmen, or factory-mass-produced. However, we know now that there was an extensive mass-production manufacture of woodenware in the United States in the early nineteenth century and that many so-called primitive artifacts of wood actually give substantial if not in many cases absolute evidence of their mass-production, factory-made origins that many have so far overlooked or deliberately shut their eyes to, and that there undoubtedly existed a great many articles and companies whose histories deserve and should receive careful study and chronicling. In the light of these realizations, there has in the last few years been considerably

more interest in wooden articles among men collectors than had ever
before been the case. Of course, there always had been a certain
interest in supposedly individually made wooden items, especially of
an animated or even semimechanical nature, such as the adjustable
candle stand with threaded-shaft, illustrated.

Another sound area of interest has long been in wood carvings of
either some substance, such as circus-wagon figures, merry-go-round
animals, and ships' figureheads, or simply in small, ingenious novelty
carvings, such as chains carved from a single piece of wood, one a
favorite project of countless whittlers. Another related specialty is the
collecting of decoys, although the most desirable decoys from an
overall collector's standpoint probably are the ones that were made
of cast iron, not wood. There are still a fair number of old wooden
decoys available, but the decoy collecting situation has become complicated in recent years by the availability—and at times they even
are entirely openly advertised—of modern decoys carved of weathered
wood. In the collecting of decoys, those made by American Indians
must not be overlooked.

The trouble with almost all wood carving is that if you enjoy it
for its inherent appeal or its history as a collector may, sooner or later
it seems there always are those who will come along and attempt to
analyze and discuss it in terms of modern artistic values or imagined
folk-art connotations that never were thought of when the pieces were
carved. To many a man, such essays in a supposed higher criticism
seem ridiculous affectations, to say the least, and, indeed, there often
is much more speculation than substance about them. Regardless of
what it may be, there is almost always someone who is ready to dissect
an artifact that is artistically good for its time and purpose and visually
satisfying today from the viewpoint of certain vague academic artistic
standards. These fellows can take a lot of fun out of not only collecting,
but of history as well, if you take them too seriously.

To a certain extent, much the same thing can be said of old pottery
items as of wood. Successful potting actually was for the most part
a mass-production business, even though actual patterns or dies were
not employed. This held true to a large extent of the so-called back-
woods potters as of the larger and better-known firms. Again, collecting
know-how and an aware approach to sound research are called for to

Interesting examples of nineteenth-century woodcarving, a four-foot-high ship's figurehead and two circus-wagon figures. The latter are believed to be from the Great Golden Globe tableau wagon, which was imported from Great Britain in 1871 for the use of Howes' Great European Circus.

G. William Holland Collection *(left)*
Ringling Museum of the Circus, Sarasota,
Florida *(right)*

enable collectors finally to put much of this material in its proper context. Unfortunately, it is always a hundred times more difficult to overcome ingrained traditions and romanticizing than to start a search for information with a clean slate in hand. Most of the early potters turned out stock sizes and styles, and these in substantial quantities. Yet the feeling somehow still widely exists that every time our fore-bears wanted a crock or jug, they went down to a clay pit, dug out some clay, and then made and fired the vessel themselves.

WEATHERVANES

Much the same concept often extends to weathervanes, its being much supposed that the average householder went out and hewed his own weathervane out of wood and metal, thereby creating more to-be-treasured folk art. Many did make their own weathervanes, of course. However, a good percentage of what is offered collectors today are somewhat weathered specimens made each year in large quantities for sale to tourists at Cape Cod and elsewhere while another substantial portion were made equally recently as manual-training-class projects. In any event, the mass-produced, factory-made weathervane was probably the greatest of overt symbols of prosperity and success available in the nineteenth century and, consciously or not, therefore mounted atop virtually every substantial residence or barn.

Many carried figures several feet long, and often three-dimensional, stamped out of sheet copper or zinc and portraying almost every possible subject, although horses, with or without vehicles, probably were the most common. There was also, in the later nineteenth century, a very frequent tie-in between the design of the weathervane and the trade of its owner; there were in effect occupational weathervanes much as there were occupational shaving mugs. Farmers for the most part favored livestock, but the catalogs of weathervane manufacturers reveal a surprising range of possibilities, although it must be admitted that simply because a man chose to adorn his house with a fire-engine weathervane, it was by no means as sure that he was a fireman as would be the fact that his shaving mug carried the picture of a fire engine. It was a good clue, however. When all is said and done, there exists an equally good chance that the fire-engine weathervane a col-

Two late nineteenth-century metal weathervanes. Top, a thirty-four-inch-long Ethan Allen Trotter weathervane. Bottom, a forty-two-inch full-dimension locomotive-and-tender weathervane. The manufacturers of these largely brass weathervanes are unidentified.

G. William Holland Collection *(top)*
Ward Kimball *(bottom)*

lector finds today may originally have been mounted not atop a private residence but on a firehouse. Similarly, a locomotive weathervane may originally have been as readily atop a railroad station as the home of an engineer. But the weathervane, as noted, was a status symbol and also in many cases an evidence of the occupation of its owner, and despite their often relatively high prices for the day, many were purchased and used by private individuals both for their personal satisfaction and to proclaim their prosperity to the world.

Probably the most famous of all weathervanes is somewhat of a fluke. It is a locomotive and tender and was intended for the use of railroads and railroaders. It is, however, in no wise an accurate depiction of a real locomotive, as is the railroad weathervane illustrated. Instead, by chance, the manufacturer, Westervelt, took a Secor toy locomotive of 1880 as the model and copied it exactly, the designers unwittingly even reproducing on the side what they evidently considered an essential appurtenance of a real locomotive but which actually represents the crank used for winding the clockwork mechanism that propelled the toy!

SCRIMSHAW AND IVORY CARVING

"Scrimshaw" is the name broadly applied to carvings of and on ivory or bone, presumably done by seafaring men and most particularly whalers. When ivory was employed, it was usually that of the teeth of whales; sometimes the tusks of walrus; the bone was customarily whalebone. There is, in point of fact, much confusion concerning the name "scrimshaw" itself, and its proper application. "Scrimshaw" seems to be a somewhat later-day corruption of earlier terms, such as "scrimshander." Actually in its broadest and probably original sense, "scrimshaw" means any nicely done example of craftsmanship or mechanical work; in a nautical sphere, it probably initially applied as readily to a neatly executed ship model made of any material as specifically to bone and ivory work. The questions remain, does "scrimshaw" in its generally understood modern usage relate only to work done by whalemen or by seafarers of all kinds? Does it apply only to work done at sea or at least while away from home for a long period, or does it apply equally to similar work done ashore? Does it apply only to whale teeth and bone, or to ivory in general, and if so, does it apply to the ivory carvings widely executed by Eskimos? If the latter, just where is a line to be drawn between that which is referred to as "scrimshaw" and to "ivory carving"? The emphasis on scrimshaw as essentially a craft afloat probably has been overdone. Certainly much of it was done in whaling ports like New Bedford by men who never put to sea and on a semicommercial scale at least, although there is at least some evidence to suggest that there was once what actually amounted to a scrimshaw industry in New Bedford and perhaps even what was, in effect, a factory! At least a measure of the carvings done by Eskimos and perhaps also by northern Indians in Alaska and the Yukon was more or less fabricated to order by traders. The traditional inclusion of a cribbage board in Eskimo-carved walrus tusks was not a natural manifestation of their folk art!

In any event, it is all collectable, and much of the work is today highly regarded. Many pieces made by sailors are semimechanical objects, such as carved whales and other animals or simply carved handles with pie-crust crimping wheels attached. Another more or less distinct group consists of teeth on which designs or pictures have been carved or scratched: ships, flags, floral patterns, ladies, or scenes of whaling or naval engagements. The scenes are often highlighted by the judicious application of ink or paint. Many other artifacts were, however, executed in ivory and customarily are classified as scrimshaw. Obviously, the creation of scrimshaw was a time-consuming and often tedious task that helped to while away long hours at sea, but it is also apparent that it was at times deliberately instigated and encouraged by ships' captains to find busy work for idle hands, as well as having been produced to a considerable extent at least with the idea of its eventual sale or at least its exchange for potables.

Ivory carving itself has long been a particular art, widely practiced, with more or less characteristic local differences in almost all parts of the world. There are, in fact, surviving ivory carvings made by cavemen. Most individuals think of ivory carvings chiefly in terms of the Oriental pieces and those produced by the Eskimos, and these are, indeed, two important and probably the best known and most popular of groupings. However, there was extensive ivory carving carried on in Africa, in Europe, and in parts of Asia other than China and Japan.

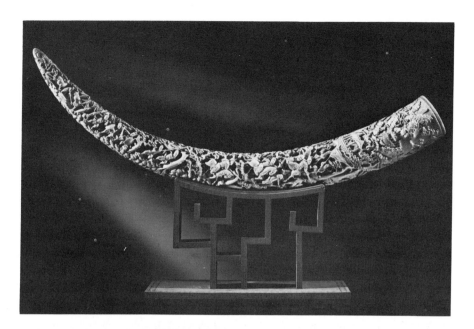

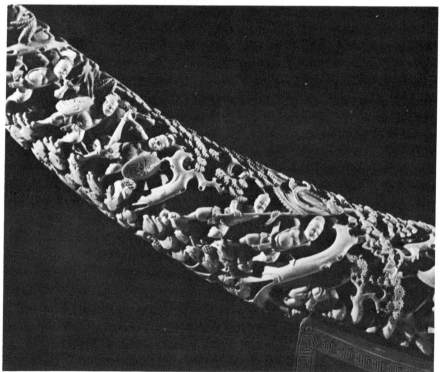

An elaborately carved elephant tusk, carved in China in the last years of the nineteenth century, together with an enlarged detail of the carving. This is an unusually fine and intricately worked specimen.

Milwaukee Public Museum

Reference already has been made in Chapter VII to the carved ivory-embellished police parade batons, which apparently are a more or less distinctly American specialty. It would also be possible, quite apart from the carving craft, for collectors of games to gather and study various artifacts, the ivory billiard ball being the most obvious. For reasons that are perhaps too complex to go into in detail here and might require deep psychological investigations, ivory as a material has always carried strong masculine connotations, and the collecting of finely carved ivory objects for centuries has been regarded as an acceptable masculine avocation. Suffice it to point out in this regard that the large, sweeping tusks of the elephant are the prerogative of the male and that female elephants usually have insignificant tusks or even no tusks at all, the tusk therefore being the symbol of masculinity in the largest of land mammals.

Despite the antiquity of many fine ivory carvings, the material that most often presents itself to the collector today, and eagerly is accepted by him, usually dates from the late nineteenth or early twentieth century. It very properly is considered by enthusiasts "old" or "antique" despite the fact that purely from a standpoint of relative age it must be considered in relation to other existent carvings that may go back hundreds of years. In this connection, it should be pointed out that the laudable efforts of conservationists now have finally practically ended the ivory trade and that the quantities of the material available in the future probably will continually diminish.

Admittedly, a considerable amount of the readily available ivory carvings are of a type made for sale to tourists, whether of Oriental or Eskimo origin, although finer pieces are not unobtainable, and, as with all things, the discerning collector appreciates specimens according to their relative merits and does not disparage anything merely because of its original cost and purpose. The photograph of the two Japanese fishermen provides an interesting comparison, however. The large figure is 19½ inches high, so large in fact that it is built up of a number of pieces of ivory. It is unusually finely detailed and dates from the nineteenth century. The small ivory fisherman shown beside it is of the type usually intended for sale to tourists. It naturally suffers from comparison with its imposing companion in the photograph, but the assembling of a collection consisting only of figures of this type can make an extremely interesting and enjoyable pursuit.

An unusually finely detailed and large Japanese nineteenth-century carved-ivory figure of a fisherman. It is nineteen and a half inches high and built up from a number of pieces of ivory. To its left is a small ivory statue of a fisherman of the size and type usually intended for sale to tourists.

Milwaukee Public Museum

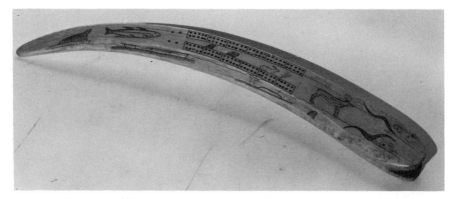

An example of an Eskimo carved and decorated walrus tusk from the first years of the twentieth century. It includes a cribbage board as well as illustrations of wildlife and objects familiar to its carvers. Note the mouth, right, with carved teeth.

George S. Indig Photograph

The Eskimo carvings are naturally of an entirely different sort, usually depicting familiar animals and objects such as seals, whales, Arctic hares, and sleds upon tusks, or actual ivory miniatures of artifacts such as spears and mallets. The Eskimo ivory often is curiously ignored or mentioned but briefly in many discussions of ivory carving, but a number of collectors feel it is, the most interesting group of all. As representatives of an overall category, specimens almost certainly are considerably scarcer than the better-known and more widely collected Oriental wares. In any event, the Eskimo carvings can be commended as being, even if almost certainly in many instances somewhat commercialized, a manifestation of one of the very few forms of true American folk art.

STATUARY

Reference has been made in various places in this volume to a number of types of statuary—wooden Indians, sports and theatrical bronzes, and cast-iron lawn figures. The subject deserves special consideration as a whole, for much that was once ignored as supposedly representative of the worst in the Victorian era now is becoming widely collected, and a good deal of the statuary that might—and in the eyes of most men, wrongly—be included in such a description is of distinctly masculine interest.

There are today in most large cities groups of men who frequent the sites where old buildings are being demolished, sometimes making pests of themselves, sometimes eliciting the interest and cooperation of demolition crews. These men are striving—and often succeed—to preserve and collect examples of architectural statuary and ornamentation, sometimes in cast iron, more often in stone carvings, and even occasionally in poured concrete. It has been realized that there exists an enormous amount of decorative embellishments incorporated into Victorian buildings, and that it is well worth saving as much of it as possible. At one time, few stone buildings were erected upon which one or more stonecutters were not called in to ply their trades. Perhaps in many or even most cases, the resulting designs, gargoyles, and similar ornamentation do not and never will rate as great, but they were nevertheless an integral part of the passing scene and are for the most part worthy of preservation. An enormous proportion of this work was destroyed over a period of many years and much more of it is destined to fall before the wrecker's ball. Time for preserving examples of material is perhaps rapidly running out, but at least an effort is being made to see to it that some of it will be saved. As is the case with so many worthwhile collectables, however, such things obviously require considerable space to house, and the unfortunate part of the situation is that most of those who are actively interested and who can manage to be on the spot when something becomes available—often a matter of very tight timing between the moment something can be removed intact and when it is smashed forever—are city dwellers themselves with relatively little storage space available.

This, at least, is not a major problem in the collecting of nineteenth- and early twentieth-century bronze statuary intended for home decoration. There are, to be sure, imposing examples, but for the most part the casts were small. Some were made by well-known artists, in some instances being copies of much earlier and often classic works; others were designed by relative unknowns or at least by men whose work may only now, through the collecting and study of these figures and groups, become properly appreciated and recorded. Most of the figures are profoundly realistic and run to animals, Roman chariots, rural scenes, stylized cavaliers, and the like. Of particular interest to many men collectors today are the allegorical feminine figures representing "Commerce," "Industry," and the like. These things were once widely regarded as Victorian horrors and melted down by the ton. Fortunately, a great many originally were made and there is a fair survival rate. Some of the later figures are not bronze at all, but bronze-finished white-metal castings.

Many of the figures of men and women originally were made and sold in pairs. Others—validly collectable for what they are—including some as much as fifteen inches or more in height, actually were not originally sold as statuary as such but were clock figures, initially mounted on the same base as a clock, either a figure on one side of the clock or a pair of figures with the clock between them. This type of large mantel clock enjoyed a vogue in the late nineteenth century. When the vogue ended, many owners removed and retained the figures, sometimes having them mounted on individual bases for continued use. In many instances, the clock manufacturers who fabricated these figures made double use of their designs and made the figures available for sale separately but with integrally cast bases as statuary pure and simple. There is no certain means of distinguishing between the clock figures and the statuary, for some of the seated figures would stand perfectly well by themselves without bases. In the case of individual standing figures, however, a base usually was necessary. If a figure has no base or is found mounted on a separate base, it probably originally was sold as part of a clock. If the same figure has an integrally cast base, it may be taken as almost certain that it originally was made and sold as statuary.

Reference should also be made to nineteenth-century plaster statuary, probably best known in the form of the figures and groups manufactured by John Rogers of New York during the latter half of the nineteenth century, although there were other manufacturers of similar pieces. This statuary is highly detailed and realistic, and also highly fragile. The company did a considerable continuing business in repairing damaged statues and in supplying materials for home repairs. Enormous quantities must have been manufactured, the usually cited estimate of 100,000 for the total production of Rogers himself appearing much too low. A good many have survived, although they have been so favored by collectors over so long a period of time now that they no longer are anywhere so readily available as they once were, and setting out to attempt to collect Rogers groups on a broad scale is hardly a project to be undertaken lightly.

CHAPTER XIII

Edged Weapons, Firearms, and Military Miscellany

The subjects of this chapter, weapons, and of the following one, covering clocks, are long-established standbys in the realm of men's collectables. One inevitable result of this has been that endless studies have been lavished upon these subjects, innumerable works of great merit and usefulness have been published as a result, and to many it no doubt will appear that substantially all that could be said of basic importance already has been said. It might perhaps justly be expected that, regardless of what may have been presented in previous chapters that was in any way new in thought or detail and thereby in value, from this point on only some sort of summation of existing material is possible.

Were this true there would be no need for chagrin in the case of such widely and firmly established categories. Nonetheless, in examining these collectables and their background and in discussing them with others, there can be perceived elements of their historical importance and of collecting approaches that have not yet been fully set forth or exploited, although in many cases more than dimly visible in the outlooks of a number of established collectors and interested potential hobbyists. The fact is that weapons—specifically firearms—and clocks can well be approached from angles not previously widely delineated. These approaches would seem to be equal in importance

Two interesting small Remington handguns. Top, a Remington-Rider .32 caliber rimfire five-shot magazine pistol, 1874–88. Bottom, a Remington Iroquois .22 caliber rimfire seven-shot revolver.

Remington Arms Company, Incorporated

and interest as most of those previously well traveled and possessing attractions certain to engage the interest of many men who previously had thought of a gun simply as a device to discharge a projectile or of a clock simply as a timekeeper.

The fact is that weapons and clocks were ever in the forefront of industrial development; they have provided us with the lead toward mass production, to machine production, and to interchangeable parts. The need for firearms being repeatedly vital if not critical, it is they more than clocks or anything else that have led us into our modern mechanical and industrial era, both directly and indirectly. It can be well submitted that, were it not for this situation, our overall industrial progress probably would be at least a hundred years behind. In fact, we might conceivably still not yet have approached its dawn. Whatever the negative attributes of firearms, it can be said that the indirect positive results of their making and refinement have had inestimably beneficial consequences, and many a collector today is just beginning to take a new look at firearms from the viewpoint of the major role they played in industrial development.

There are relatively few cases recorded of the literal carrying out of the axiomatic conversion of swords into plowshares, but in effect there have been enormously broad results tantamount to precisely this, which is not to disparage the firearm as an often necessary article of defense, or its collecting from the conventional standpoint, but rather to suggest the almost limitless fascination of approaching both its history and its collecting and study from another aspect. The possibilities of what the interested collector-investigator can uncover in these spheres are virtually illimitable and tie in with many other areas of collecting. The whole thing, it should be noted, goes far beyond the usual and oft-cited matter of the development of interchangeable parts for firearms manufacture, although that in itself is an integral and vital part of the overall picture.

The first type of what is now known as the "universal milling machine"—there were earlier types of machines to which this name previously had been applied—is illustrated in Chapter VII. This type of machine came into being to fill a need for a machine to make tools for the mass production of the great quantities of muskets called for by the outbreak of the Civil War. In 1861 the Providence Tool Company of Providence, Rhode Island, was awarded a contract for the manufacture of Springfield muskets. Making the nipples for these muskets was a machine-tool operation, but the twist drills employed to drill the holes in the nipples had to be made by hand, as all such drills were then produced, workmen using rat-tail files to file the spiral flutes. This was as recently as 1861, bear in mind, and was then the only way known to produce twist drills. The superintendent of the plant wondered if it were not possible to make the drills by machine and asked Brown & Sharpe to try to develop such a machine. The direct result was the first universal milling machine, a machine tool capable of spiral milling. The first machine was sold to the Providence Tool Company in March 1862, marking the start of the production of universal milling machines. The universal milling machine has had incalculable effects on the broad spectrum of industrial progress, but it is only necessary to consider what would be the state of the mechanical arts today if twist drills could still be produced only by hand filing.

A detailed study of the history of manufactures will reveal that an enormous number of the milestone developments of machine tools and manufacturing techniques were brought into being under the exigencies and pressures of the requirements of firearms manufacture. However, before exploring the subject of firearms themselves at length, consideration should now be given to an earlier form of weaponry, the edged weapon.

EDGED WEAPONS

Although there are instances and examples to dispute this as a definitive overall statement, edged weapons other than the sword, the bayonet, and the hunting knife played a relatively minor role in events on the American continents, as also did body armor. The armored horsemen of the early Spanish conquerors may have played an important psychological role in contending with men who had never seen a horse, but the deep woods that most of the early explorers and colonists encountered obviously precluded the practical deployment of armored men and made such standard European weapons of the day as the halberd and the pike useless in the type of fighting that was encountered. By this time the forces of the great European powers were engaged in their struggles in North America, the firearm had become the chief weapon of war. As a consequence, Americans in general and American weapons collectors in particular have no great tradition of armor and edged weapons comparable to those of Europe and Asia. There are many American collectors of European and Oriental armor and edged weapons, but for the most part the interest of American collectors naturally centers around the swords carried by members of the military establishment of the United States, a field broad and interesting enough to content most.

Peculiarly enough, however, while the pike and the storied pikemen of European warfare seem utterly alien to the American experience, there are two specific American pikes that are of tremendous historical and collector's interest and therefore, and especially as they are often confused, require special mention here. These are the John Brown Pike, and the Joe Brown or Georgia Pike. Although both are of astoundingly late origin as pikes go, genuine specimens of both are extremely desirable and difficult to obtain; it is difficult to speculate on how problematical it would be for a collector to secure one or both, although it can hardly be said to be impossible.

The John Brown Pikes were manufactured in Collinsville, Connecticut, in 1857 on an order from John Brown, a thousand being made supposedly to arm Kansas free-soilers who were unable to afford firearms, but were held at Collinsville until instructions were received to ship them to one Isaac Smith at Chambersburg, Pennsylvania. Smith was really Brown, who secretly had them moved to a farm he had rented near Harpers Ferry, Virginia, in preparation for his assault on the arsenal there. It was Brown's intention to arm freed slaves (who were not familiar with firearms) with the pikes. After Brown was captured, most of the pikes were recovered, either at the farm or at the arsenal, where they were stored until Harpers Ferry was captured by the Confederate forces and the pikes moved farther south. In the closing days of the war, they were issued to a Texas regiment and eventually were recovered by the United States government at the close of the war. Most of these seem to have subsequently been destroyed by fire while stored in a United States arsenal. The genuine surviving specimens appear to have been examples presented to friends by Virginia officials in 1859 shortly after Brown's capture.

The Joe Brown Pikes, naturally enough with so close a similarity of names, frequently are confused with the John Brown Pikes. Joseph E. Brown was the wartime Governor of Georgia. Foreseeing a shortage of firearms in the Confederacy, he issued a proclamation in July 1862 calling for the manufacture of 10,000 "Georgia Pikes" and offering to furnish the design to anyone capable of making a quantity. About 2,500 appear to have been fabricated, not all of an identical pattern, and they were eventually issued at the time of Sherman's approach. As recently as 1904, the United States Army sold 1,200 of these captured pikes at an auction of surplus material. Genuine Joe Brown Pikes are far more common than John Brown Pikes, and in a number of instances collectors have secured the former under the impression it was the latter.

Of European and Oriental armor and edged weapons little need be said here, save to note that the Oriental specimens almost invariably differ in every way from their European counterparts and form a distinct classification and group of collectables in themselves.

Much, on the other hand, could be said with pertinence concerning the swords of the United States forces, which are of so extensive an interest to collectors. While it is true that for lengthy stretches of time in our early history our regular military and naval establishments were small, it must be borne in mind that they were ever conducted on formal lines of organization, prescribing at each period the specific and appropriate saber, sword, or cutlass for each arm and rank of the service. For example, contrast the illustrated United States Light Cavalry Saber, Model 1850, and the United States Light Artillery Saber, Model 1840, or the United States Naval cutlasses of 1826 and 1860, illustrated. Furthermore, although the actual numbers of men in service, particularly in the Army, may have been relatively low between early wars, it was ever the policy of the government to keep adequate supplies of the proper arms on hand for the rapid expansion of any unit in time of trouble; it was only in the cases of unexpected conflicts of monumental proportions, such as the Civil War, when prodigious supplies of additional weapons had to be manufactured with great speed. Still further, the militia establishment was always very strong and the state governments saw to it that their troops were properly equipped with adequate reserve supplies on hand. The collector of United States swords, therefore, not only has a field of enormous potential variety, but also of at least a fair measure of availability of specimens.

In addition to the regulation models, the collector of American military swords has available to him the wide variety of nonregulation swords. These were often the result of necessity, as naturally was the case with many Revolutionary War swords, and often the result of the early regulations being loosely drawn, leaving much to the choice of the individual in the case of officers who were not issued their swords by the government but purchased them individually from various sources. There are, of course, collectors who specialize in either enlisted men's or officers' swords. In addition to such more or less semi-standardized regulation swords, there are also the swords resulting from the long-favored custom of various government and private sources honoring distinguished officers with special elaborate presentation swords.

THE DEVELOPMENT OF FIREARMS

The progression of firearms is best basically traced by systems of ignition. Firearms, as far as the average collector is concerned, comprise hand guns and shoulder guns, a field broad enough to satisfy

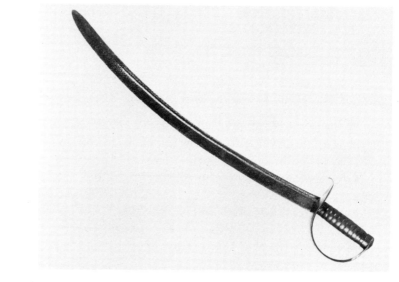

Top, a United States naval cutlass, Starr contract of 1826. Bottom, a United States naval cutlass, Model 1860.

United States Naval Academy Museum

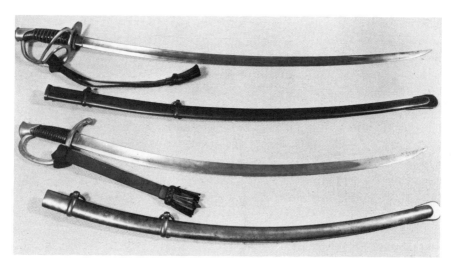

Top, a United States Light Cavalry saber, Model 1850. Bottom, a United States Light Artillery saber, Model 1840.

West Point Museum

almost every enthusiast, although, if only for the sake of completeness, it is necessary not entirely to write off artillery as a collectable. However, in most cases the average enthusiast will not have occasion to be concerned actively with it as a collector's item. Cannon, of course, preceded individual firearms. The gun as such is variously recorded to have first appeared in Europe between the middle of the thirteenth and early in the fourteenth century; the earliest ones may well have been some form of what more properly might be designated a rocket than a gun. The subject is rather uncertain and somewhat speculative, yet it is claimed that guns were used at the Siege of Seville in 1247, a date much earlier than that generally cited, and there are records of guns and gunpowder being exported to England from the Low Countries as early as 1314. It is possible that firearms appeared in Europe somewhat earlier than usually has been suggested.

In any event, it appears certain that the first firearms designed for use by an individual, that is to say, a personal and more or less portable gun, appeared in the latter part of the fourteenth century. They were essentially hand cannon which were fired by touching off the charge with a glowing match applied by hand in the same manner as a regulation cannon of the day. In modern parlance, a hand gun is one that can be held and fired in one hand, a pistol or revolver. All of the earliest personal firearms were in a sense hand guns, for regardless of their form, size, and weight, the user would have available only one hand with which to hold the weapon, his other hand of necessity being engaged in holding and at the proper moment applying the slow match to the touchhole.

It can thus safely be asserted that for all intents and purposes the personal firearm as we think of it today could not come into being until the invention of the gun lock, actuated by a trigger or other means, whereby a musketeer could not only use both hands to hold and manipulate his weapon but concentrate his attention on aiming his piece without having to shift his glance at the last moment to assure ignition. From this point on, the development of ignition methods may be summarized as matchlock, wheel lock, snaphance, miquelet lock, flintlock, percussion cap, and, finally, fixed ammunition in the form of a cartridge containing its own primer. This is the progression usually given, but it is by no means so simple and clear-cut as it may seem

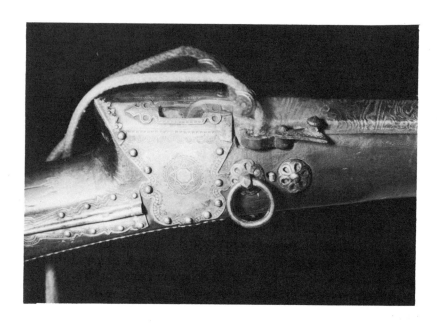

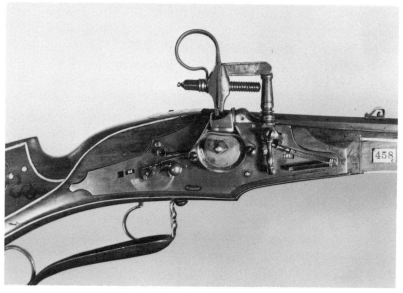

Early types of gun locks. Top, a late fifteenth-century matchlock, in this instance a Moorish piece. The photograph is a dual exposure showing the lighted match in position before firing and after being triggered into the opened pan. Bottom, an early sixteenth-century wheel-lock action.

Remington Arms Company, Inc.

at first glance, for there was much overlapping, and certain primitive forms continued to be widely favored in other parts of the world long after they had been abandoned in Europe.

In the matchlock, a lighted match was held in position above the flashpan, which normally was covered to protect the priming powder and prevent it from falling out. Prior to firing, the flashpan was uncovered, aim taken, and the trigger pulled, thereby lowering the match into the flashpan and firing the piece. The matchlock was developed in the latter part of the fifteenth century and, crude and archaic as it now appears, held sway in European military arms for about two centuries. The matchlock continued in widespread use in Asia well into the eighteenth century, and, in any event, if someone offers the average collector a matchlock today and it is genuine, the chances are it is from India or points east and not, as many will try to tell you, from one of d'Artagnan's buddies or a Pilgrim father.

As suggested, charts that attempt to trace the development of the gun by a sequence of lock designations can be somewhat misleading. The wheel lock developed after the matchlock, to be sure; it was an obvious great advance and improvement and has an inherent appeal to the mechanical-minded, but it did not replace the matchlock in any sense. The wheel lock was developed early in the sixteenth century. Basically it consisted of a steel wheel with roughed edges which lay adjacent to the flashpan and, in fact, protruded slightly into the bottom of the flashpan, and a doghead which held a piece of pyrite and was pressed against the top of the firing pan (in the illustration there is no piece of pyrite in position in the jaws of the doghead). The wheel was wound up with a key. When the trigger was pulled, the wheel spun, the top of the flashpan moved away, allowing the pyrite to be forced directly against the edge of the wheel, producing sparks which ignited the priming powder and fired the gun. The wheel lock was expensive, easy to put out of order, and difficult to repair. Some were used on military pistols in fact; the wheel lock for the first time served to make the pistol practical; but as far as is known, no ruler cared to go to the expense of equipping his musketeers with wheel locks, and the use of the wheel lock remained generally reserved for gentlmen's ornate personal weapons and hunting pieces.

The snaphaunce was a step toward the realized flintlock and appeared in the Low Countries toward the end of the sixteenth century. At first glance, the snaphaunce looks much like a flintlock; the flint is held in what was by then generally known as a "cock," which obviously derived from the doghead of the wheel lock. When the trigger is pulled, the flint strikes against and throws back a steel surface—the battery—creating a shower of sparks which ignite the priming powder in the flashpan. However, the battery was entirely separate from the flashpan, and the flashpan had a separate sliding cover that opened simultaneously with the descent of the cock by means of a separate cover-opening mechanism.

The miquelet lock was an Iberian invention of approximately the same date as the snaphance. It very closely approached what is usually termed a "true flintlock" and remained the standard lock of many Mediterranean gunsmiths during the entire era that the flintlock reigned supreme in northern Europe and in America. The miquelet lock combined the battery and the flashpan cover; when the flint struck the battery and threw it backwards, the same action uncovered and exposed the flashpan, which was located under the battery; in short, the horizontal section of the L-shaped battery formed the cover of the flashpan. In a snaphance, the mechanism was housed and protected inside the lock, while in a miquelet lock, the main spring was located on the outside of the lock, where it could easily be damaged. The flintlock, which appeared in the first decades of the seventeenth century, in effect combined the best features of the snaphance and miquelet locks and eliminated their weak points, as well as, in time, adding a few special improvements of its own. However, in essence, the flintlock was a lock with an L-shaped battery that formed the cover of the flashpan and with an internal mechanism.

The flintlock remained the standard gun lock in America and in most of Europe until it gradually gave way to percussion methods of ignition in the early nineteenth century. The flintlock, however, it should be emphasized, far from disappeared from either use or manufacture elsewhere in the world and among peoples who did not care to be dependent upon factory-made percussion caps or fixed ammunition, and to whom, also, these seemed a useless additional expense. Whereas, in the United States and Europe, innumerable existing flintlocks were converted to percussion in the earlier decades of the nineteenth century, following the Civil War tens of thousands of then surplus percussion muskets were sold to Europe, where they were converted to flintlocks for use in trade in Africa and the Near East. Flintlocks were, in fact, standard articles of manufacture for this trade up to the start of World War I. When the German Army occupied Belgium in 1914, they confiscated large stocks of flintlocks then in the process of manufacture for this trade in the fear that they would be used against them by patriotic snipers. It is apparent that even today rather large supplies of flintlocks—the locks alone, not the entire firearm—still exist in North Africa and the Near East and that a considerable business is being conducted in making these locks up into complete guns, which are offered for sale to novice collectors.

Early in the nineteenth century a number of individuals turned their attention toward methods of firearm ignition by means of striking a sharp blow directly on a small quantity of fulminate of mercury or fulminate of potassium chlorate and directing the resulting sparks directly into the powder load in the gun, thereby eliminating the necessity of an exterior flashpan as well as the flint, which had to be renewed after every dozen shots or so. The realized form of this invention was the percussion cap, a thin casing of metal that enclosed a charge of fulminate and was placed over a nipple that served as an anvil and also as a means of conducting the sparks into the barrel. The percussion cap was an obvious major improvement and remained popular long after the idea was further developed into the pin-fire, rim-fire, and center-fire metallic cartridges.

A word concerning cartridges, which are a collector's specialty in themselves, countless enthusiasts seeking examples of the literally thousands of types of cartridges that have been manufactured at different times and places. The metallic cartridge with its self-contained primer is an invention of the mid-nineteenth century, but the concept of the cartridge itself is almost as old as the personal firearm. Going into battle or going hunting with a supply of measured powder charges wrapped, with a ball, in paper that itself served as wadding was an obvious convenience, and such cartridges were widely adopted at a comparatively early date. In loading, the paper was bitten open at the powder end, the powder allowed to flow out into the barrel, and the paper and ball then driven home on top of the powder charge. Only the priming powder for the flashpan was carried in a container and a small amount poured into the pan for each shot. During the percussion-cap era, a number of types of paper and foil cartridges were manufactured and sold, particularly in connection with early revolvers. Naturally, such cartridges are today generally highly prized by cartridge collectors who, although they confine their efforts to commercial cartridges, by no means restrict them to metallic cartridges alone.

Interchangeable Parts

Four major topics deserve special comment now, both from the standpoint of firearm history and the collector of firearms, and because of their direct and indirect impact upon manufactures in general; interchangeable parts, the breechloader, the revolver, and other forms of repeating firearms. There is, of course, a distinction between mass production, machine production, and interchangeable parts, although today they have more or less blended into one thing; when we hear that something is being mass-produced, we assume it is being machine-made, and we likewise assume that anything made in this manner will possess interchangeable parts. Initially, however, mass production—although it was not called by that name—simply meant making a great many more or less similar articles. Given enough armorers and gunsmiths, a sixteenth-century ruler could rapidly have produced enough pikes and matchlocks to equip an army; similarly, given enough men, an American Indian chief could mass-produce arrowheads. There is nothing arcane about this.

In any event, for better or worse, depending on how you may personally want to look at it, whenever and wherever you trace and follow this industrial progression, it will almost invariably be found to be instigated, initially developed, and carried through in some connection with weaponry. This is not to say that all of these endeavors were devoted to the manufacture of weapons themselves. Maritime powers long required great stocks of ship's fittings. The machinery for mass-producing interchangeable ship's blocks that was installed at the Royal Navy Yard at Portsmouth, England, at the very beginning of the nineteenth century frequently is cited as an example of the dawn of machine production of great quantities of identical articles. Yet the very figures cited in connection with this plant, that when in full operation in 1808 it turned out over 130,000 blocks annually, with ten men doing the work formerly performed by one hundred thirty, in itself indicates that for many decades previously there must have been mass production, if not machine production and interchangeability, of more or less standard sizes and designs of blocks to meet the vast requirements of the Royal Navy.

On the other hand, the manufacture of guns with interchangeable parts had itself long attracted the attention of farsighted men who appreciated the savings in time and money that could be effected by such an arrangement. It was not uncommon for a great power in the eighteenth century, such as France or Great Britain, to have over 100,000 flintlock muskets out of service at any one time awaiting repairs that could be accomplished only by hand-forging individual parts to fit. An effort was made to manufacture muskets with interchangeable parts in France in 1717, and again in 1785, Thomas Jefferson, who was then Minister to France, endeavoring unsuccessfully to have the United States engage the artisan in charge. The musket in question would have been the French Charleville, of which thousands were supplied by France during the American Revolution, which were, in effect, thereby the standard musket of the Continental Army and which provided the pattern from which the earliest regulation muskets made in the United States for the Army were copied.

The first two United States contracts for firearms were given to Eli Whitney, for muskets in 1798, and to Simeon North, for pistols in 1799. Whitney set up a new plant which became the famous Whitney Arms Company of Whitneyville, Connecticut. North already had his own factory, at Berlin, Connecticut. North started fulfilling his contract for 1,500 pistols at once, at first following his usual methods of manufacture but gradually developing machinery and working toward a complete interchangeability of parts. Whitney was supposed to deliver 10,000 muskets in two years but he waited to begin production until he had designed and built the machinery required and did not complete the order for eight years. From their combined efforts evolved what was to become known throughout the world as the "American system" of manufacture, mass-production by machinery, the machinery often designed and built to perform a specific task, and interchangeability of parts. Historians have been hard put to differentiate between the roles played in this by North and Whitney, although, as Joseph Wickham Roe points out, Whitney was better known and had greater influence in promoting the acceptance of the principles involved among other manufacturers and in the setting up of his system of manufacture in the government's own arms-manufacturing work at Harpers Ferry, Virginia, and Springfield, Massachusetts.

It goes without saying that most early North and Whitney firearms are regarded as highly desirable and have always been much sought by gun collectors. The reasons for which they usually have been sought are still entirely valid, but it should also be remembered that they are all the more collectable and interesting because of the role they played in the development of the entire art of the manufacturing process.

The Breechloader

It is a favorite parlor game during peacetime to sit around and denigrate the military as being unbelievably hidebound and traditionalist when it comes to the adoption of new ideas and to endeavor to substantiate this by their supposed slowness in adopting various and seemingly advantageous inventions. An examination of industrial history suggests that this is not by any means the case. The state of technical development of manufacturing was simply not up to the point of successfully producing many seemingly premature inventions and, furthermore, it must always rightly be the aim of the military establishment in any country to see that the equipment issued is of such a nature that it will stand up under the rigors of combat conditions, something that obviously is better known to the army than to civilian inventors and manufacturers; a firearm mechanism that may prove satisfactory when used by a sportsman may fail utterly when employed by an army in the field.

The development of the breechloading firearm is a good case in point. The idea was almost as old as the personal firearm and its advantages were readily recognized. For one thing, a breechloader obviously could be loaded faster than when the charge and missile had to be rammed down a long barrel. For another thing, most military men were aware that, in the excitement of battle, many soldiers forgot that

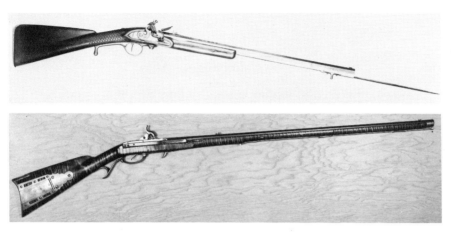

Early military breechloaders. Top, a Ferguson flintlock breechloading rifle of the 1770s used to a limited extent by the British Army. Bottom, a Hall breechloader, first manufactured as a flintlock and shown here converted to or built as a percussion firearm in the 1830s or early 1840s. The Hall was the first breechloader used by the United States Army.

West Point Museum *(top)*
Old Sturbridge Village Photo *(bottom)*

their pieces had not been discharged after loading and rammed successive loads into their barrels; a breechloader could be designed to preclude this. The trouble was that for years it was simply impossible to make breeches that would open and then close tight enough to prevent the escape of so much gas as to reduce materially the impetus of the discharge of the projectile. In short, workmen simply were unable to work to close enough tolerances.

There were several passable eighteenth-century flintlock breechloaders, all of which seem to have tried to reduce the escape of gas to a minimum by using not a hinged breech but a screw plug attached to the trigger guard, which served as a handle. The best known of these was the Ferguson, some British soldiers actually going into action in the American Revolution armed with Ferguson breechloaders by virtue of being under the command of the inventor, Major Patrick Ferguson, who supplied his men with the firearm of his invention. It is believed that this was the first time that breechloaders were ever actually used in a battle, that of King's Mountain on October 7, 1780, although there has always been some question as to just how many of the breechloaders were employed. Major Ferguson was killed in the action and, although his breechloader was subsequently still improved, nothing more came of it. A Ferguson breechloader has long been considered a prime collector's item.

Although, because of its use at King's Mountain, the Ferguson often is considered by way of being an American piece, the first reasonably successful breechloader actually manufactured in the United States and the first adopted in any way by the United States Army was the Hall. This was invented by Captain John H. Hall and patented in 1811, and initially was manufactured in the form of pistols and sporting arms. Finally, in 1817 the government ordered one hundred Hall rifles for test purposes and two years later Hall was given a contract for one thousand with the provision that the manufacturing was to be done in a United States armory. From 1820 until his death in 1841, Hall continued at the Harpers Ferry Armory, designing and building much important machinery. A number of Hall breechloaders were also manufactured on contract by Simeon North, perhaps 40,000 rifles and carbines being manufactured in all for the Army, later models having percussion ignition rather than being flintlocks. The Halls obviously were serviceable, but were still deficient in muzzle velocity as compared to muzzleloaders, due to leakage of gas at the breech. Much has been made of Hall's machinery and his contribution to industrial progress; some have attempted to claim for him the origination of interchangeable parts. But the point generally overlooked, and it is the really vital point, is that, by the time of the Hall breechloaders, manufacturing techniques had reached a point of being able to adhere to sufficiently close tolerances as to make a breechloader practical if not wholly satisfactory.

Breechloaders were used in the Civil War, but it was not until after that war that the breechloader became standard in the United States Army and that in general the principle finally was accepted for the vast majority of firearms, although a number of breechloaders had been in manufacture and use from the 1840s onward. It would require an assemblage of many dozens of specimens, a number of them rather scarce, adequately to illustrate the basic development of the breechloader, and such a collection could be expanded almost indefinitely.

The Revolver

As was the case with the breechloader, the concept of the multishot weapon was very old, generally taking the form of a number of revolv-

This very unusual American .52 caliber revolver was fabricated in the late seventeenth or early eighteenth century. The lock plate is marked "J. Pim of Boston, N.E. Fecit." The cylinder was revolved by hand, each chamber having its own flashpan, a construction made practicable by the employment of the snaphance-type lock.

Winchester Gun Museum—Olin—New Haven, Connecticut

ing barrels in the general shape of what, in the mid-nineteenth century, was popularly known as a pepperbox, or on occasion a single barrel with a revolving cylinder, or true revolver. The chief difficulty was that flintlock revolvers usually required a separate flashpan and battery for each barrel, which made for great clumsiness, or else the pan had to be recharged with priming powder after each shot. This difficulty was overcome in the snaphance revolver illustrated, a remarkable firearm made by a Boston, Massachusetts, gunsmith, J. Pim, late in the seventeenth century. Pim cleverly reverted to the then largely obsolete snaphance design in order to be able to employ a single battery and to provide each cylinder with an individual flashpan. This forerunner is probably one of the most important and interesting antique firearms known.

Essentially, of course, the real story of the revolver starts with Samuel Colt's invention, which was patented in the United States in 1836, Colt subsequently stating that at the time he was entirely unaware of anything ever having previously been designed in the way of a revolving firearm. In any event, the important part of Colt's invention was the automatic sequential turning, indexing, and locking when the hammer was cocked, all previous revolving firearms seemingly having been turned and locked by hand. A subsidiary but perhaps equally important feature of the early Colts was the separate recessing of the nipples for the percussion caps in an effort to preclude accidental multiple ignition.

The first Colt revolvers—handguns and revolving rifles, carbines, and shotguns—were manufactured in Paterson, New Jersey, by the Patent Arms Manufacturing Company. So-called Paterson Colts have become something of a symbol of rarity and desirability among firearms collectors, and their status as such certainly cannot be denied. However, a good many more were manufactured than the general impression has it. The Paterson factory was active from 1836 to 1842 and, at a minimum, manufactured 5,000 firearms, although in the end it was a financial failure. There has always been some question as to whether any of the so-called Walker Colts, a model named after Captain Samuel H. Walker of the Texas Rangers, were manufactured at Paterson. However, when the Mexican War broke out, Colt secured an order for a thousand revolvers, which he had made on contract by the Whitney Arms Company, and it was the Walker model that was then produced, some 2,000 "Whitneyville Walkers" being manufactured in all. From that point on, the success of the Colt was assured; a new company, Colt's Patent Fire Arms Manufacturing Company, was established, and a factory set up in Hartford, Connecticut.

The Colt revolver has, of course, become part of American legend; many of the early models were five-shot, incidentally, and not "six-shooters," including the first repeating rifles purchased by the United States government, a few five-shot .56 caliber rifles in 1857. The revolver did not long remain an exclusive prerogative of Colt's, numerous other types being produced ranging from the prepossessing models made by Remington (who began manufacturing revolvers in 1857), Whitney, and others to those who fabricated revolvers just as cheaply as they possibly could and thereby brought into the argot the expression "hotter than a two-dollar pistol." This was somewhat of a misnomer because, before the cheap manufacturers were through, they were turning out revolvers that retailed for as little as seventy-five cents—smoothbores, it should be added, for, after all, who could expect rifling at such a price?

Such junk guns apart, although it would seem now that they would be well worth collecting and preserving as examples of precisely what they were, there was a well established and accepted chart of values

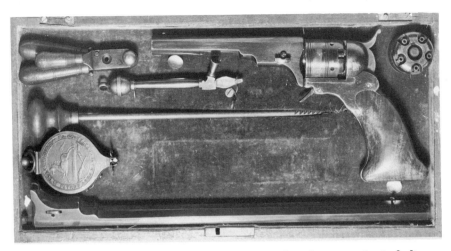

A Colt Paterson five-shot belt pistol ca. 1836 cased with accessories including an extra cylinder (upper right) and extra twelve-inch barrel (bottom). The powder flask is missing from its place in the case but the outfit is otherwise complete.

Colt Industries, Colt's Firearms Division

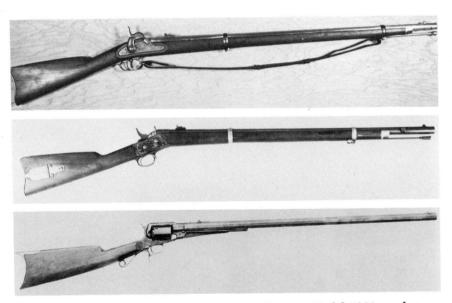

Three interesting rifles. Top to bottom: United States Model 1861 musket, one of 25,000 made on contract by the Norwich Arms Company, Norwich, Connecticut in 1864; a Remington muzzleloader converted to breechloading using the Remington rolling-block system, ca. 1865–70; and a Remington Beals revolving rifle, .36 caliber, 1866–72.

Old Sturbridge Village Photo (*top*)
Remington Arms Company, Inc. (*center and bottom*)

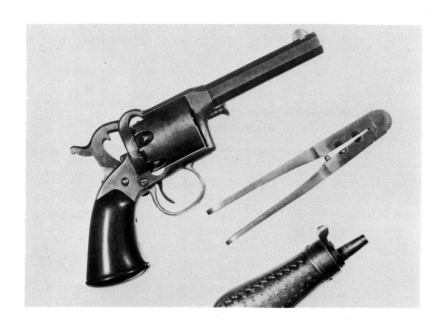

Two Remington cap-and-ball revolvers. Top, Remington Beals pocket revolver, .31 caliber, first model, together with bullet mold and powder flask. This 1857 model was the first revolver made by Remington. Bottom, a Remington Model 1861 .36 caliber Navy revolver.

Remington Arms Company, Inc.

on the Western frontier as to exactly how much a revolver was worth in a poker game—$22.00 for a Colt, $18.50 for a Remington, and $16.00 for other makes.

All of the early revolvers were, of course, percussion ignition or, as they were generally referred to by their owners, "cap-and-ball guns." With the advent of cartridge revolvers, there was a continuing demand, for perhaps two decades after the Civil War, for the conversion of percussion revolvers to fire the new type of ammunition, and many types of such conversion revolvers, Colts, Remingtons, and others are known. It should not be assumed that everyone immediately desired a cartridge firearm, however. Even as late as 1888, manufacturers were still cataloging and selling revolvers with optional cap-and-ball cylinders. Not every cap-and-ball revolver is therefore by any means necessarily as old as it may seem. As an even more important precautionary note, it should be observed that today Colt is manufacturing the single-action .45 caliber revolver first introduced in 1871.

The Repeater

The revolver was patently a repeater. It quickly became widely popular as a handgun but never attained great success or favor as a form of repeating long gun, although at first thought it might appear to have been an ideal solution to the problem, as least where five or six successive shots would have been sufficient. To provide an authentic answer to why the revolving rifle died aborning is a task that really defies absolutely satisfactory solution. Much is speculative. There is an answer that may involve mainly questionable elements, although it is not without some interest even if it involves legend. It is built on the theory that, regardless of safeguards, there always was danger of chain ignition in a cap-and-ball revolving weapon, a highly undesirable happening when in such close proximity to a shooter's face as would inevitably be the case with a rifle, but tolerable in a handgun if the shooter could train himself to aim accurately enough without sighting along the barrel. Thereby, we are told, arose the custom of "shooting from the hip" with all its concomitant elements of American Western folklore. While on the subject of Western legend, it should also be remarked that, despite all the fabled lore of the revolver, the deadly and feared weapon of the old West was the shotgun. It was not for nothing that the guards on stagecoaches carried this weapon called by its name, and town marshals who knew their business and wanted to stay alive patrolled with a shotgun, usually sawed off, in their hands, rather than relying on handguns as do the heroes of a thousand Western motion pictures.

The idea of a repeating long gun was in the air long before the advent of the revolver, and a number of experimental types were constructed. Simeon North made one or more for proposed military use in 1825. It was a ten-shot flintlock, the ten loads being rammed home on top of each other, each adjacent to a separate touchhole with a cover, the flintlock lock sliding along in a groove beneath them. To fire the first load, the lock was positioned next to it, primed, and the cover of the touchhole raised, the lock being moved slightly rearward and the flashpan reprimed for each successive shot. At the tenth shot, the lock was as far to the rear as it would go, in substantially the same position it would permanently occupy on a conventional single-shot flintlock.

A number of repeating percussion weapons were developed and manufactured prior to the Civil War, some as early as the late 1840s. It is not possible to go into the matter here at any great length, and it is hardly necessary to point out that here again there is an almost endless specialty for the firearms collector. However, the Jennings-Smith & Wesson-Volcanic-Henry-Winchester complex is in many ways the basic and most important one and is illustrative of so many of the points that have figured in this book that it deserves mention here.

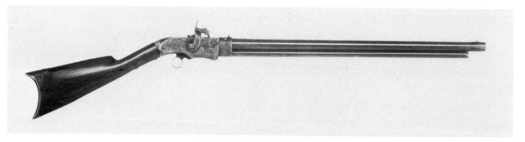

The Jennings rifle, the first moderately successful tubular-magazine repeating rifle. It fired twenty shots without reloading, using a hollow ball containing the powder charge. These rifles were manufactured on contract by Robbins & Lawrence of Windsor, Vermont, in 1850 and 1851.

Winchester Gun Museum—Olin—New Haven, Connecticut

Early Smith & Wesson metallic cartridge handguns. Top, the .44 caliber single-action "American" model, introduced in 1869. Wild Bill Hickok was carrying a pair when he was killed. Bottom, the .22 caliber single-shot target pistol, model of 1891.

Smith & Wesson of Bangor Punta

The Jennings rifle, invented by Lewis Jennings, was the first moderately successful tubular-magazine repeating rifle, firing twenty shots without reloading, using a hollow ball containing the powder charge, a popular early form of cartridge among pioneers in repeating firearms. Robbins & Lawrence of Windsor, Vermont, was one of the leading firearms manufactories of the day, and, in 1850, they contracted to make 5,000 Jennings rifles—some being made as repeaters and others, rather curiously and for reasons that have never satisfactorily been explained, being turned out as single-shot rifles. Among the skilled workmen at Lawrence & Robbins who worked on the Jennings rifles was one Benjamin Tyler Henry, whose thread we will pick up again.

In 1852 a partnership was formed by Horace Smith and Daniel Baird Jennings to manufacture magazine pistols and rifles that were an improvement on the Jennings and on a slightly earlier repeating rifle that had been merchandised as the Volitional. The new repeater was named the Volcanic, and in 1855 it was taken over by a new company formed in New Haven, Connecticut, which included Oliver F. Winchester among its stockholders, the Volcanic Repeating Arms Company, Daniel Wesson for a time acting as the plant superintendent. In 1856 Wesson rejoined Smith in Springfield, Massachusetts, in the manufacture of a revolver using rimfire cartridges. The Smith & Wesson revolvers broke open for loading, and inasmuch as it controlled the patent for the boring of the chambers all the way through the cylinder, the company was able rapidly to establish itself in a paramount position in revolver manufacture, particularly after it introduced its first heavy revolver. This was the .44 caliber center-fire "American" model brought out in 1869. It was followed shortly thereafter by a slightly modified model known as the Russian Model, of which large quantities were manufactured for the Russian Imperial Army. The role of the big Smith & Wessons on the American frontier has been somewhat overshadowed by the publicity garnered by other makes. Wild Bill Hickok was carrying a pair of the .44's when he was killed and the gun belt that Jesse James foolishly took off at Bob Ford's suggestion shortly before Ford killed him with a Smith & Wesson .44 that Jesse himself had given him carried a mixed pair, a Smith & Wesson .44 and a .45 caliber Colt. Frank James, on the other hand, always favored Remingtons and is believed never to have carried any other make.

To pick up the two divergent threads of the repeating-rifle matter, the Volcanic Repeating Arms Company became insolvent in 1857 and, when the smoke cleared away, it was owned by Oliver F. Winchester and reorganized as the New Haven Arms Company, although still making arms that bore the Volcanic name. Winchester brought Benjamin Tyler Henry in to take charge of things and see what he could develop. Henry picked up the old Jennings and Volcanic threads and developed the improved firearm that was introduced in 1860 as the Henry rifle, which was manufactured until 1866. In 1865 Winchester undertook to change the name of the company to the Henry Repeating Arms Company, but about this time Winchester evidently decided it would be a good idea to have his own name on the company and the product, and when the new company was incorporated in 1866, it became the Winchester Repeating Arms Company, the first rifle to bear the Winchester name being the Model 1866 or 66, to be followed in turn by the Model 73, Model 76, and so on, all three of the first models being manufactured simultaneously for some time. Oliver Winchester was by way of being a gun collector himself, or at least had an appreciation of the advantages of building up a sample collection for factory reference.

In 1871 he traded Richard S. Lawrence of the by then defunct firm of Robbins & Lawrence a Winchester Model 66 in exchange for the Jennings rifle illustrated on page 380.

MILITARY MISCELLANY

It will be apparent that the collecting of weapons and of firearms in particular can be directed into many directions as a specialty. One obvious one concerning which little specific has been said is the collecting of military firearms. Probably this appears an obvious byway, particularly when it is channeled toward the collecting of military weapons of one's own country, or of one's country and its allies. In this connection, one firearm in particular should be mentioned here as of interest to both American and British collectors, simply because, although it is comparatively recent and is, in fact, a World War I rifle, and 2,193,429 were manufactured in 1917 and 1918, its existence is unknown to many novice collectors. This is the U.S. Rifle Model 1917, or the U.S. Enfield Magazine Rifle Model 1917, often dubbed the "American Enfield." It is a largely forgotten rifle, popular memory and tradition marking the Springfield '03 as the rifle of the United States services in World War I, the mighty Springfield '03 by now having become one of the legendary rifles of American history—although the story that there were doughboys who could fire aimed shots with it so rapidly the Germans thought they were facing machine guns can probably be discounted. The Enfield was, of course, originally a British rifle, the successor to the Lee-Enfield, and in the early years of World War I quantities of Enfield .303 caliber rifles were manufactured on contract in the United States by Remington and others. When the United States entered the war, there were only two plants tooled up to make the Springfield '03, the United States armories at Springfield, Massachusetts, and Rock Island, Illinois. Accordingly, to fill the need for large quantities of rifles in a hurry, the Enfield was adopted as a United States arm with a few slight changes, the major one being the change to use American .30–06 caliber ammunition. Hence, the "American Enfield," which did good service in the war but which was dropped immediately thereafter, the modified Springfield '03 remaining the standard United States rifle and, in fact, the rifle with which the United States entered World War II.

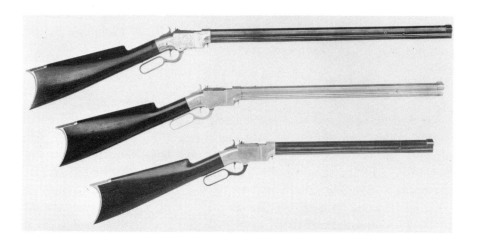

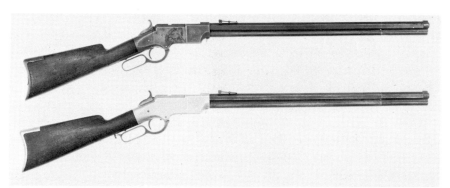

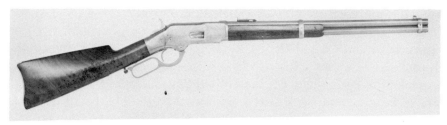

Steps in the development of the Winchester repeating rifle. The first three arms are Volcanic Rifles, manufactured by the Volcanic Arms Company and the New Haven Arms Company, 1856–60. The next two are Henry rifles, with iron frame (1861) and brass frame (1861–66), and, finally, bottom, the first Winchester, the Model 1866 or 66.

Winchester Gun Museum—Olin—New Haven, Connecticut

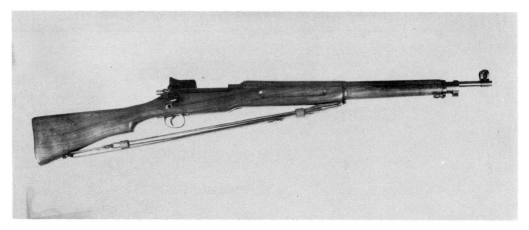

America's forgotten military rifle, the U. S. Enfield 1917 rifle, caliber .30-06 of which over two million were manufactured on contract in 1917 and 1918 to supplement Springfield '03 rifle production. They were mainly used in the United States but some were carried in France.

Remington Arms Company, Inc.

A specialization in military arms can readily lead to, or suggest as independent hobbies, other forms of military collecting. Two associated or distinct hobbies, depending on the inclinations of the individual, are the collecting of military-uniform buttons, badges, and insignia of rank, and the collecting of medals and orders. The latter hobby is considered by many a numismatic one or at least very closely related to numismatics—many medals being struck in the same manner as were coins. In any event, the hobby is carried on by real enthusiasts with considerable studiousness. However, another precautionary note is necessitated by this reference to the collecting of medals and orders. So popular has the hobby become, albeit often not carried on with a proper degree of care and seriousness, that a number of reproductions of medals and orders, complete with reproduction ribbons where called for, are being manufactured and even totally spurious decorations of what to some appear evidently "appropriate" designs are being created and fabricated for sale to unwary enthusiasts, a substantial number of whom have seemingly provided sufficient evidence of their undiscriminating susceptibility to this sort of thing to warrant production.

CHAPTER XIV

Clocks
and Watches

This account has now come full circle, back to Chauncey Jerome, a passage from whose autobiography was quoted almost at the very beginning of the book. Jerome was probably the greatest figure in all clockmaking; very likely he should be considered the true archetype of the man of the mass-production manufacturing scene, the individual who, more than anyone else, led the way toward so much that made life easier and better, and the man thereby indirectly responsible for many of the things that today are so avidly collected by men. Jerome has always had to be mentioned in even the briefest account of old clocks and clockmaking—the story simply cannot be told without him—but it is evident that references to him have not always been accompanied by much enthusiasm on the part of either teller or reader. This may seem all the more strange when it is considered that Jerome is one of the very few of the important old-time artisan-inventor-manufacturers who left behind any sort of a biographical record of their lives and work. There are two main reasons for this seemingly peculiar situation:

For one thing, in the eyes of many, Jerome made far too much of a good thing out of mass production. To some, as suggested in Chapter I, he is the man who started a revolution that destroyed forever the supposedly endearing old craft ways. To others, his manufacturing revolution was responsible for a host of social ills whose solutions are yet far from being fully in sight. These people are all happy to find an ally in P. T. Barnum, for, perhaps even more important in the long run, given the accepted mores of the American fabric, Jerome had the misfortune to run afoul of Barnum.

For one thing, Barnum, who has become an authentic American folk hero, sold somewhere over a million copies of his autobiography, and there were editions in print even in the late 1920s, almost forty years after his death. Of Jerome's book, published in 1860, there were perhaps at best a few thousand copies printed. As was pointed out in Chapter IX, one of the things that Jenny Lind has continually had going for her memory was her sponsorship by Barnum, which resulted in favorable mention over the decades in his book. On the other hand, if Barnum put you down as a bad one, much of the tar inevitably could not help but stick, and Jerome was undoubtedly Barnum's favorite villain. In Reverend Samuel Orcutt's otherwise conventional and staid book published in 1887, *A History of the City of Bridgeport, Connecticut,* the reader usually is startled to find a denunciation of the Jerome Clock Company as a "rotten concern." The mystery of the Reverend's departure from his usual style is cleared up when it is realized that "rotten concern" is Barnum's designation and that the whole account is in fact a paraphrase from Barnum's autobiography, *Struggles and Triumphs; or, Forty Years' Recollections of P. T. Barnum.*

The peculiar thing about the whole affair is that, seemingly, no one has ever bothered to investigate the whys and wherefores of the matter in any depth, Barnum's statements being taken at face value. This is rather strange because, according to Barnum, he was a sucker who himself was humbugged. The affair took place in 1855, when Jerome Clock Company and the Terry & Barnum Clock Company were merged, both Jerome and Barnum claiming that the other's company was secretly insolvent at the time. It would appear, however, that for several years previous Barnum had fallen under the spell of the seemingly illimitable possibilities of making money through mass-production Connecticut clockmaking and was determined to get his share of the pie one way or another, building up a fictitious edifice with which he may well have duped both himself and Jerome's son, who brought the Jerome Clock Company into the merger.

That P. T. Barnum should have allowed himself to become engrossed in the Connecticut clock business as it had been developed to a stage of marvelous perfection by Jerome need not be surprising. It was precisely the sort of thing calculated to interest any man. Jerome did not write his account until several years after the fiasco, but it is worth quoting from him again here both to give more of the contemporary flavor of the business and also to provide a suggestion of precisely the type of thing that, personally witnessed, would have made Barnum or anyone else certain there was a fortune in the mass production of clocks:

It may not be uninteresting to a good many to know how the brass clocks at the present day are made. It has been a wonder to the world for a long time, how they could possibly be sold so cheap and yet answer so good a purpose. And, indeed, they could not, if every part of their manufacture was not systematized in the most perfect manner and conducted on a large scale. I will describe the manner in which the O-G. case is made (the style has been made a long time, and in larger numbers than any other,) which will give some idea with what facility the whole thing is put through. Common merchantable pine lumber is used for the body of the case. The first workman draws a board of the stuff on a frame and by a movable circular saw cuts it in proper lengths for the sides and top. The knotty portions of it are sawed in lengths suitable for boxing the clocks when finished, and but little need be wasted. The good pieces are then taken to another saw and split up in proper widths, which are passed through the plancing [sic] machine. Then another workman puts them through the O-G. cutter which forms the shape of the front of the case. The next process is the glueing on of the veneers—the workman spreads the glue on one piece at a time and then puts on the veneer of rosewood or mahogany. A dozen of these pieces are placed together in handscrews till the glue is properly hardened. The O-G. shapes of these pieces fit into each other when they are screwed together. When the glue is sufficiently dry, the next thing is to make the veneer smooth and fit for varnishing. We have what is called a sand-paper wheel, made of pine plank, its edge formed in the O-G. shape, and sand-paper glued to it. When this wheel is revolving rapidly, the pieces are passed over it and in this way smoothed very fast. They are then ready to varnish, and it usually takes about ten days to put on the several coats of varnish, and polish them ready for mitering, which completes the pieces ready for glueing in shape of the case. The sides of the case are made much cheaper. I used to have the stuff for ten thousand of these cases in the works at one time. With these great facilities, the labor costs less than twenty cents apiece for this kind of case, and with the stock, they cost less than fifty cents. A cabinet maker could not make one for less than five dollars. This proves and shows what can be done by system. The dials are cut out of large sheets of zinc, the holes punched by machinery, and then put into the paint room, where they are painted by a short and easy process. The letters and figures are then printed on. I had a private room for this purpose, and a man who could print twelve or fifteen hundred in a day. The whole dial cost me less than five cents. The tablets were printed in the same manner, the colors put on afterwards by girls, and the whole work on these beautiful tablets cost less than one and a half cents: the cost of glass and work was about four cents. Every body knows that all of these parts must be made very cheap or an O-G. clock could not be sold for one dollar and a half, or two dollars. The weights cost about thirteen cents per clock, the cost of boxing them about ten cents, and the first cost of the movements of a one-day brass clock is less than fifty cents. I will here say a little about the process of making the wheels. It will no doubt, astonish a great many people to know how rapidly they can be made. [Here follows the section quoted in Chapter I.]

It will be seen from his reference to weights that what Jerome is speaking of here in the 1850s is still a weight-driven clock. Men commonly talk of clockwork and whether it is used to drive a clock or some other device, and what they refer to is a spring-operated mechanism, usually one with a coil spring, although the Ives brothers were to become famous as the makers of a clock actuated by a leaf spring, the so-called wagon-spring clock. For many years the spring-operated clock was regarded as a special type of article designated a "marine clock" because such a mechanism was a necessity on a rolling ship. Ashore many, well past the middle of the nineteenth century, regarded a marine clock as somewhat of a useless affectation. It was, in fact, a dispute over this point that led to the formation of Seth Thomas Sons and Company in 1866 as a distinct entity from the Seth Thomas Clock Company. A number of the stockholders in the older company, evidently including Edward Thomas, one of the sons of the founder, wanted no part in making marine clocks. As a result, the other two brothers, Aaron and Seth, with others, founded the new firm especially to make marine clocks. This new venture proved most successful and, finally, in 1879, it was brought within the original company by an exchange of stock.

By "O-G.," Jerome referred to what, as he said, was a style that had by then proved the most popular of all, a plain flat-topped case with an O-G., or O.G., or ogee molding around the front. An ogee is a molding consisting of two curves, one concave and the other convex. It also may be called a "cyma," and may be demonstrated by the letter S, although the relative flow of the shape was usually not so sharp in woodworking practice. The weight-operated O.G. clock remained a standard type for decades, examples still being found in the lines of Connecticut clock manufacturers in the 1890s. "Tablets" referred to the decorated panel that customarily filled the door of a clock under the dial.

Jerome's career is so pertinent to clocks and clock collecting and so perfectly illustrative of many of the themes of this book that there is a temptation to dwell upon it unduly. His was not the whole story, of course, and in any event, properly to understand his achievements and contributions, it is necessary to go back further in the history of American clocks and clockmaking.

EARLY AMERICAN CLOCKS

There were numerous clockmakers in the Colonies prior to the American Revolution. A clock was a luxury then, but by no means quite the luxury that tradition tells us. Some of the clockmakers imported mechanisms from Europe, some brought over parts which they assembled here, but most made their own components, although it appears that in many instances there was a distinct difference between those who actually made the works and those who made the cases. The usual cased clock was long the tall clock or what so frequently is referred to as a "grandfather's clock." The other common type of clock was an uncased wall clock consisting merely of mechanism, dial, weights, and pendulum, the type commonly referred to, but probably not by its contemporaries, as a "wag-on-the-wall"—it was called simply a "hang-up clock" by its makers. If the wag-on-the-wall mechanism was put in a free-standing case tall enough to accommodate the drop of the weights and just wide enough in the waist to take the swing of the pendulum, you had, in essence, the grandfather's clock. This is probably exactly what happened in a number of instances; the standard wag-on-the-wall mechanism was cased to order. As the eighteenth

Early American tall or grandfather's clocks. Left, a maple case clock with twelve-inch arched brass dial, made by Nathaniel Mullikan of Lexington, Massachusetts, ca. 1760. Right, a carved top mahogany case clock with eight-day brass movement made by Caleb Wheaton, ca. 1780.

Old Sturbridge Village Photos

century drew on, there was ever more demand for a cased clock for that finished look, and less for the crude and by then obviously unfinished-appearing wag-on-the-wall.

As a result, there were a great many tall clocks manufactured—a great deal more than many people would like to admit. There were clockmakers throughout the Colonies and the early Republic, but there were particular centers in Connecticut and Massachusetts in the North, and in Pennsylvania. Most of the earlier clocks had brass gears and other brass components, but the material was expensive and not easily come by at best. An important early innovation—it was to prove really only a temporary departure—both to reduce cost and to speed up production, was the use of wooden gears in the movements. You can make a pretty good clock with a wooden mechanism so long as the wood is well seasoned and the clock is operated in a fairly consistent and dry climate. It is not really important whether or not clocks with wooden works had previously been made in Europe, as some claim, or whether the American clockmakers invented or merely borrowed the idea. What is important is the obvious aim behind the idea even in the eighteenth century: more and cheaper clocks. Every clockmaker had what he termed his "engine"—"engine" then being a word that meant substantially what "machine" means today—on which he could cut gears. In fact, it was usually the final task of the apprentice clockmaker, before he could become a journeyman and literally start on his journey some place away from his master, to construct a satisfactory engine of his own. Many of these early clockmakers built engines on which they could cut a dozen or so identical gears at the same time.

There is a theory that has been sketched out at times but never fully developed that equates clockmaking and gunmaking, primarily because the Pennsylvania area that was so much a center of clockmaking in the eighteenth century also was the center of the manufacture of the Pennsylvania rifle, the long gun usually referred to with less accuracy as the "Kentucky rifle." There is a connection between clockmaking and gunmaking, but it is not to be found in Pennsylvania, but rather in Connecticut. The clockmakers there, who early in the nineteenth century started to mass-produce clocks and to make the parts of first hundreds, and then thousands and tens of thousands interchangeable, were either aware of what Eli Whitney was doing at

Whitneyville, Connecticut, and what Simeon North was doing at Berlin and, later, Middletown, Connecticut, or were by an amazing and seemingly almost impossible coincidence paralleling their ideas and work on their own. Mass-produced firearms with interchangeable parts in the quantities required to fill military orders were one thing, of course; mass-produced clocks or anything else with interchangeable parts for eventual sale to individual customers was something else altogether. It was in this clockmaking activity that we really finally arrive at the modern concept of manufacturing.

Most accounts of early clockmaking more or less imply, if they do not come right out and say it, that grandfather's clocks were never mass-produced; that each and every one of them was—as, indeed, some were—an absolutely individualistic, one-of-a-kind, custom-made affair. The same accounts then usually go on to tell the story of Eli Terry. Terry stands very high in clockmaking history, and any of his clocks is regarded as highly desirable today and justly so. Terry was born in East Windsor, Connecticut, in 1772, served his apprenticeship, and in 1793 moved to Plymouth, Connecticut, and set up in business for himself. In the early 1800s Terry was operating a clock shop where he was using water power to operate some of his equipment, in itself an innovation at the time. In 1807 he sold this factory to Heman Clark and bought another building, which he started to fit up with water-powered machinery of more advanced design. He also entered into a contract with Porter Brothers in Waterbury, Connecticut, to supply them with 4,000 clock mechanisms in the next three years, a contract which he fulfilled by delivering one thousand in 1809 and three thousand in 1810. Porter Brothers were casers of clock movements, buying from numerous clockmakers in the area, casing the mechanisms, and selling them as completed clocks, grandfather's clocks. In other words, Terry and Porter Brothers were mass-producing grandfather's clocks, and this is what the famous contract was all about!

Terry had some interesting apprentices and workmen whose names were to bulk large in subsequent clock history as manufacturers on their own. There had been Heman Clark, to whom he sold his old shop; there were Silas Hoadley and Seth Thomas in the new shop; and still a little later there was to be Chauncey Jerome. In or about 1810 Terry sold the shop where he had made the 4,000 movements for

Porter Brothers to Hoadley and Thomas. Hoadley and Thomas made mostly completely cased clocks, and in 1813 Thomas sold out his interest to Hoadley and started his own company in what was then Plymouth Hollow but which has since become Thomaston. Eli Terry was also to have a community named for him—Terryville, Connecticut.

It should be said here that there were other types of clocks developed and brought into use around this time, tall and often ungainly shelf clocks, and rather delicately wrought wall clocks of the types designated as "banjo," "lyre," and "girandole" clocks. These were all essentially low-production and fairly costly clocks, although their whole story, too, probably has not yet been told. They are highly desirable and collectable, but somehow they have never had the basic appeal for most men collectors as have the simpler, sturdy, mass-produced clocks that were about to burst upon the world in profusion from Connecticut and make that state the undoubted clock center of the world.

THE GREAT CLOCK BOOM

The mainstream of clockmaking from this point on was the search for designs and the manufacture of a continually cheaper clock that could be mass-produced in ever larger quantities. The vehicle in the form of which this innovation was to appear was to be a smaller, cheaper shelf or mantel clock that would be completely cased, a case being a necessity for any free-standing clock. A great deal has been written, much loosely and by hearsay and without too much examination of actual designs, as to the first step in this direction being the so-called pillar-and-scroll clock, a shelf clock about twenty inches high that took its name from the form of ornamentation at the top of the case. It would appear that the proper name for this type of clock and the one under which it was merchandised at the time is not "pillar-and-scroll clock," as it is usually known to collectors, but "pillar scroll-top case clock." In any event, the pillar-and-scroll business has diverted attention from the really great improvement of the day and confused the whole issue.

If the accompanying photographs are studied, it will be seen that the traditional design for a shelf clock in the later eighteenth and early

Two early American mantel or shelf clocks, both with cases in two parts. Left, a clock of about 1785 with engraved brass nameplate under the dial, made by Aaron Willard, Roxbury, Massachusetts. Right, a clock made about 1810 by E. Tabor, also of Roxbury. Note the almost identical configuration of the glass panels in the doors of these two clocks.

Old Sturbridge Village Photos

The customary relationship of the early two-part case shelf clock to the grandfather's clock with the center section eliminated is graphically demonstrated in these two clocks of about 1810. The tall clock was made by Simon Willard of Boston, Massachusetts; the shelf clock, by David Wood of Newburyport, Massachusetts.

Old Sturbridge Village Photos

A Seth Thomas wooden-works striking shelf clock in one-part box-like case, ca. 1816. The label reads "E. Terry's Patent Clock. Made and Sold by Seth Thomas, Plymouth, Conn." This would appear definitely to evidence that at least one of Terry's patents was not on the pillar scroll-top case.

Old Sturbridge Village Photo

Two early examples, both ca. 1816, of the famous pillar scroll-top-case shelf clock. That at the left was manufactured by Eli Terry; that at the right, by Seth Thomas, both of Plymouth, Connecticut. Seemingly endless controversy rages over who actually developed this beautiful type of clock case.

Old Sturbridge Village Photos

nineteenth century—and there were some shelf clocks built in this period, probably more than tradition has it—was simply a truncated grandfather's clock. They were, in most instances, simply grandfather's clocks with the narrow waist eliminated, and the cases were made in two parts, usually each with its own door, the upper one, over the face, of glass, the lower one of wood. It was, in effect, two cases in one and the case cost almost as much to make as the case of a grandfather's clock.

This should have "bugged" any forward-looking man into making a clock that could be sold for less money by being turned out faster and cheaper, and it did bug some clockmaking genius sometime around 1810, whether Eli Terry, Heman Clark, or someone else. The solution was so simple that when we see it, accustomed as we are to traditional accounts of clockmaking history, we completely overlook the basic monumental innovation and look elsewhere for explanations. The great invention was not the pillar scroll-top case, which was an incidental or coincidental point of decoration, obviously aimed at an endeavor to retain a continuing relationship to the tops of many grandfather's clocks but in cheaper form, nor was the thing that struck early nineteenth-century clockmakers as great and revolutionary any new movement. The really important new idea was to house a clock completely in one case with straight sides and front, essentially a mere box, with but one glass door covering the entire front and opening to expose the entire clock, the glass left clear over the dial and painted in its lower portion (the tablet) to take the place of the solid covering on the lower section of the traditional two-part case shelf clocks. Once this single case and door concept was worked out everything else— decorated top, cheaper and smaller works—was secondary, and a great deal that hitherto has been confusing becomes clear.

This is not to say that there are no mysteries left to the story. Tradition has it that the pillar scroll-top case was introduced by Eli Terry in 1814, and that Terry patented the clock. There is no way of ascertaining if it was patented or what any patent that may have been issued in connection with it covered, as all the early records of the United States Patent Office were destroyed by fire in 1836. There undoubtedly was one or more Terry clock patents in this period, but whether on movements, as seems most likely, or on the design of the case—as most commentators have assumed on no particular basis whatsoever other than it is the form the case eventually took that gave the clock its name—or if there might even conceivably have been a patent or patents on some feature or features of the new machinery built and installed for the mass-production of the new one-door shelf clocks.

The new clocks were an instant success, greatly cutting into the sale of tall clocks because making the case in this size and form enabled it to be manufactured for less than half the cost of even a cheap tall clock case. Thomas is supposed to have paid Terry a thousand dollars for the right to manufacture the new clock, the demand being too great for Terry to hope to handle it by himself, or so the story goes, and according to Jerome they each started by making approximately 6,000 clocks a year but afterwards production increased to 10,000 to 12,000 annually for each. But supposing Thomas paid for the rights to manufacture, did he buy the rights to a mechanism or to a case, and, if a case, was it necessarily the pillar scroll-top case, or was it for a license based on the one-door case idea? Endless controversy—some of it valid and pertinent, much manifestly ridiculous and useless—has swirled around the pillar scroll-top case clock, its invention, the rights to its manufacture, and the supposed patent or patents. A fair argument has been made out for the fact that it, or at least the case design or the mechanism, but not necessarily both, was originated not by Eli Terry but by Heman Clark.

After studying what evidence seemingly is available on these matters, it seems logical to conclude that much of the enduring confusion is due to the custom of assuming that the pillar scroll-top style clock cases and the mantel clock movements are inextricably linked together, and of completely overlooking the fact that the important development actually was neither of these but, rather, the single-unit, one-door case. It seems virtually impossible that even in the evidently somewhat confused and uncertain state of the patent system in the second decade of the nineteenth century a single patent would have been issued that would have covered both a mechanism, a mechanical improvement, and a case, a design. If the one-patent concept is abandoned and the whole matter looked at from the viewpoint that the basic one-door case idea, the movement or movements, and the pillar scroll-top case design are entirely separate things, then everything becomes much clearer and the seemingly irreconcilable begin to fall into logical and nonconflicting positions.

In any event, a pillar scroll-top case clock is a beautiful and important antique. Those manufactured by Eli Terry not unnaturally are preferred, despite the fact that in recent years the thought has repeatedly been heard advanced by dealers that a Thomas is "just as good." Just what this means is unclear, unless anyone is so crass as to suggest that those who propound it do not have Terry clocks but do have Thomas specimens to sell.

Just how much of a real monopoly Terry and Thomas enjoyed with the pillar scroll-top case clocks is not clear, but it is certain that even during the prime period of this type of clock, from its introduction into the later 1820s, the rest of the clockmaking business did not simply stand still and wither. There was a good market for clocks of all types, and plenty of clockmakers seeking to make something cheaper, better, or at least novel. An inexpensive shelf clock still sold for fifteen or eighteen dollars retail, and no one had yet really plumbed the depths of the mass-production clock market, although it no doubt seemed to many that the ultimate had been reached, what with tens of thousands of pillar scroll-top case clocks being manufactured each year. The mass-produced clocks of this period, whether pillar scroll-top cased or not, were mostly of the thirty-hour type with wooden movements, although some eight-day clocks, usually with brass movements, and naturally more expensive, were produced. There were numerous clock factories of various size scattered throughout New England, but mainly in northwestern Connecticut. Bristol Township, which includes Forestville, was to become a particular center.

Chauncey Jerome got into the clock business on his own after leaving Terry, settling in Bristol, making cases and sometimes complete clocks, using movements he secured from others for the most part. Finally he went into business with his brother, Noble, and Elijah Darrow and started making complete clocks. Around 1826 he created his own revolution in clockmaking with the seemingly simple and obvious idea of placing a mirror in the lower half of the door instead of the tablet. These clocks were called by him "bronze looking-glass clocks," although there was no actual bronze involved. Mirrors were not too

Two looking-glass clocks, the type that next succeeded the pillar scroll-top case clock in enormous popularity, the idea of securing both a clock and a mirror in one purchase being almost irresistible. That at the left was made by William C. Emerson ca. 1830; on the right, by Jason Rawson, ca. 1840.

Old Sturbridge Village Photos

common then and the idea of a household being able to secure both a clock and a mirror in the same purchase evidently was irresistible to most prospective buyers. The bronze looking-glass clock, which was made by a number of manufacturers, gave the clock business a great impetus into the middle 1830s, sales finally falling off due to the panic of 1837. It was then that Jerome got his next and greatest idea. Up to then, inexpensive clocks had been one-day or thirty-hour clocks with wooden movements, while virtually all the more costly clocks had had eight-day brass works. Jerome conceived the idea of a one-day clock with brass works. It was not exactly the sudden flash it has been pictured; Jerome had long been thinking of the possibilities of exporting cheap clocks, but the wooden works were likely to swell up on an ocean voyage and become useless, and rolled brass was by then being cheaply produced in Connecticut.

From this point on, the clock-manufacturing business rapidly evolved to the point pictured by Jerome in his autobiography, with many manufacturers thinking in terms not of tens of thousands of clocks but of hundreds of thousands, and inexpensive Connecticut clocks with brass movements going all over the world by the millions, and the prices continually coming down. The rolling of inexpensive brass was soon followed by the production of inexpensive spring steel, and the makers of so-priced clocks were no longer dependent on weights for the operation of their products and were able to manufacture smaller clocks. In studying both the clocks themselves and the catalogs of their manufacturers, the most impressive point is the seemingly almost unending variety of styles and sizes that were produced, many of them remaining in production in substantially the same form up to around the turn of the century. No one apparently has ever estimated the total number of models manufactured in this period, but it cannot be doubted that it runs up into many thousands. Furthermore, in time, most of the models were offered with one-day movements, optionally with or without strike or alarm, and eight-day movements with strike, but optionally with or without alarm.

The overall total of basic models thereby unquestionably runs into five figures; what it could be in terms of major variations alone is incalculable. The clock collector can have a veritable field day with all these, collecting and housing as many as he can afford. In doing so, he

A mantel clock of the so-called Double Gothic type. It was manufactured by Daniel Pratt, Jr., of Bristol, Connecticut, about 1850 and is equipped with an eight-day brass movement with wagon-type spring. The tablet is of engraved glass.

Old Sturbridge Village Photo

Two nineteenth-century Bristol, Connecticut, clocks. At the left is a so-called acorn-style or Charter Oak clock, made by the Forestville Manufacturing Company; right, a clock with a figure-eight door, manufactured by the Atkins Clock Company, probably in the 1870s.

Old Sturbridge Village Photo *(left)*
George S. Indig Photograph *(right)*

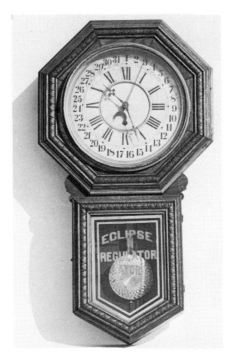

A railroad-station clock, one used for many years by the Southern Pacific, and measuring thirty-three inches in height. It was manufactured by the Sessions Clock Company of Forestville, Connecticut. Note the third hand is not a second hand but indicates the day of the month.

Ward Kimball

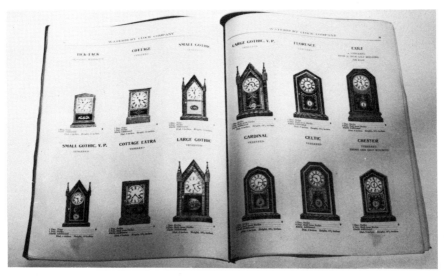

A double-page spread from the 1895–96 catalog of the Waterbury Clock Company of Waterbury, Connecticut, showing twelve wooden-cased clocks of styles often believed to be, or at least sold as, of much earlier date.

George S. Indig Photograph

Late nineteenth-century small brass-cased French coach or portable clock. The actual manufacturer is unknown; this was one of a number furnished bearing the name of Tiffany, the New York jewelers.

George S. Indig Collection

A classic-design, early twentieth-century Seth Thomas mantel clock with beveled glass and brass case and decorated porcelain face. There is also an equally interesting basic type of similar design with exposed escapement on the face.

George S. Indig Photograph

will be making a satisfying contribution to the study and preservation
not only of the clock industry in particular but also to that of American
manufacture as a whole, for this was manifestly the business that
showed the way to virtually all other manufacturing endeavors. It was
once often said, snobbishly, that there was little or nothing in this
period of clock manufacture starting at roughly 1840 that was meritorious or worthy of collecting, which, of course, was and is ridiculous,
not only for what is there and what they represent, but because it is
only in this period and with these clocks that the average collector can
gather enough specimens to make a significant study and contribution
to clock knowledge—which is not by any means to sell the idea of
having but one old clock in working order in use both to tell the time
and for its decorative value.

Following the Civil War there was a considerable influx of French
clocks into the United States, and many American manufacturers
turned to producing similar styles in order to compete with them.
Furthermore, there was in many cases a general gingerbreading up of
styles in accord with the prevailing Victorian standards of decoration.
Many of the earlier clocks, with their relatively simple lines attuned
to mass production as a matter of fact, accord much better with our
present concepts of good design than do many of the ornate clocks
introduced in the last third of the nineteenth century, but these, too,
form an integral part of the overall industrial picture and should not
be neglected by collectors merely on superficial grounds. They are eminently collectable as a specialty, and many enthusiasts are starting
seriously to collect and study them, as they are the clocks of the early
twentieth century. It should not be forgotten, either, that all through
this period of inexpensive mass-produced clocks and down to the present day, there have been manufactured beautiful and imposing tall or
grandfather's clocks and these units of the later nineteenth and early
twentieth century should certainly not be ignored or neglected, either.

Neither, certainly, although the idea may at first seem a little startling to more traditional-thinking clock collectors, should the electric
clock. Electric clocks are, in fact, quite interesting to many collectors,
both of clocks and of electric antiques. In theory, the electric clock
dates back well beyond the turn of the century and there are some
nineteenth-century examples to be found. As a widely accepted and

manufactured article, the electric clock is, of course, comparatively recent, but even now it can be said with reasonable certainty that any pre-World War II electric clock definitely is a collectable, and any such time limitation that may be imposed will, of course, continually move forward as it does with other groups of collector's items.

One group of nineteenth-century clocks of especial interest to men collectors are those with animated figures, which may take widely varying shapes and forms and range from clocks in cast-iron cases in the form of a man or woman whose animation is limited to a blinking of the eyes as the clock ticks, to clocks with three-dimensional figures that parade or go through some other sequence of motion. The cuckoo clock is perhaps the best-known and most extensively produced of animated clocks; in fact, its production was enormous and vastly overshadows that of all other types combined. The cuckoo clock is one of the few essentially European types of clocks that enjoy a considerable popularity among American collectors, although a great many eschew the type altogether as playing no part in the development of the American clock industry, and an enormous amount of work still re-

Representatives of a group of clocks of especial interest to many collectors, models of machinery. Left, a French clock in the form of a steam hammer. Right, a clock representing the front of a locomotive, manufactured by the Ansonia Clock Company of Ansonia, Connecticut, in the 1880s and 1890s.

Mrs. L. W. Slaughter *(left)*
Ward Kimball *(right)*

mains to be done in ascertaining the details of its history and manufacture. Still, most men who collect clocks probably would enjoy including at least one good cuckoo clock among their assemblage.

Another clock specialty of great interest to men comprises clocks that are mounted in whole or partial models of machinery, such as the locomotive clock and the steam-hammer clock illustrated, steam engines, and so on. The locomotive clock is American, made of cast brass, and manufactured by the Ansonia Clock Company of Ansonia, Connecticut, in the 1880s and 1890s. Clocks of this general type are, however, known to have been manufactured later, even in the 1920s. The steam-hammer clock is French, clocks falling into this general grouping having been made in both the United States and Europe. Obviously, they were men's clocks to start with and are prime masculine antiques today.

Probably more clocks were originally manufactured than any other major and fairly substantial widely popular collectable. And probably more old clocks still remain to be uncovered by and for collectors than do specimens of any other group of a similar nature and stature among hobbyists. Concurrently, probably more reproduction or faked clock parts, including artificially yellowed and aged-appearing dials are readily available than for any other category of antiques. Put these three facts together and take caution! Complete clocks are, of course, also reproduced, and there have even been do-it-yourself home assembly kits for fabricating what appear at first glance to be old-style American clocks marketed in the hobby trade in recent years.

WATCH COLLECTING

Watch collecting is related to and not dissimilar from clock collecting, although a good many watches can obviously be housed in a much smaller compass than an equal number of clocks. On the other hand, watch collections usually lack the visual impact and potential decorative value of clock collections. The history of watches and most particularly of the American watch-manufacturing industry in many ways closely parallels that of clocks and clockmaking save that, while it is known that there was a great deal of clockmaking in the Colonies prior to the American Revolution, many doubt whether there actually was any fabricating of watches in the Colonies or even any in the United States prior to the nineteenth century. This is negative speculation, based on the denigrating assumption that a number of gentlemen who advertised themselves as watchmakers prior to 1801 actually imported their products and merely placed, or had placed, their names upon them.

The story of American nineteenth-century watchmaking is much that of clockmaking; a search for ways to mass-produce watches of ever greater quality and at ever lower cost. Efforts in this direction began very early in the nineteenth century—which in itself is very suggestive of the fact that watches had previously been fabricated in the United States—but it was not until the middle of the century that machine-made mass production of watches with interchangeable parts became a really working reality. The result was that, for a while, the United States became the world center for watchmaking, as it was for ever, known to have been manufactured later, even in the 1920s. The clocks. The story of American watchmaking is a rather lugubrious one, as evidenced by the fact that of the at least sixty different companies that have at one time or another manufactured fine watches in the United States, today only three survive.

Watches are, of course, collected as complete units, movements and cases, but they may be classified either by the case or by the movement. Many fine watches were sold by their manufacturers prior to the early 1900s as movements only and were cased to suit the requirements of the purchaser by individual jewelers, the design of the watch case frequently revealing the occupation or interests of its owner. The developing exigencies of mail-order selling gradually bringing on the custom of offering watches as complete, cased units. The so-called hunting case is, of course, one with a hinged cover over the dial, the alternate style of case being referred to as an "O.F. case," simply the initials of "open face." By and large, the railroad watches were the finest of pocket watches, and they form an interesting specialty both among watch collectors in general and among collectors of railroadiana, early cases depicting locomotives being especially sought. As is generally known, the wristwatch was slow in achieving acceptability among men, until it proved itself overseas during World War I. Comparatively little is yet heard of wristwatch collecting, but it obviously is an im-

Top, nineteenth-century railroad watches, showing four examples of early cases with railroad motifs from the period when many watches were sold uncased and the buyer purchased a case separately. The second watch from the left dates from 1855. Also pictured (bottom) are the faces of Hamilton movements No. 1 and No. 2, from the 1890s.

Ward Kimball *(top)*
Hamilton Watch Company *(bottom)*

portant and worthwhile form of watch collecting and by now many specimens certainly are old enough to warrant the attention of collectors.

Another interesting and historically important watch-collecting specialty is the collecting of cheap American watches. The story of the American dollar watch, an artifact that now has completely vanished from the marts of trade, is really an industrial epic in itself and one deserving of full preservation and study. The first dollar "watches" were somewhat on the lines of what most today would consider a small clock, but it was not too long before their size if not their quality approached that of the usual pocket watch. As examples of industrial progression they well deserve retention and commemoration.

In sum, this holds true of every category of collectables. While there will perforce always be wide variations of relative desirability and value, if we lose sight of the fact that everything that once played a part in contemporary life merits preservation and study, and, hopefully, the recording of the results of such investigations as are undertaken, we are limiting our own potential for enjoyment. There awaits a worthwhile individual pathway in antiques collecting for every man whose interests and inclinations tend in this direction.

Index